Brave the exam elements with CGP!

The current GCSE AQA Geography climate is tougher than ever.
But don't worry, this CGP book creates a perfect revision environment...

It's packed with clear notes for the whole course, plus bang-up-to-date case studies,
exam-style questions, geographical skills and more. It'll brighten up your day!

CGP — still the best! ☺

Our sole aim here at CGP is to produce the highest quality books —
carefully written, immaculately presented and dangerously close to being funny.

Then we work our socks off to get them out to you
— at the cheapest possible prices.

Contents

Unit 2: Challenges in the Human Environment

Section A: Urban Issues and Challenges

Unit 2A — Urban Issues and Challenges

Section B: The Changing Economic World

Unit 2B — The Changing Economic World

Section C: The Challenge of Resource Management

Unit 2C — Resource Management

Unit 2C — Food

Unit 2C — Water

Unit 2C — Energy

Unit 3: Geographical Applications

Section A: Issue Evaluation

Unit 3A — Issue Evaluation

Section B: Fieldwork

Unit 3B — Fieldwork

Geographical Skills

Don't Forget

You <u>don't</u> need to study <u>all</u> of the content in Units 1B, 1C and 2C — some themes are optional. See page 1 for more details.

Published by CGP

Editors: Claire Boulter, Tom Carney, Zoe Fenwick, Katharine Howell, Becca Lakin, David Maliphant, David Ryan.

Contributors: Sophie Anderson, Paddy Gannon, Jack Gillett, Meg Gillett, Barbara Melbourne.

Proofreading: Claire Plowman, Karen Wells.

ISBN: 978 1 78294 610 6

With thanks to Ana Pungartnik for the copyright research.

Printed by Elanders Ltd, Newcastle upon Tyne
Clipart from Corel®

Based on the classic CGP style created by Richard Parsons.

Structure of the Course

Don't stumble blindly into your GCSE course — this page tells you what you're facing...

You'll have to do Three Exams

You'll study three units, and then sit three exams at the end of the course.

Geographical skills will be tested in every paper.

Unit 1: Physical Environment

Unit 1 is divided into three sections (A, B and C):

Section A: The Challenge of Natural Hazards

- Natural Hazards
- Tectonic Hazards
- Weather Hazards
- Climate Change

Section B: The Living World

- Ecosystems
- Tropical Rainforests
- EITHER Hot Deserts OR Cold Environments

Section C: Physical Landscapes in the UK

- UK Physical Landscapes
- TWO FROM Coastal Landscapes, River Landscapes OR Glacial Landscapes in the UK

Here's how Paper 1 is structured:

1 hour 30 minutes	88 marks in total	35% of your final mark

Unit 2: Human Environment

Unit 2 is divided into three sections (A, B and C):

Section A: Urban Issues and Challenges

Section B: The Changing Economic World

Section C: The Challenge of Resource Management

- Resource Management
- EITHER Food OR Water OR Energy

Here's how Paper 2 is structured:

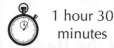

1 hour 30 minutes	88 marks in total	35% of your final mark

Unit 3: Geographical Applications

Unit 3 is divided into two sections:

Section A: Issue Evaluation

You'll get some material 12 weeks before the exam. You have to analyse and interpret it, then answer questions on related issues in the exam.

Section B: Fieldwork

In the exam, you'll have to write about general fieldwork techniques, as well as geographical enquiries (i.e. fieldwork) that you have done yourself.

You have to answer all the questions in this exam. Here's how Paper 3 is structured:

1 hour 15 minutes	76 marks in total	30% of your final mark

There's more about this paper on pages 121-123.

Use the Stamps to Help Guide Your Revision

Throughout this book, there are stamps to show you what you're revising. They look like this:

Example and Case Study stamps show where you need to know a real-world example. You might have studied a different place or event — if you revise that instead, make sure you know the same kind of information that's given in this book (times, places, impacts etc.).

In the exams, you'll be tested on skills like map reading and data analysis. This stamp shows sections on relevant skills.

At the bottom of some pages you'll find a practice question. Answering these is a great way to prepare for the exam.

May the course be with you...

It's worth knowing all this so nothing comes as a shock. Now you're fully briefed, onward to the joys of Unit 1A.

Natural Hazards

You often see natural hazards on the news — but that's not an excuse to watch telly instead of revising.

A Natural Hazard is a Threat to People or Property

Give it a rest Keith, there's nobody around

1) A natural hazard is a natural process which could cause death, injury or disruption to humans, or destroy property and possessions.

2) A natural disaster is a natural hazard that has actually happened.

3) Extreme events which do not pose any threat to human activity are not counted as hazards (e.g. a drought in an uninhabited desert or an avalanche in Antarctica).

There are Two Main Types of Natural Hazard

Most natural hazards can be divided up into two main categories:

1 Geological Hazards

Geological hazards are caused by land and tectonic processes.

They include volcanoes and earthquakes (see p.3-8), landslides and avalanches.

2 Meteorological Hazards

Meteorological hazards are caused by weather and climate.

Examples include tropical storms (p.10-12) and other extreme weather (p.13-14), e.g. heatwaves and cold spells.

Climate change (p.15-18) may increase the risk of meteorological hazards.

Different Factors Affect the Hazard Risk from Natural Hazards

Hazard risk is the probability of people being affected by a hazard in a particular area. There are several factors that can affect hazard risk:

Vulnerability

1) The more people that are in an area exposed to natural hazards, the greater the probability they will be affected by a natural hazard.

2) For example, an area with high population density on a flood plain (like much of Bangladesh) is very vulnerable to flooding caused by extreme weather, and a city at the base of a volcano (like Naples, Italy) is very vulnerable to volcanic eruptions.

Capacity To Cope

1) The better a population can cope with an extreme event, the lower the risk of them being severely affected.

2) For example, higher income countries (HICs) are better able to cope with flooding because they can afford to build flood defences and evacuate people.

Nature of Natural Hazards

1) Type — the risk from some hazards is greater than others.
E.g. tropical storms can be predicted and monitored, giving people time to evacuate.
But earthquakes happen very suddenly, with no warning, so it's much harder to protect people.

2) Frequency — natural hazards that occur more often may carry a higher risk.

3) Magnitude — more severe natural hazards tend to have the greatest effects.
E.g. a magnitude 9.0 earthquake that struck Japan in 2011 killed over 15 000 people, whereas a 6.3 magnitude earthquake in L'Aquila, Italy, in 2009 killed around 300 people.

EXAM QUESTION

Another natural hazard — forgetting to wear deodorant for PE...

There's more about natural hazards on the way, but before you rush off, have a crack at this question:

1) Outline one factor that can affect the risk from natural hazards.   [2]

Natural Hazards — Effects and Responses

Now it's time to find out how natural hazards <u>affect</u> people and how people <u>respond</u> to them.

Natural Hazards Have Primary and Secondary Effects...

1) The <u>primary effects</u> of natural disasters are the <u>immediate impacts</u> caused by the hazard itself:

- Buildings and roads are <u>destroyed</u> by earthquakes, volcanic eruptions or tropical storms.
- People are <u>injured</u> or <u>killed</u>, e.g. when buildings collapse.
- <u>Crops</u> and <u>water supplies</u> can be damaged or contaminated.
- Electricity cables, gas pipes and communication networks can be damaged, <u>cutting off supplies</u>.

2) The <u>secondary effects</u> happen <u>later</u> on, often as a <u>result</u> of the primary effects.

> Examples of the effects and responses to specific hazards can be found on pages 6, 7 and 11.

- The <u>initial</u> hazard can trigger <u>other</u> hazards, e.g. earthquakes can trigger tsunamis (enormous waves caused by seawater being displaced).
- Aid and emergency vehicles <u>can't get through</u> because of blocked roads or bridges — this can cause <u>more deaths</u>.
- A shortage of <u>clean water</u> and a lack of proper <u>sanitation</u> makes it easier for <u>disease</u> to spread.
- <u>Food shortages</u> can occur if crops are damaged, livestock are killed or supply lines are blocked.
- The country's <u>economy</u> can be weakened — damage to businesses can cause <u>unemployment</u>, and the <u>reconstruction</u> process can be very <u>expensive</u>.

...Which Also Lead To Immediate And Long-Term Responses

Some effects have to be dealt with <u>before</u>, <u>during</u> or <u>immediately after</u> the natural disaster to stop further loss of life, injuries or damage to property. Others are dealt with in the <u>longer term</u>:

Immediate Responses

1) <u>Evacuate</u> people (before the hazard occurs if possible).
2) Treat the <u>injured</u> and <u>rescue</u> anyone cut off by damage to roads or bridges.
3) <u>Recover</u> dead bodies to prevent disease spreading.
4) Provide temporary supplies of <u>electricity</u> and <u>gas</u> if regular supplies have been damaged.
5) Provide <u>food</u>, <u>drink</u> and <u>shelter</u> to people without homes.
6) Foreign governments or charities may send <u>aid workers</u>, <u>supplies</u> or <u>financial donations</u>.

Long-Term Responses

1) <u>Repair</u> homes or <u>rehouse</u> people who have lost their homes.
2) <u>Repair</u> or rebuild buildings, roads, railways and bridges.
3) <u>Reconnect</u> broken electricity, water, gas and communication connections.
4) <u>Improve</u> forecasting, monitoring and evacuation plans.
5) Improve <u>building regulations</u> so that buildings can <u>withstand</u> similar hazards in the future.
6) Boost <u>economic recovery</u>, e.g. by promoting tourism.

Learning this page will have a positive effect on your marks...

I know, I know... there's quite a lot of stuff you need to learn here. But the better you know this stuff, the better you'll understand the examples coming up. And trust me... there are some humdingers lined up for you.

Tectonic Plates

The Earth's surface is made of huge floating <u>plates</u> that are <u>constantly moving</u>... Rock on.

The Earth's Surface is Separated into Tectonic Plates

1) The Earth's <u>crust</u> (its outer layer) is divided into slabs called <u>tectonic plates</u> that float on the <u>mantle</u> (a layer of semi-molten rock).

2) Plates are made of 2 types of crust:
   - <u>Continental</u> crust is thicker (30-50 km) and less dense.
   - <u>Oceanic</u> crust is thinner (5-10 km) and more dense.

3) The plates are moving because of <u>convection currents</u> in the mantle.

4) The places where plates meet are called <u>plate margins</u> or <u>plate boundaries</u>.

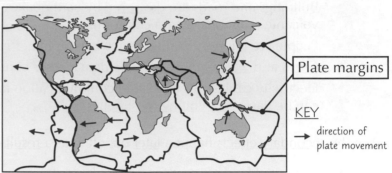

Plate margins

KEY

→ direction of plate movement

There are Three Types of Plate Margin

1 Destructive Margins

These are where two plates are moving <u>towards</u> each other.

Where an <u>oceanic</u> plate meets a <u>continental</u> plate, the denser oceanic plate is <u>subducted</u> (forced down into the mantle) and destroyed, creating gas-rich magma. <u>Volcanoes</u> and <u>ocean trenches</u> occur here.

Where <u>two continental</u> plates meet, the ground is <u>folded upwards</u>, creating <u>fold mountains</u>.

Example: along the west coast of South America, the oceanic <u>Nazca</u> plate is being subducted beneath the continental <u>South American</u> plate, creating the <u>Atacama Trench</u>.

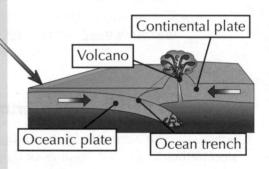

Continental plate

Volcano

Oceanic plate

Ocean trench

2 Constructive Margins

Constructive margins are where two plates are moving <u>away</u> from each other. Magma <u>rises</u> from the mantle to <u>fill</u> the gap and cools, creating <u>new</u> crust.

Example: the movement of the <u>Eurasian</u> plate and the <u>North American</u> plate away from one another is forming the mid-Atlantic ridge.

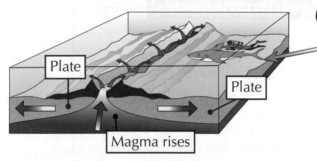

Plate

Plate

Magma rises

3 Conservative Margins

Conservative margins are where two plates are moving <u>sideways</u> past each other, or are moving in the <u>same direction</u> but at <u>different speeds</u>. Crust isn't created or destroyed.

Example: at the San Andreas Fault, the <u>Pacific</u> plate is moving in the <u>same direction</u> as the <u>North American</u> plate but <u>faster</u>.

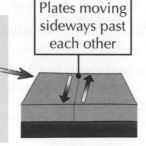

Plates moving sideways past each other

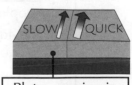

SLOW QUICK

Plates moving in the same direction at different speeds

Giant plates whacking into each other — smashing stuff...

Make sure you understand what tectonic plates are and the different boundaries that they can create, or you'll really struggle to work constructively through the rest of the section. I find sketching diagrams can be useful...

Volcanoes and Earthquakes

Where plates meet, <u>volcanoes</u> and <u>earthquakes</u> occur. If only the waiter would carry them more carefully.

Volcanoes Occur at Destructive and Constructive Plate Margins

1) At <u>destructive</u> margins, the denser oceanic plate moves down into the <u>mantle</u>, where it <u>melts</u>. A pool of <u>magma</u> forms, which then rises through cracks in the crust called <u>vents</u>. The magma (called <u>lava</u> when it reaches the surface) <u>erupts</u>, forming a volcano.

2) At <u>constructive</u> margins, the magma <u>rises</u> up into the gap created by the plates moving <u>apart</u>, forming a volcano.

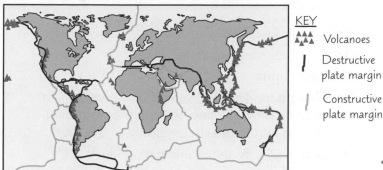

KEY
▲▲▲ Volcanoes
| Destructive plate margin
| Constructive plate margin

3) Some volcanoes also form over parts of the mantle that are really hot (called <u>hotspots</u>), e.g. in Hawaii.

4) When a volcano erupts, it emits <u>lava</u> and <u>gases</u>. Some volcanoes emit lots of <u>ash</u>, which can cover land, block out the sun and form <u>pyroclastic flows</u> (super-heated currents of gas, ash and rock).

Earthquakes Occur at All Three Types of Plate Margin

1) Earthquakes are caused by the <u>tension</u> that <u>builds up</u> at all three types of plate margin:

- <u>Destructive margins</u> — tension builds when one plate gets <u>stuck</u> as it moves past the other.
- <u>Constructive margins</u> — tension builds along <u>cracks</u> in the plates as they move <u>away</u> from each other.
- <u>Conservative margins</u> — tension builds up when plates that are <u>grinding past</u> each other get <u>stuck</u>.

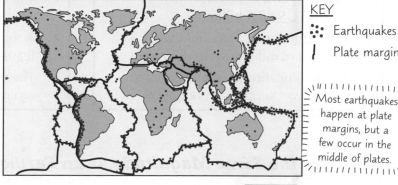

KEY
∴ Earthquakes
| Plate margin

Most earthquakes happen at plate margins, but a few occur in the middle of plates.

2) The plates eventually jerk past each other, sending out <u>shock waves</u>. These vibrations are the earthquake.

3) The shock waves spread out from the <u>focus</u> — the point in the Earth where the earthquake <u>starts</u>. The waves are <u>stronger</u> near the focus and cause more damage.

4) The <u>epicentre</u> is the point on the Earth's <u>surface</u> straight <u>above</u> the focus.

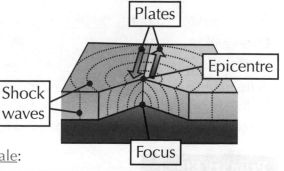

Plates
Epicentre
Shock waves
Focus

5) Earthquakes are measured using the <u>moment magnitude scale</u>:

- The <u>moment magnitude scale</u> measures the amount of <u>energy</u> released by an earthquake (called the <u>magnitude</u>).
- It is a <u>logarithmic</u> scale — so a magnitude 7 earthquake would cause <u>ten times</u> as much ground shaking as a magnitude 6 earthquake.
- Earthquakes of magnitude 6 and below normally only cause <u>slight damage</u> to buildings, although they can be <u>worse</u> in very <u>built up</u> areas.
- Earthquakes of magnitude 7 and above can cause <u>major</u> damage and deaths.

Damage after a 7.8 magnitude earthquake in Nepal in 2015.

EXAM QUESTION

Tension, jerks, major damage — sounds like my dance moves...

1) Explain how volcanoes form at destructive plate margins. [3]

Tectonic Hazards in Contrasting Countries

The effects of and responses to tectonic hazards can vary depending on a country's wealth. You need to know about two tectonic hazards in contrasting countries — they could be earthquakes or volcanic eruptions.

New Zealand Suffered a 7.8 Magnitude Earthquake in 2016...

See p.3 for more on the effects of hazards and how people respond to them.

Place: Kaikoura, New Zealand

Date: 14th November, 2016

GDP per capita: US $40 331

Plate boundary: Destructive and conservative — the Pacific plate is subducting beneath the Australian plate to the north, and sliding past it to the south.

Magnitude: 7.8 on the moment magnitude scale

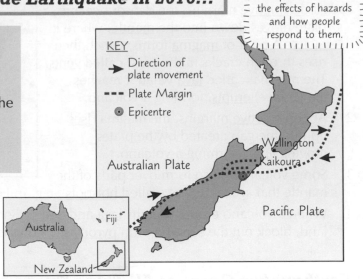

Primary Effects

- 2 people died and over 50 people were injured.
- Tens of thousands of homes were damaged, and some were destroyed.
- 60 people needed emergency housing.
- The total cost of damage was around US $8.5 billion.
- Over 200 km of road and over 190 km of rail line were destroyed.
- Communications, water, sewerage and power supplies were cut off.

Secondary Effects

- The earthquake triggered up to 100 000 landslides, which blocked major road and rail routes.
- A major landslide blocked the Clarence River, leading to flooding and the evacuation of 10 farms.
- The earthquake generated a tsunami with waves of around 5 m, leaving debris up to 250 m inland.

...this was the Same Magnitude as an Earthquake in Nepal in 2015

Place: Gorkha, Nepal

Date: 25th April, 2015

GDP per capita: US $690

Plate boundary: Destructive — the Indo-Australian plate is being subducted beneath the Eurasian plate.

Magnitude: 7.8 on the moment magnitude scale

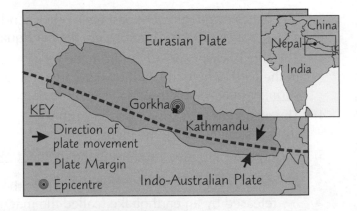

Primary Effects

- Around 9000 people died and more than 22 000 were injured.
- An estimated 800 000 buildings were damaged or destroyed.
- 4 million people were left homeless.
- The cost of damage was over US $5 billion.
- Roads and bridges were destroyed.
- Water tanks and pipes were destroyed, leaving 2 million people without access to clean water and sanitation.

Secondary Effects

- The earthquake triggered avalanches on Mount Everest which killed 18 people.
- Many mountain roads were blocked by landslides, preventing emergency aid from reaching remote areas.
- A lack of clean water caused outbreaks of typhus, which killed at least 13 people.

Tectonic Hazards in Contrasting Countries

New Zealand Responded Quickly to the Earthquake

Whether you've studied earthquakes or volcanic eruptions, make sure you know the effects and responses.

Immediate Responses

- A tsunami warning was issued quickly, and residents of coastal areas were told to move to higher ground.
- Hundreds of people were housed in emergency shelters and community centres.
- 200 of the most vulnerable people were evacuated from Kaikoura by helicopter within 24 hours of the earthquake.
- Power was restored to most places within a few hours. Temporary water supplies were set up.
- International warships were sent to Kaikoura with supplies such as food, medicine and portable toilets.

Long-Term Responses

- $5.3 million of funding was provided by the Kaikoura District Council to help with rebuilding the town's water systems and harbour.
- Most road and rail routes were repaired and reopened within 2 years.
- The Kaikoura Mayoral Earthquake Relief Fund was set up to help residents who couldn't afford basic supplies, and donations were received from around the world.
- By March 2017, a permanent water main had been laid in Kaikoura. The new pipe was designed to move with any future earthquakes so it won't break.

Large cracks in roads needed to be repaired after the earthquake.

© Nigel Spiers / Alamy Stock Photo

Nepal's Response was Slower and Less Effective

Immediate Responses

- India and China sent teams to help residents rescue people trapped by debris, but a lack of tools and machinery slowed down rescue efforts.
- People tried to recover the dead and treat the injured, but damaged roads made it hard for emergency workers and aid to get through.
- Charities such as Oxfam provided medicine, food and temporary water supplies.
- The Red Cross set up emergency shelters for 130 000 families who had lost their homes.

Long-Term Responses

- The World Bank Group financed $500 million worth of projects to build earthquake-resistant housing, and repair roads and irrigation systems. Some projects are still ongoing.
- The road from Nepal into Tibet was reopened 2 years after the earthquake, but many other routes remain damaged.
- Many heritage sites were reopened in June 2015 to encourage tourists back to the area.
- Water supply is being restored, but two years after the event, many people still didn't have access to clean water.
- NGOs are working with residents to increase their resilience to disasters, for example by providing alternative energy sources.

People needed rescuing from collapsed buildings

Money money money — always helpful when responding to hazards...

It wasn't just lack of wealth that made Nepal more vulnerable than New Zealand — it also has a much higher population density, so the risk was higher. Whatever examples you've learnt, make sure you know them well.

Unit 1A — Tectonic Hazards

Living With Tectonic Hazards

Because they keep quiet most of the time, plenty of people <u>live</u> in areas affected by tectonic hazards...

Lots of People Live in Areas at Risk from Tectonic Hazards

1) Many people <u>live close</u> to volcanoes or in areas vulnerable to earthquakes. Some people don't have a <u>choice</u> in this — for example, they may not be able to <u>afford</u> to move, or they may not know the risks.

2) However, many people <u>choose</u> to live in a hazardous region, e.g. around 1 million people live close to Mount Etna in Italy. People may make this choice for many <u>reasons</u>:

- They've <u>always</u> lived there — moving means <u>leaving</u> their <u>jobs</u> or <u>families</u>.
- In wealthier countries, effective <u>monitoring</u> and evacuation plans can <u>minimise</u> risk.
- They're confident that their <u>government</u> will <u>support</u> them after an earthquake or volcanic eruption. In 2001, the Italian government provided <u>financial aid</u> and <u>tax breaks</u> for local residents when Mount Etna erupted.
- The <u>minerals</u> from volcanic <u>ash</u> makes volcanic <u>soil</u> very <u>fertile</u>, attracting farmers. For example, the <u>mineral-rich</u> soil around Mount Etna is ideal for producing grapes.
- Volcanoes are <u>tourist attractions</u>, so lots of people live nearby to work in the tourist industry — Mount Etna receives <u>hundred of thousands</u> of visitors when it is erupting.

Management can Reduce the Effects of Tectonic Hazards

<u>Management strategies</u> can reduce the number of people killed, injured, made homeless or left unemployed.

Monitoring

1) <u>Earthquakes</u> — <u>seismometers</u> and <u>lasers</u> monitor earth movements, and can be used in <u>early warning systems</u> to give a small but vital amount of <u>warning</u> before a large earthquake occurs.

2) <u>Volcanic eruptions</u> — scientists can monitor the tell-tale signs that come before an eruption, such as tiny <u>earthquakes</u>, escaping <u>gas</u>, and changes in the <u>shape</u> of a volcano.

Prediction

1) <u>Earthquakes</u> — <u>cannot</u> be reliably <u>predicted</u>, but scientists can <u>forecast</u> where they may occur by monitoring the <u>movement</u> of tectonic plates.

2) <u>Volcanic eruptions</u> — can be predicted if scientists <u>monitor</u> volcanoes closely.

Planning

<u>Similar</u> methods are used to plan for earthquakes and volcanic eruptions:

1) Future developments can <u>avoid high-risk</u> areas.

2) <u>Emergency services</u> can <u>prepare</u>, e.g. by <u>practising</u> rescuing people from collapsed buildings.

3) People can be <u>educated</u> so that they know what to do in the event of a hazard.

4) Governments can <u>plan evacuation routes</u> to get people away quickly and safely.

5) <u>Emergency supplies</u> like blankets, clean water and food can be <u>stockpiled</u>.

Protection

1) <u>Earthquakes</u> — new buildings can use reinforced concrete that <u>absorb</u> an earthquake's <u>energy</u>. Existing buildings and bridges can be <u>strengthened</u> with steel frames so they're less likely to collapse. Automatic <u>shut-off switches</u> can turn off gas and electricity supplies to <u>prevent fires</u>.

2) <u>Volcanic eruptions</u> — buildings can be <u>strengthened</u> so that they're less likely to <u>collapse</u> under the weight of ash. <u>Trenches</u> and <u>barriers</u> have been used to try to <u>divert lava</u> away from settlements, but with <u>little success</u>.

Volcano? For many people, it's more like volcaYES...

Make sure you know how monitoring, prediction, protection and planning can help to reduce the risks from earthquakes and volcanoes. It's easy to get them muddled up, so try writing out a few points from each box.

Global Atmospheric Circulation

This might not be as exciting as volcanoes, but it's still important stuff. And what a pretty page it is...

Air Circulates between High and Low Pressure Belts as Surface Winds

1) Global atmospheric circulation is the transfer of heat from the equator to the poles by the movement of air.

2) Air moves due to differences in air pressure — winds blow from high pressure areas to low pressure areas.

3) The global atmospheric circulation system is divided into loops (called cells) — each cell has warm rising air that creates a low pressure belt and cool sinking air that creates a high pressure belt.

4) Each hemisphere has three cells. Here's how air moves in these cells:

- The sun warms the Earth at the equator, causing the air to rise. This creates a low pressure belt.

- As the air rises it cools and moves away from the equator.

- 30° north and south of the equator, the cool air sinks, creating a high pressure belt.

- At the ground surface, the cool air moves either back to the equator (as trade winds) or towards the poles (as westerlies). These winds curve because of the Earth's rotation — this is called the Coriolis effect.

- 60° north and south of the equator the warmer surface winds meet colder air from the poles. The warmer air rises, creating low pressure.

- Some of the air moves back towards the equator, and the rest moves towards the poles.

- At the poles the cool air sinks, creating high pressure. The high pressure air is then drawn back towards the equator.

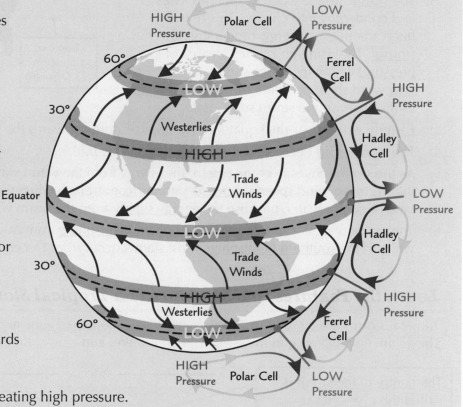

Global Atmospheric Circulation Affects Weather Around The World

Global atmospheric circulation influences weather and climate. For example:

1) At the equator, the sun is directly overhead — this means the Earth's surface receives a lot of solar radiation, so it's hot. Warm, moist air rises and forms clouds, so it rains a lot.

2) By the time air reaches 30° north and south of the equator, it has released most of its moisture as rain. The dry air means there are few clouds and little rainfall, so deserts are often found at this latitude.

3) The UK lies close to the low pressure zone at 60° north. Warm rising air brings lots of cloud cover and rainfall, often as low pressure systems carried from the Atlantic by westerly winds.

And I thought baked beans were the main cause of wind patterns...

...sorry, that lowered the tone. Best focus on the three air circulation cells between the equator and the poles. You need to know how these cause the wind patterns that give the world its weather and climate.

Tropical Storms

Tropical storms (a.k.a. <u>hurricanes</u> in the North Atlantic and Northeast Pacific, <u>typhoons</u> in the Northwest Pacific, or <u>cyclones</u> in the South Pacific and Indian Ocean) are <u>low pressure</u> weather systems with intense rain and winds.

Tropical Storms Develop over Warm Water

1) Tropical storms develop between 5 and 30° north and south of the equator, when:

 - sea temperature is <u>27 °C</u> or <u>higher</u>.
 - wind shear (the <u>difference</u> in <u>wind speed</u>) between higher and lower parts of the atmosphere is <u>low</u>.

2) The <u>warm</u> surface water evaporates, rises and condenses into clouds. This releases huge amounts of <u>energy</u>, producing powerful <u>storms</u>. The rising air creates an area of <u>low pressure</u>, which <u>increases</u> surface winds. <u>Low</u> wind shear prevents clouds <u>breaking up</u> as they rise, so the storm stays intact.

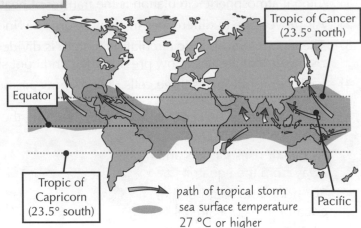

3) <u>Easterly</u> winds near the equator move tropical storms towards the <u>west</u>.

4) The storms <u>spin</u> because of the <u>Coriolis effect</u> (see p.9).

5) As the storm moves over the ocean, the energy from the warm water <u>strengthens</u> the storm, so wind speeds <u>increase</u>. Storms <u>lose</u> strength when they move over land or cooler water, because the <u>energy supply</u> from the warm water is <u>cut off</u>.

6) The majority of storms occur in the <u>northern hemisphere</u> from August to October, while in the <u>southern hemisphere</u> most storms occur from December to April.

Tropical storms occur at different times of year in different areas depending on when sea temperatures are highest.

Learn the Features and Structure of a Tropical Storm

Tropical storms are <u>circular</u> in shape, <u>hundreds of kilometres wide</u> and usually last <u>7-14 days</u>. They spin <u>anticlockwise</u> in the <u>northern</u> hemisphere, and <u>clockwise</u> in the <u>southern</u> hemisphere.

The <u>centre</u> of the storm is called the <u>eye</u> — it's up to <u>50 km</u> across and is caused by <u>descending</u> air.

There's <u>very low pressure</u>, <u>light winds</u>, <u>no clouds</u>, <u>no rain</u> and a <u>high</u> temperature in the eye.

300 km

Descending air

Eyewall

Rising air

West ← Storm movement → East

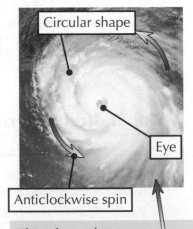

Circular shape

Anticlockwise spin

Eye

The eye is surrounded by the <u>eyewall</u>, where there's <u>spiralling rising air</u>, <u>very strong winds</u> (around <u>160 km</u> per hour), <u>storm clouds</u>, torrential <u>rain</u> and a <u>low</u> temperature.

Towards the <u>edges</u> of the storm the <u>wind speed falls</u>, the clouds become <u>smaller</u> and more scattered, the rain becomes <u>less intense</u> and the temperature <u>increases</u>.

This photo shows <u>Hurricane Katrina</u> passing over the Gulf of Mexico in <u>2005</u>. It made landfall in the USA on <u>29th August</u>.

Forget warm water, you're in hot water when one of these turns up...

Make sure you know how storms develop and what their characteristics are. It'll be a whopping great help if you know them inside out and back to front for the exam. And you know that I'd never lie. I pinky promise.

Tropical Storms — Typhoon Haiyan

EXAMPLE

It's time to apply what you've learnt to another <u>real-world</u> example. Don't say I don't spoil you.

Typhoon Haiyan was One of the Most Powerful Storms Ever Recorded

1) Typhoon Haiyan made landfall in the Philippines on <u>8th November 2013</u>.

2) <u>Tacloban</u> and <u>Cebu</u> were among the <u>worst</u> affected areas, with up to <u>280 mm</u> of <u>rain</u> and <u>winds</u> reaching a maximum of <u>314 km/hour</u>.

3) A <u>storm surge</u> with waves of up to <u>2.3 m</u>, combined with a <u>high tide</u>, meant that Tacloban was hit by waves of up to <u>5 m</u>.

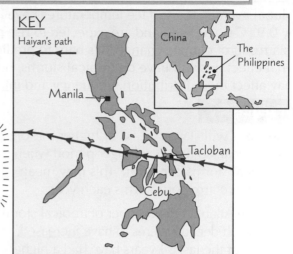

KEY
Haiyan's path

A storm surge is a temporary rise in water level caused by wind pushing waves onshore.

Primary Effects

1) <u>8000</u> people were <u>killed</u>.

2) Over <u>1 million homes</u> were severely damaged or destroyed.

3) <u>1.9 million</u> people were made <u>homeless</u>.

4) Strong winds damaged <u>electricity lines</u>, and <u>water supplies</u> were <u>contaminated</u> by <u>salt water</u> from the storm surge.

5) The heavy rain and storm surges flooded <u>600 000 hectares</u> of farmland.

6) The cost of <u>damage</u> was estimated at approximately <u>US $13 million</u>.

Secondary Effects

1) Flooding triggered several <u>landslides</u>, which blocked roads and delayed the arrival of aid.

2) <u>5.6 million</u> workers lost their <u>jobs</u> after businesses and agricultural land were destroyed.

3) The <u>lack</u> of clean water caused outbreaks of <u>diseases</u> such as dysentery.

The Philippines and the Wider World Responded Quickly

Immediate Responses

1) <u>PAGASA</u> (the Philippines' meteorological agency) broadcast <u>warnings</u> about Typhoon Haiyan two days before it made landfall. This led to the <u>evacuation</u> of <u>800 000</u> residents before the storm. Unfortunately, some of these people <u>died</u> when evacuation centres <u>flooded</u>.

2) <u>Fishermen</u> were warned not to go to sea.

3) The Philippines declared a <u>state of emergency</u>, which led to many charities offering <u>aid</u> in the form of <u>food</u>, <u>shelter</u> and <u>clean water</u>.

4) Plan International constructed <u>pit latrines</u> for <u>100 000</u> people to help <u>prevent</u> the spread of <u>disease</u>.

Long-Term Responses

1) The UN appealed for over <u>$300 million</u> to help fund rebuilding and relief.

2) Charities built new <u>storm-resistant houses</u> for those who lost their homes.

3) The Philippines' <u>tourism board</u> encouraged people to <u>visit</u> the country after the storm by emphasising that <u>most</u> areas were <u>unaffected</u> and that money from tourism would help with the <u>rebuilding</u> process.

Many homes needed rebuilding after Typhoon Haiyan

The facts on Haiyan make for grim reading, that's no joke.

You might not have studied this exact tropical storm (I'll try not to be too offended), but you still need to know these facts for the one you've studied. Best make sure you've got some effects and responses locked down.

Tropical Storms — Climate Change and Management

Climate change may make tropical storms more severe, so we need to find ways to manage their impacts.

Climate Change May Affect Tropical Storms

Global average sea surface temperatures have risen by 0.9 °C since 1880 and are expected to rise more as a result of climate change. It's hard to predict what effect this will have on tropical storms, but it may affect their distribution, frequency and intensity.

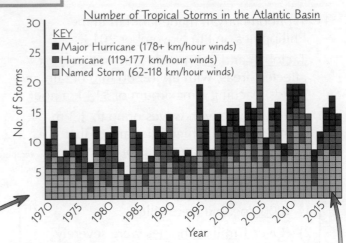

Number of Tropical Storms in the Atlantic Basin

KEY
■ Major Hurricane (178+ km/hour winds)
■ Hurricane (119-177 km/hour winds)
■ Named Storm (62-118 km/hour winds)

No. of Storms / Year

Frequency

Oceans will stay at 27 °C or higher for longer each year, so there's a longer period when tropical storms can form. This may mean that there are more storms each year.

In the Atlantic, the number of tropical storms each decade seems to have increased. 16 of the last 24 years have had a higher than average number of hurricanes.

Distribution

As the average ocean temperature rises, more of the world's oceans could be above 27 °C — this may mean that tropical storms can form in areas that haven't experienced them before, e.g. at higher latitudes.

Intensity

Higher sea surface temperatures are likely to result in more evaporation and increased cloud formation, so more energy is released. This could mean storms become more powerful.

In the Atlantic, the number of major hurricanes has increased since 1970. 2014-2018 had almost twice as many major hurricanes as 1970-1975.

There Are Many Ways To Reduce The Effects Of Tropical Storms

Prediction and Monitoring

1) Storms can be monitored using radar, satellites and aircraft. Computer models can then be used to calculate a storm's predicted path.

2) Predicting where and when a tropical storm is going to happen gives people time to evacuate and protect their homes and businesses.

Example: during Typhoon Haiyan, predicting the storm's path helped authorities decide which areas needed to be evacuated.

Planning

1) Future developments, e.g. new houses, can avoid high-risk areas, such as low-lying coastal zones.

2) Governments can plan evacuation routes to ensure people can get away quickly.

3) Emergency services can prepare for disasters by practising rescuing people from flooded areas.

Example: after Typhoon Haiyan, volunteers started rescue simulations so they were better prepared for future storms.

Protection

1) Buildings can be designed to withstand tropical storms. Buildings can also be put on stilts so they're safe from floodwater.

2) Flood defences can be built along rivers (e.g. levees) and coasts (e.g. sea walls).

Example: mangrove forests are being planted in the Philippines to act as a natural flood defence.

Prediction, planning and protection prevent poor performance...

EXAM QUESTION

Check you're clear on how the impacts of tropical storms can be reduced, then try this exam question:
1) *Explain how effective planning can reduce the impacts of a tropical storm.* [4]

UK Weather Hazards

Weather hazards are quite <u>common</u> in the UK — and it's not just about <u>rain</u>, either...

The UK Experiences Lots of Different Weather Hazards

Hazard	Impacts	Example
Strong Winds	• Strong winds (gales) can <u>damage</u> properties and <u>disrupt transport</u>. • Uprooted trees and debris can <u>injure</u> or <u>kill</u> people.	In 2018, <u>Storm Ali</u> killed two people when <u>100 mph</u> winds blew over several trees.
Heavy Rainfall	• Too much rain can cause <u>flooding</u>, which can damage homes, disrupt transport networks and drown people. • <u>Recovering</u> from flooding can cost <u>millions</u> of pounds.	Parts of South Wales flooded in 2018 after over <u>180 mm</u> of rain fell in <u>48 hours</u> during <u>Storm Callum</u>.
Snow and Ice	• Snow and ice can cause <u>injuries</u> due to slipping and <u>deaths</u> due to the cold. • Schools and businesses can be forced to <u>shut</u>, and <u>disruption</u> to <u>travel</u> can have <u>economic impacts</u>.	In March 2018, the '<u>Beast from the East</u>' brought up to <u>50 cm</u> of snow, causing <u>major disruption</u> to traffic and schools.
Drought (a lack of precipitation)	• <u>Water</u> supplies can run <u>low</u>, causing <u>economic</u> impacts such as <u>crop failures</u>. • Rules to <u>conserve</u> water (like banning hosepipes) have to be introduced.	From April 2010 to March 2012, southern and eastern England only received <u>75%</u> of their average <u>monthly rainfall</u>. By spring 2012, <u>groundwater</u> levels were very <u>low</u>.
Thunderstorms	• Heavy <u>rain</u>, strong <u>winds</u> and lightning can all occur during thunderstorms. • Lightning can cause <u>fires</u>, which can damage property and the environment, and can occasionally kill people.	In July 2014, a series of thunderstorms struck southern and central England, with <u>lightning</u> strikes causing <u>power cuts</u> and <u>delaying flights</u>.
Heat Waves	• During long periods of hot weather, pollution builds up in the air. This can cause <u>heat exhaustion</u> or <u>breathing difficulties</u>, which can kill people. • Disruption to <u>transport</u> from rails buckling or roads melting can cause <u>economic impacts</u> — but the <u>tourism</u> industry may <u>benefit</u> from the better weather.	2018 was one of the <u>hottest</u> summers on record, with temperatures reaching <u>35 °C</u> in Kent. 

Weather in the UK is Becoming More Extreme

The UK's weather is naturally <u>variable</u>, but extreme events seem to be becoming more <u>common</u> and <u>severe</u>:

1) <u>Temperature</u>: The UK's ten <u>warmest</u> years have all occurred <u>since 1990</u>, and 2018 was the joint hottest summer on record. Extreme <u>cold</u> events seem to be more frequent too — <u>seven</u> of the UK's <u>eleven coldest</u> recorded temperatures have occurred <u>since 1980</u> and December 2010 was the coldest month for over 100 years.

2) <u>Rainfall</u>: More rainfall records were <u>broken</u> between <u>2010</u> and <u>2014</u> than in any decade on record. Major <u>flooding</u> events have become <u>more frequent</u> over the past ten years — December 2015 was the <u>wettest</u> month ever recorded, and severe flooding occurred in many areas of the UK.

Many roads were impassable after the 2015 floods.

Heat waves, thunderstorms, snow — just a regular day in Cumbria...

The weather hazards affecting the UK probably don't seem as bad as volcanoes, earthquakes or hurricanes. But when your sofa's bobbing around in three feet of water, or a tree crashes into your roof, it's still pretty rough.

UK Weather — Somerset Levels Flooding

On the whole, UK weather isn't <u>THAT</u> extreme, but it has its moments. You need to know an <u>example</u> of an extreme weather event, and how <u>management strategies</u> reduced the risk from it.

Storms Flooded the Somerset Levels in Winter 2013-2014

1) From December 2013 to February 2014, Somerset experienced <u>three times</u> the average amount of <u>rainfall</u> for those months.

2) Lots of rain fell on already <u>saturated</u> ground, and coincided with <u>high tides</u> and <u>storm surges</u>. This caused extensive flooding of the Levels, an area of <u>low-lying</u> land criss-crossed by <u>rivers</u>.

3) <u>Human activities</u> also played a part — the rivers hadn't been <u>dredged</u> (cleared of sediment) regularly for 20 years, which reduced their capacity.

Much of the area is a flood plain (see p.53).

Social Impacts

- More than <u>600</u> homes were <u>flooded</u>, and many people were forced to evacuate.
- <u>Villages</u> such as Muchelney were <u>cut off</u> by road, and the only way in or out was by boat.
- Major <u>transport links</u>, including the A361 and some train lines, were <u>closed</u> or <u>disrupted</u>.
- <u>Insurance</u> prices <u>soared</u>, and some residents were unable to insure their homes against future flooding.

Environmental Impacts

- <u>11 500 hectares</u> were flooded, including farmland — this destroyed many crops.
- <u>Standing water</u> made the ground <u>toxic</u> and <u>unproductive</u> for over a year. Loss of nutrients and damage to soil structure decreased the long-term <u>fertility</u> of land.
- <u>Tonnes</u> of mud and <u>debris</u> were left by the floods, damaging vegetation.

Economic Impacts

- The total cost of <u>damage</u> to the Somerset Levels was estimated at over <u>£80 million</u>.
- Local companies lost more than <u>£1.2 million</u> in business.
- Loss of tourism cost the county <u>£200 million</u>.

Management Strategies Have Been Used to Reduce Flood Risk

You can rein it in now...

1) <u>Before</u> the flood, individuals and organisations took action to <u>limit its impacts</u>:

- <u>Warning systems</u> gave people time to <u>prepare</u>, e.g. the <u>Met Office</u> warned people to find <u>emergency accommodation</u> in case they had to leave their homes.
- Individuals and local authorities used <u>sandbags</u> and <u>flood boards</u> to try and limit flood damage to homes.

2) <u>Since</u> the flood, the government has set up the 'Somerset Levels and Moors Flood Action Plan' — a <u>20-year plan</u> which aims to limit the risk of <u>future flooding</u>. <u>£100 million</u> will be spent on:

- Turning temporary <u>pumping stations</u> into <u>permanent</u> ones.
- Regular <u>dredging</u> of the rivers Parrett and Tone.
- Building a <u>tidal barrage</u> at Bridgwater.
- <u>Widening</u> the River Sowy's channel and King's Sedgemoor Drain.

Dredging of the River Parrett started in March 2014

Manage your revision strategies — have a go at this question...

1) With reference to a named example, explain how management strategies can reduce the impacts of extreme weather in the UK. [6]

Climate Change — The Evidence

We British like to talk about the weather, so global climate change should give us plenty to go on...

The Earth is Getting Warmer

Climate change is any significant change in the Earth's climate over a long period.
The climate constantly changes, it always has, and it always will.

1) The Quaternary period is the most recent geological time period, spanning from about 2.6 million years ago to the present day.

2) In the period before the Quaternary, the Earth's climate was warmer and quite stable. Then things changed a lot.

The Quaternary period includes the whole of human history.

3) During the Quaternary, global temperature has shifted between cold glacial periods that last for around 100 000 years, and warmer interglacial periods that last for around 10 000 years.

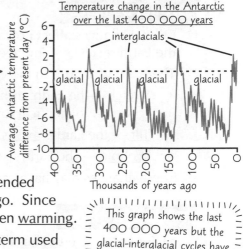

Temperature change in the Antarctic over the last 400 000 years

4) The last glacial period ended around 15 000 years ago. Since then the climate has been warming.

5) Global warming is the term used to describe the sharp rise in global temperatures over the last century. It's a type of climate change.

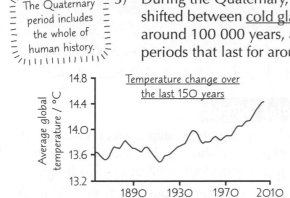

Temperature change over the last 150 years

This graph shows the last 400 000 years but the glacial-interglacial cycles have been repeating throughout the Quaternary period — there have been at least 20.

Evidence for Climate Change Comes from Many Sources

Scientists can work out how the climate has changed over time using a range of methods. For example:

Ice and Sediment Cores

1) Ice sheets are made up of layers of ice — one layer is formed each year.

2) Scientists drill into ice sheets to get long cores of ice.

3) By analysing the gases trapped in the layers of ice, they can tell what the temperature was each year.

4) One ice core from Antarctica shows the temperature changes over the last 400 000 years (see graph above).

5) The remains of organisms found in cores taken from ocean sediments can also be analysed. These can extend the temperature record back at least 5 million years.

Tree Rings

1) As a tree grows it forms a new ring each year — the tree rings are thicker in warm, wet conditions.

2) Scientists take cores and count the rings to find the age of a tree. The thickness of each ring shows what the climate was like.

3) Tree rings are a reliable source of evidence of climate change for the past 10 000 years.

Pollen Analysis

1) Pollen from plants gets preserved in sediment, e.g. at the bottom of lakes or in peat bogs.

2) Scientists can identify and date preserved pollen to show which species were living at that time.

3) Scientists know the conditions that plants live in now, so preserved pollen from similar plants shows that climate conditions were similar.

Temperature Records

1) Since the 1850s, global temperatures have been measured accurately using thermometers. This gives a reliable but short-term record of temperature change.

2) Historical records, like harvest dates or newspaper weather reports can extend the record of climate change further back.

Glacial cycles — as used by the polar bears in the Tour de Greenland...

Climate change is a really hot topic (sorry), so make sure you learn this stuff inside and out before your exam.

Climate Change — Causes

Climate change goes back long before humans roamed the Earth. Some natural factors cause climate change, but in the last 150 years or so human activities have begun to change the climate too.

Some Natural Factors are Possible Causes of Climate Change...

1 Orbital Changes

1) Orbital changes affect how much solar radiation (energy) the Earth receives — more energy means more warming.

2) There are variations in the way the Earth orbits the Sun:
   - Stretch —the Earth's orbit around the Sun varies from circular to elliptical (oval-shaped). This is also called eccentricity.
   - Tilt — the Earth's axis is tilted at an angle as it orbits the Sun.
   - Wobble — the Earth's axis wobbles like a spinning top (this is also known as precession).

3) These changes may have caused the glacial and interglacial cycles of the Quaternary period.

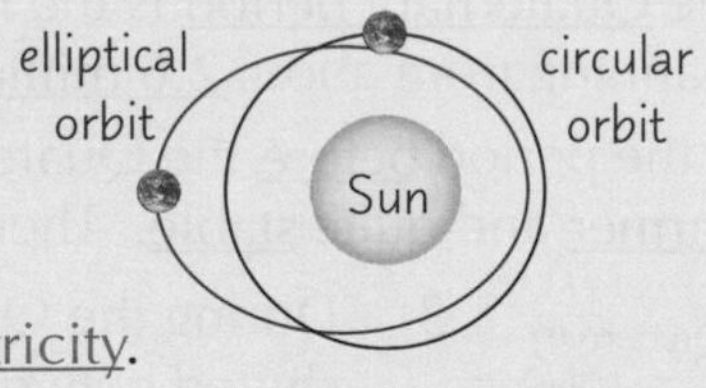

elliptical orbit *circular orbit* *Sun*

2 Volcanic Activity

1) Major volcanic eruptions eject large quantities of material into the atmosphere.

2) Some of these particles reflect the Sun's rays back out to space, so the Earth's surface cools.

3) Volcanic activity may cause short-term changes in climate, e.g. the Earth cooled by about 0.5 °C after Mount Pinatubo erupted in 1991.

3 Solar Output

1) The Sun's energy output isn't constant — it changes in short cycles of about 11 years, and possibly cycles hundreds of years long as well.

2) Reduced solar output means that the Earth's climate may become cooler in some areas.

3) Solar output isn't thought to have a major effect on global climate change.

... and so are Human Activities

1) In recent years, global temperature has risen sharply. This is called global warming.

2) There's a scientific consensus that human activity is causing global warming through the greenhouse effect.

3) The greenhouse effect takes place when greenhouse gases, such as carbon dioxide (CO_2) and methane, absorb outgoing heat from the Earth, so less is lost to space. It's essential for keeping the planet warm.

4) However, if greenhouse gas levels increase, more energy is trapped and the planet warms up even more.

5) Humans are increasing the concentration of greenhouse gases in the atmosphere through:

Burning Fossil Fuels

CO_2 is released into the atmosphere when fossil fuels like coal, oil, natural gas and petrol are burnt, e.g. in thermal power stations or cars.

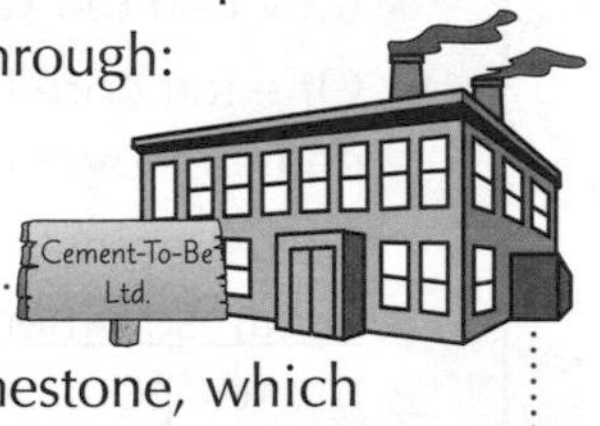

Cement Production

Cement-To-Be Ltd.

Cement is made from limestone, which contains carbon. When cement is produced, lots of CO_2 is released into the atmosphere.

Farming

1) Farming livestock produces a lot of methane — cows love to fart...

2) Rice paddies contribute to global warming, because flooded fields emit methane.

How very dare you!

Deforestation

1) Plants remove CO_2 from the atmosphere and convert it into organic matter using photosynthesis.

2) When trees are cut down, they stop taking in CO_2.

3) CO_2 is also released into the atmosphere when trees are burnt as fuel or to make way for agriculture.

EXAM QUESTION

The greenhouse effect — an irresistible urge to throw stones...

1) Explain how deforestation contributes to the greenhouse effect.   [2]

Effects of Climate Change

Whether it's <u>human</u> or <u>natural</u> factors to blame, climate change seems to be having an <u>impact</u>...

Climate Change Affects the Environment...

<u>Temperatures</u> are expected to rise by <u>0.3</u> to <u>4.8 °C</u> between 2005 and 2100.
This is already causing some major <u>effects</u> on the <u>environment</u>, and will continue to do so:

1) Warmer temperatures are causing <u>glaciers</u> to <u>shrink</u> and <u>ice sheets</u> to <u>melt</u>. Melting land ice, like the Greenland and Antarctic ice sheets, means that <u>water</u> stored on <u>land</u> is <u>returning</u> to the oceans, causing <u>sea levels</u> to <u>rise</u>.

2) <u>Sea ice</u> is also <u>shrinking</u>, leading to the loss of polar habitats.

3) Rising sea levels mean <u>low-lying</u> and <u>coastal</u> areas, like Miami in the USA, will <u>flood</u> more regularly. <u>Coastal erosion</u> will <u>increase</u> with sea level rise and some coastal areas will be <u>submerged</u>, so habitats will be lost.

4) Other species are <u>declining</u> due to warming, e.g. <u>coral reefs</u>, like the Great Barrier Reef in Australia, are suffering from <u>bleaching</u> (rising sea temperatures make coral expel the algae that lives in them, causing them to starve and die).

5) <u>Precipitation</u> patterns are changing — global warming is affecting how much rain areas get.

6) The distribution and quantity of some species could change and <u>biodiversity</u> could <u>decrease</u>:
   - Some species now live at <u>higher latitudes</u> (further from the equator) due to warming temperatures.
   - Some habitats are being <u>damaged</u> or <u>destroyed</u> because of climate change — species that are adapted to these areas may become <u>extinct</u>, e.g. climate change may limit <u>bamboo</u> growth, leading to the decline in numbers of <u>giant pandas</u> that rely on bamboo as a food source.

...and it Affects People Too

Rising temperatures and <u>climate change</u> don't only affect the environment — there are <u>impacts</u> on <u>people</u> too.

1) In some places, <u>deaths</u> due to <u>heat</u> have <u>increased</u> — but deaths due to <u>cold</u> have <u>decreased</u>.

2) Some areas could become so <u>hot</u> and <u>dry</u> that they're <u>difficult</u> or impossible to <u>inhabit</u>. Low-lying <u>coastal areas</u>, e.g. the Maldives, could be <u>lost</u> to the sea or <u>flood</u> so often that they also become <u>uninhabitable</u>. This may lead to <u>migration</u> and <u>overcrowding</u> in other areas.

3) Some areas are <u>struggling</u> to supply enough water for their residents due to problems with <u>water availability</u> caused by changing rainfall patterns. This can lead to <u>political tensions</u>, especially where rivers cross borders.

4) Climate change is affecting <u>farming</u> in different ways around the world:
   - <u>Globally</u>, some <u>crops</u> have <u>suffered</u> from climate change (e.g. warming in recent years has caused smaller yields in Argentina's wheat crops).
   - But some farmers in <u>high-latitude</u> countries are finding that their crops <u>benefit</u> from the warmer conditions and produce higher yields.

5) <u>Lower crop yields</u> could increase <u>malnutrition</u>, <u>ill health</u> and <u>death</u> from starvation, particularly in lower latitudes.

6) Climate change means the <u>weather</u> is getting more <u>extreme</u>. This means more money has to be spent on <u>predicting</u> extreme weather events, <u>reducing</u> their impacts and <u>rebuilding</u> after they take place.

The effects of not learning this page include declining mark availability...

Well, that was a cheerful read — loads of ways that climate change can affect people and the environment. But these are exactly the sorts of things that might turn up in your exam, so you'd better learn them. Hop to it.

Managing Climate Change

People have come up with lots of ways of coping with climate change, and you need to know about them.

Mitigation Strategies aim to Reduce the Causes of Climate Change

Various strategies aim to reduce the causes of climate change, by reducing the concentration of greenhouse gases in the atmosphere:

Planting Trees

Planting trees increases the amount of CO_2 that is absorbed from the atmosphere through photosynthesis.

Carbon Capture

1) Carbon Capture and Storage (CCS) is designed to reduce emissions from power stations burning fossil fuels.

2) CCS involves capturing CO_2 and transporting it to safe places where it can be stored, e.g. deep underground.

Alternative Energy Production

1) Replacing fossil fuels with nuclear or renewable energy can help reduce greenhouse gas emissions.

2) In the UK, more offshore wind farms are being built, e.g. in East Anglia, and several wave, tidal and nuclear power projects have been planned.

International Agreements

1) The Paris Agreement aims to reduce greenhouse gas emissions and limit global warming. It came into force on 4th November 2016 and has been signed by 195 parties, including the European Union (EU). It encourages developed countries to help developing countries put mitigation strategies into place.

2) Each country has submitted a pledge which indicates how much they will try to reduce their greenhouse gas emissions by. The EU and the UK agreed to reduce their emissions by at least 40% from their 1990 levels by 2030.

Adaptation Means Responding to the Effects of Climate Change

Here are some of the ways that people are adjusting to the effects of climate change:

Changing Agricultural Systems

Changing rainfall patterns and higher temperatures will affect the productivity of existing systems.

1) It may be necessary to plant new crop types that are more suited to the new climate conditions in an area, e.g. soya, peaches and grapes may be grown in southern England.

2) In some regions, biotechnology is being used to create new crop varieties which are more resistant to extreme weather events, e.g. drought-resistant millet is being grown in Kenya.

Managing Water Supply

Dry areas are predicted to get drier, leading to more water shortages — so people need to use water resources more efficiently.

1) Water meters can be installed in homes to discourage excessive water use.

2) Rainwater and waste water can be collected and recycled.

Coping with Rising Sea Levels

At current rates, sea levels are predicted to rise about 65 cm by 2100 — this would flood many islands and coastal areas.

1) Better flood warning systems are being put in place, and physical defences such as flood barriers are being built. E.g. the Thames Barrier in London can be closed to prevent sea water flooding the city.

2) In areas that can't afford expensive flood defences, e.g. Bangladesh, people are building raised flood shelters and building houses on embankments.

When I need alternative energy, I reach for the cookie jar...

Make sure you know the difference between mitigation and adaptation and you'll be flying come exam day. Mitigation means taking action to reduce the risk, and adaptation means trying to adjust to new conditions.

Revision Summary

Well, you just survived a very hazardous section. It may be all about disasters, but get a load of these questions down you and there won't be any kind of disaster in the exam. I know it looks like there's a lot of stuff here, but you'll be surprised how much you just learned. Try them out a few at a time, then check the answers on the pages. Once you can answer them all standing on your head and juggling five balls, move on to the next section. You'll enjoy the view when you get there...

Natural Hazards (p.2-3) ☑

1) What is a natural hazard?
2) How does the magnitude of a hazard affect the risk to people?
3) What's the difference between a primary and a secondary effect? Give an example for each.
4) Give one immediate and one long-term response to a natural hazard.

Tectonic Plates (p.4-5) ☑

5) Name the type of plate margin where two plates are moving towards each other.
6) Name the type of plate margin where two plates are moving sideways past each other.
7) Why do volcanoes form at destructive plate margins?
8) At which types of plate margins can earthquakes occur?

Tectonic Hazards (p.6-8) ☐

9) a) Give an example of an earthquake in a wealthier part of the world.
    b) Describe two effects of the earthquake and two responses to it.
10) a) Give an example of an earthquake in a less wealthy part of the world.
    b) Describe two effects of the earthquake and two responses to it.
11) Why do people live in areas prone to tectonic hazards?
12) Briefly describe the four management strategies that can reduce the effects of tectonic hazards.

Global Atmospheric Circulation and Tropical Storms (p.9-12) ☑

13) How does global atmospheric circulation lead to high and low pressure belts?
14) Describe the distribution of tropical storms.
15) What conditions are required for a tropical storm to develop?
16) Describe two characteristics of the eye of a tropical storm.
17) Using an example, describe three effects of and three responses to a tropical storm.
18) How might climate change affect tropical storms?
19) How can a city be protected against a tropical storm?

Weather Hazards in the UK (p.13-14) ☑

20) List the types of weather hazard that can be experienced in the UK.
21) Give two pieces of evidence for the weather becoming more extreme in the UK.
22) a) Give an example of one extreme UK weather event and explain what caused it.
    b) Describe the social, economic and environmental impacts of the extreme weather event.

Climate Change (p.15-18) ☑

23) What is the Quaternary period?
24) Give four sources of evidence for climate change over the Quaternary period.
25) What are the natural factors that can cause climate change?
26) What is the greenhouse effect?
27) Give four ways that human activities can increase the concentration of greenhouse gases in the atmosphere.
28) Give one effect of climate change on the environment.
29) How might alternative energy production reduce the causes of climate change?

Ecosystems

Welcome to a lovely new topic. Take your coat off, sit down and make yourself at home.
Do have a slice of cake — I made it myself. Just relax and I'll tell you all the gossip about ecosystems.

An Ecosystem Includes all the Living and Non-Living Parts in an Area

1) An ecosystem is all the biotic (living) parts (e.g. plants and animals)
   and the abiotic (non-living) parts (e.g. soil and climate) of an area.

2) The organisms in ecosystems can be classed as producers, consumers or decomposers:

   • A producer (e.g. grass) uses sunlight energy to produce food.

   • A consumer gets its energy by eating other organisms. They can eat
   producers (e.g. rabbits eat grass) or other consumers (e.g. foxes eat rabbits).

   • A decomposer is an organism that gets its energy by breaking down
   dead material, e.g. dead producers (e.g. fallen leaves) and dead
   consumers (e.g. animal remains). Bacteria and fungi are decomposers.

The Nutrient Cycle Shows How Nutrients Move Through an Ecosystem

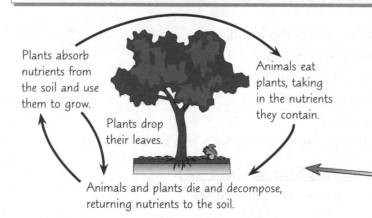

Plants absorb nutrients from the soil and use them to grow.

Plants drop their leaves.

Animals eat plants, taking in the nutrients they contain.

Animals and plants die and decompose, returning nutrients to the soil.

1) When dead material decomposes,
   nutrients are released into the soil.

2) The nutrients are then taken up
   from the soil by plants. The plants
   may be eaten by consumers.

3) When the plants or consumers die,
   the nutrients are returned to the soil.

4) This transfer of nutrients is
   called nutrient cycling.

Food Chains and Food Webs Show What Organisms Eat

1) A food chain shows what eats what.

2) A food web shows lots of food chains
   and how they overlap.

3) Each part of an ecosystem depends on
   other parts, e.g. consumers may depend on
   producers as a habitat and a source of food.

4) If one part changes, it affects all the other
   parts that depend on it. For example:

   If the blackberry bushes are cut back,
   there is less food for greenfly, so their
   population may decline. Animals that
   depend on greenfly for food, such as
   ladybirds and spiders, also have less to
   eat, so their populations may decline too.

Blackberry ⟶ Sparrow ⟶ Sparrowhawk

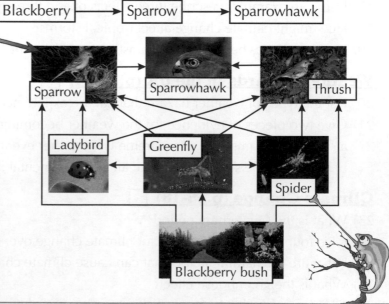

Sparrow • Sparrowhawk • Thrush • Ladybird • Greenfly • Spider • Blackberry bush

I like food chains — especially ones that sell burgers...

*You may be asked how a change in an ecosystem affects the other parts. To help you figure out the answer,
draw a food web so you can clearly see what will have more food, less food, a reduced habitat and so on.*

UK Ecosystem — Slapton Ley Reed Beds

Time to look in more detail at a <u>UK</u> ecosystem. Grab a cuppa and a scone — we're off to <u>Devon</u>.

The Slapton Ley Reed Beds in Devon are a Small-Scale Ecosystem

1) Slapton Ley in South Devon is a freshwater <u>lagoon</u>, separated from the sea by a shingle barrier. It contains one of the largest <u>freshwater reed beds</u> in Devon.

2) The lagoon is a Site of Special Scientific Interest (<u>SSSI</u>) and a National Nature Reserve (<u>NNR</u>), so it's <u>protected</u> from over-development.

3) The reed beds provide a <u>habitat</u> for lots of plants and animals. For example:

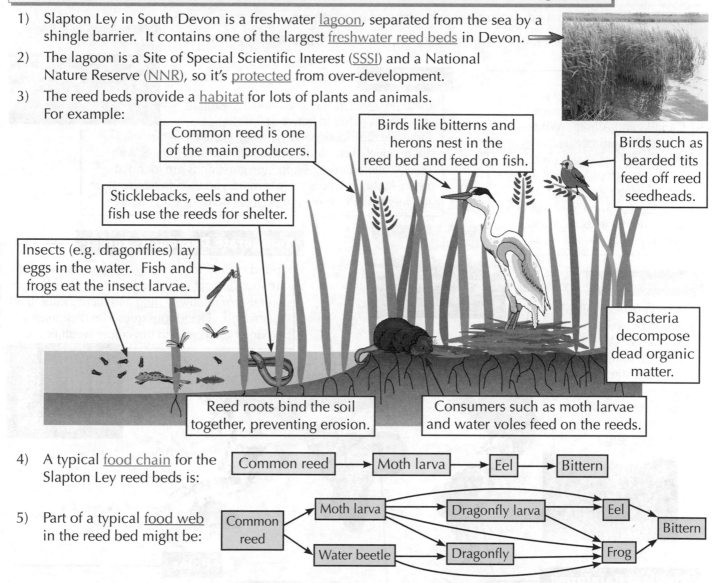

Common reed is one of the main producers.

Birds like bitterns and herons nest in the reed bed and feed on fish.

Birds such as bearded tits feed off reed seedheads.

Sticklebacks, eels and other fish use the reeds for shelter.

Insects (e.g. dragonflies) lay eggs in the water. Fish and frogs eat the insect larvae.

Bacteria decompose dead organic matter.

Reed roots bind the soil together, preventing erosion.

Consumers such as moth larvae and water voles feed on the reeds.

4) A typical <u>food chain</u> for the Slapton Ley reed beds is:

Common reed → Moth larva → Eel → Bittern

5) Part of a typical <u>food web</u> in the reed bed might be:

Common reed → Moth larva → Dragonfly larva → Eel → Bittern
Common reed → Water beetle → Dragonfly → Frog → Bittern

A Change to One Part of the Reed Beds has an Impact on Other Parts

1) The Slapton Ley reed beds are an <u>interdependent</u> ecosystem — all the components depend on each other.

2) Changing one component can have a <u>knock-on effect</u> on other components. For example:

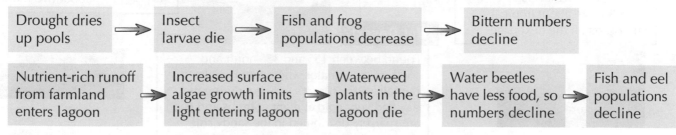

Drought dries up pools → Insect larvae die → Fish and frog populations decrease → Bittern numbers decline

Nutrient-rich runoff from farmland enters lagoon → Increased surface algae growth limits light entering lagoon → Waterweed plants in the lagoon die → Water beetles have less food, so numbers decline → Fish and eel populations decline

Reed beds — the latest in organic sleeping arrangements...

You may well have studied a different small-scale UK ecosystem. Whether you learn the details of that example or this one, make sure you can name some of the producers, consumers and decomposers in the ecosystem.

Global Ecosystems

Time for a whistle-stop tour of the world's ecosystems. All aboard...

You Need to Know the Characteristics of Global Ecosystems

1) The climate in an area determines what type of ecosystem forms.
2) The map shows the global distribution of seven major types of ecosystem.

Tundra

Found at high latitudes (above 60° N) in Northern Europe, Canada and Alaska. Winters are very cold, summers are brief and there is little rainfall. There are hardly any trees — vegetation includes mosses, grasses and low shrubs. There's a layer of permanently frozen ground called permafrost (see p.34).

Grassland

There are two types of grassland. Savannah grasslands are found between the tropics. There are distinct dry and wet seasons, although rainfall is still relatively low. Most of the vegetation is grasses with a few scattered trees. Temperate grasslands are found at higher latitudes where there is more variation in temperature and less rainfall. There are no trees here — just grasses.

Temperate Deciduous Forest

Found mainly in the mid-latitudes where there are four distinct seasons. Summers are warm, winters are relatively mild and there's rainfall all year round. Deciduous trees lose their leaves in winter to cope with the colder weather.

Boreal Forest

Also known as taiga. Found between 50-60° N. Winters are cold and dry, and summers are mild and moist. Trees are coniferous — they are evergreen and have needles.

Tropic of Cancer, 23.5° N

Equator

Tropic of Capricorn, 23.5° S

Polar

Found around the north and south poles. They are very cold, icy and dry. Not much grows at all (see p.34). They remain dark for several months each year so the growing season is very short — about two months.

Tropical Rainforest

Found around the equator, between the tropics, where it's hot and wet all year round. This is an area of lush forest, with dense canopies of vegetation forming distinct layers. There's more about tropical rainforests on the next page.

Hot Desert

Found between 15° and 35° north and south of the equator where there's little rainfall (see p.30). It's very hot during the day and very cold at night. Shrubs and cacti are sparsely distributed in the sandy soil.

Global echo-systems — they go round and round and round...

Aah, lovely. Don't just gaze at the pretty pictures though — you need to know where these ecosystems are found and what they're like. You'll be pleased to know there's more on some of them coming up next. Hurrah.

Tropical Rainforests

If you want to set the scene for this page, I recommend a hot shower and a CD of shrieking monkey noises...

Tropical Rainforests are Hot and Wet All Year Round

Climate

1) The climate is the <u>same all year</u> round — there are no definite seasons.
2) It's <u>hot</u> (the temperature is generally between <u>20-28 °C</u> and only varies by a few degrees over the year). This is because the <u>sun's</u> energy is more intense near the equator as it is <u>overhead</u> all year round.
3) <u>Rainfall</u> is very <u>high</u>, around 2000 mm per year. It rains every day.

Plants

1) Most trees are <u>evergreen</u> to help them take advantage of the continual growing season.
2) Many trees are really <u>tall</u> and the <u>vegetation</u> cover is <u>dense</u> — very little light reaches the forest floor.
3) There are lots of <u>epiphytes</u> (plants that grow on other living plants and take nutrients and moisture from the air), e.g. orchids and ferns.

Orchid

Fern

Soil

The soil <u>isn't</u> very <u>fertile</u> as heavy rain washes nutrients away. There are <u>surface nutrients</u> due to decayed leaf fall, but this layer is very <u>thin</u> as decay is fast in the warm, moist conditions.

Animals

Rainforest ecosystems are believed to contain more <u>animal species</u> than any other ecosystem. Gorillas, jaguars, anacondas, tree frogs, sloths and howler monkeys are all found here, and there are also many species of insects and birds.

Tree Frog

Anaconda

People

Many <u>indigenous</u> people have adapted to life in the rainforests. They make a living by <u>hunting</u> and fishing, gathering nuts and berries, and <u>growing vegetables</u> in small garden plots.

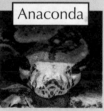

Rainforests Have Very High Biodiversity

1) Biodiversity is the <u>variety</u> of organisms living in a particular area — both <u>plants</u> and <u>animals</u>.
2) Rainforests have extremely <u>high biodiversity</u> — they contain around <u>50%</u> of the world's plant, animal and insect species, and may contain around <u>half</u> of <u>all life</u> on Earth.
3) Rainforests are <u>stable</u> and <u>productive</u> environments because their climate is constant — it's <u>hot</u> and <u>wet</u> all the time. Plants and animals don't have to cope with changing conditions and there is always plenty to eat.
4) Many organisms have <u>evolved</u> to <u>depend</u> on just a few other species for survival — they are <u>specific</u> to a particular <u>habitat</u> and <u>food</u> source. Many species are also only found in a small area.
5) <u>Deforestation</u> (see p.26) and <u>uncontrolled development</u> of the rainforest are likely to lead to the <u>extinction</u> of many species and the loss of biodiversity. The number of threatened species in Brazil increased from 628 in 2008 to 1182 in 2014.

I hate change.

Tropical Rainforests

Rainforests are Interdependent Ecosystems

All the parts of the rainforest (climate, water, soils, plants, animals and people) are <u>dependent</u> on one another — if any <u>one</u> of them changes, <u>everything</u> else is affected. For example:

1) The <u>warm</u> and <u>wet</u> climate helps fungi and bacteria on the forest floor to <u>decompose</u> dead plant material <u>rapidly</u>. This makes the surface soil <u>high</u> in <u>nutrients</u>, meaning plants can <u>grow easily</u>.

2) Plants <u>pass on</u> their <u>nutrients</u> when <u>eaten</u> by animals. The dense vegetation provides lots of <u>food</u>, so animal populations are <u>high</u>. When the animals <u>die</u>, their <u>nutrients</u> are transferred back to the <u>soil</u>, making it <u>richer</u> and encouraging lots of <u>vegetation</u>. This is a key part of the <u>nutrient cycle</u> (see p.20).

3) Many plant and animal species have formed <u>symbiotic relationships</u> (where they each depend on the other for survival). For example:

Agouti (a rodent) are one of the only animals that can <u>crack</u> open the hard seed pod of the <u>Brazil nut</u> to eat the nut inside. Sometimes, the agouti <u>bury</u> the nuts — these can <u>sprout</u> into new seedlings. If the agouti became <u>extinct</u>, Brazil nut tree numbers would <u>decline</u> and so could the populations of all the other animals that depend on Brazil nut trees for food or shelter. <u>People</u> who <u>sell</u> Brazil nuts to make a living could also be affected.

<u>Cecropia trees</u> have hollow stems and produce an energy-rich <u>foodstuff</u> at the base of their leaves. This makes the trees an ideal home for <u>Azteca ants</u>, who rely on the trees for <u>food</u> and <u>shelter</u>. Without Cecropia trees, the Azteca ants could struggle to survive.

The ants <u>fight</u> off other insects that try to feed on the tree. They also <u>attack lianas</u>, which <u>compete</u> with the Cecropia for <u>sunlight</u> by winding vines around their stems. Without the Azteca ants, Cecropias would be much more vulnerable to predators.

But Humans are Interfering with these Ecosystems

1) <u>Changes</u> to one part of the rainforest ecosystem can have <u>knock-on effects</u> on the whole ecosystem. For example, cutting down trees (deforestation) can contribute to climate change.

2) Trees <u>intercept</u> and take up lots of water, and <u>release</u> it back into the atmosphere, providing moisture for further rainfall. <u>Reducing</u> tree cover may <u>increase</u> the risk of <u>drought</u>, affecting the plants and animals that live in the rainforest ecosystem.

3) Trees <u>stabilise</u> soil with their roots and provide some <u>nutrients</u> when they <u>drop</u> their <u>leaves</u>. With fewer trees, the soil would have less protection from heavy rainfall, the few <u>nutrients</u> present would <u>wash away</u> more easily and plants would <u>struggle</u> to grow.

For more on deforestation turn to p.26-27.

Rainforests — hot, wet and full of creepy bugs, eugh...

Check you know the characteristics of a rainforest ecosystem and how those characteristics are interdependent.
Cover the page, write down what you know, then check you've got it all. Now drip on over to the next page for...

Tropical Rainforests — Adaptations

It can be difficult to <u>survive</u> in tropical rainforests, so plants and animals have <u>adapted</u> to make life easier.

Plants Have Adapted to the Physical Conditions

Plants in the rainforest are adapted to <u>high rainfall</u>, <u>high temperatures</u> and <u>competition for light</u>.

1) Trees <u>compete</u> for <u>sunlight</u> by growing tall.

2) Plants have <u>thick</u>, <u>waxy leaves</u> with pointed <u>drip-tips</u>. These <u>channel</u> rainwater to the point, encouraging <u>runoff</u> so the weight of the water <u>doesn't damage</u> the plant. This also means there's <u>no standing water</u> for fungi and bacteria to grow in. The leaves' waxy coating also helps to <u>repel</u> the rain.

3) Climbing plants, such as <u>lianas</u>, use tree trunks to <u>reach</u> sunlight.

4) Many trees have <u>smooth</u>, <u>thin bark</u> as there's no need to protect the trunk from cold temperatures. The smooth surface also helps <u>water</u> to <u>run off</u> easily.

5) Large, stable <u>buttress roots</u> support the tall trees' trunks.

6) Plants <u>drop</u> their <u>leaves</u> gradually throughout the year, meaning they can go on growing <u>all year</u> round.

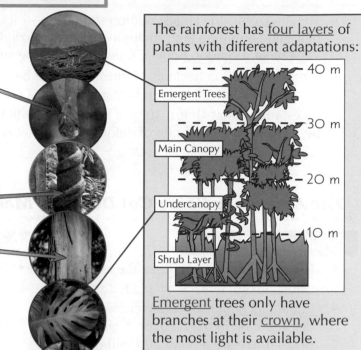

The rainforest has <u>four layers</u> of plants with different adaptations:

Emergent Trees — 40 m
Main Canopy — 30 m
Undercanopy — 20 m
Shrub Layer — 10 m

<u>Emergent</u> trees only have branches at their <u>crown</u>, where the most light is available.

Some <u>undercanopy</u> plants have <u>large leaves</u> to absorb as much sunlight as possible.

Animal are Adapted To Finding Food And Escaping Predators

Many animals spend their entire lives high up in the <u>canopy</u>. They have <u>strong limbs</u> so that they can move around their habitat quickly and easily, e.g. howler monkeys.

Some birds have <u>short</u>, pointed <u>wings</u> so that they can easily <u>manoeuvre</u> between the dense tangle of trees, e.g. the harpy eagle.

<u>Suction cups</u> help some animals climb, e.g. tree frogs. Others have <u>flaps</u> of <u>skin</u> that help them <u>glide</u> between trees, e.g. flying squirrels.

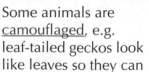

Some animals are <u>camouflaged</u>, e.g. leaf-tailed geckos look like leaves so they can <u>hide</u> from <u>predators</u>.

Some animals are adapted to the <u>low light</u> levels on the rainforest floor, e.g. anteaters have a sharp sense of <u>smell</u>, so they can <u>detect predators</u> without seeing them.

Many animals are <u>nocturnal</u>, e.g. sloths. They feed at night when it's <u>cooler</u> — this helps them to <u>save energy</u>.

Many animals can <u>swim</u>, e.g. jaguars. This helps them cross river channels.

What's a tree's favourite drink? Root beer...

You may be given a picture in the exam and asked to describe how an organism is adapted to its environment. Don't panic if you don't know what it is — think how the features shown might be adaptations to help it survive.

Deforestation in the Amazon

CASE STUDY

Deforestation is the <u>removal</u> of <u>trees</u> from forests. It's happening in many tropical rainforests, like the Amazon.

The Amazon Has Experienced Large-Scale Deforestation

1) The <u>Amazon</u> is the <u>largest</u> rainforest on Earth — it covers an area of around <u>8 million km²</u>, including parts of Brazil, Peru, Colombia, Venezuela, Ecuador, Bolivia, Guyana, Suriname and French Guiana.

2) Almost 18 million hectares of forest were lost between 2001 and 2012 — an average of <u>1.4 million hectares</u> were lost per year in this period.

3) It's estimated that almost <u>30%</u> of the Amazon will have been deforested by <u>2030</u> if the <u>current rate</u> of deforestation is not reduced.

Key
□ The Amazon

The Amazon is Being Cut Down for Many Reasons

Commercial Farming

- Forest is cleared to make space for <u>cattle grazing</u> or for huge <u>plantations</u>.
- <u>Cattle ranching</u> is the main cause of deforestation in the Amazon — in Brazil, there are around <u>200 million</u> cattle on about <u>450 000 km²</u> of pasture.
- <u>Soy</u> is another commercially farmed crop — up to <u>250 000 km²</u> of former forest has been used for its production. <u>Rice</u>, <u>corn</u> and <u>sugar cane</u> are also grown.

Subsistence Farming

- Forest is cleared by small-scale farmers who need land to grow food for <u>themselves</u> and their <u>families</u>.
- Many <u>indigenous</u> people are subsistence farmers.

Commercial Logging

The Amazon is full of valuable <u>hardwood trees</u> such as <u>mahogany</u>, which makes <u>logging</u> extremely tempting to both <u>legal</u> and <u>illegal</u> businesses.

Other

MINERAL EXTRACTION

<u>Gold</u>, <u>iron ore</u> and <u>copper</u> are mined and exported to help boost countries' <u>development</u>. Explosives are sometimes used to clear earth, and deep pits have to be dug to reach the mineral deposits.

ENERGY DEVELOPMENT

Building hydroelectric dams <u>floods</u> large areas of forest. The construction of the <u>Balbina Dam</u> (near Manaus, Brazil) flooded <u>2400 km²</u> of rainforest.

POPULATION GROWTH

<u>Population growth</u> and <u>migration</u> to the area is putting <u>pressure</u> on the Amazon rainforest, especially as the Brazilian government offers land in the rainforest to poor people from overcrowded cities, e.g. many farmers have been settled along the <u>Trans-Amazonian Highway</u>.

ROAD BUILDING

- The 4000 km <u>Trans-Amazonian Highway</u> connects the Brazilian coast to Peru, Colombia and Ecuador, through the Amazon.
- <u>New roads</u> built for logging have <u>opened</u> up areas that were previously too hard to get to, <u>destroying</u> and <u>threatening</u> more of the forest.

5-10%

20-25%

65-70%

2-3%

1-2%

Causes of Deforestation in the Amazon Rainforest (2000–2005)

KEY
■ Cattle Ranching
□ Other Commercial Farming
▨ Subsistence Farming
▨ Commercial Logging
▨ Other Causes

95% of deforestation in the Amazon occurs within 50 km of roads or rivers.

Deforestation in the Amazon

CASE STUDY

Deforestation in the Amazon has Environmental and Economic Impacts

Climate Change

1) Trees <u>remove CO$_2$</u> from the atmosphere — the Amazon stores around <u>140 billion tonnes</u> of <u>carbon</u>. Deforestation <u>releases</u> some of this as <u>CO$_2$</u>, which causes <u>global warming</u> (see p.16).

2) Up to <u>75%</u> of <u>Brazil's</u> CO$_2$ <u>emissions</u> come from deforestation.

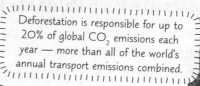
Deforestation is responsible for up to 20% of global CO$_2$ emissions each year — more than all of the world's annual transport emissions combined.

Economic

1) <u>Economic development</u>, farming in particular, has brought <u>wealth</u> to many Amazonian countries. E.g. in March 2018, Brazil exported almost <u>$600 million</u> of <u>beef</u>. Brazil is also the world's <u>second largest</u> exporter of <u>soy beans</u>.

2) The mining industry creates <u>jobs</u> for lots of people, e.g. the Buenaventura mining company in Peru employs over 8000 people.

3) <u>Logging</u> contributes a huge amount to Brazil's <u>economy</u>, but it can destroy <u>resources</u> that countries <u>depend</u> on, e.g. timber, and <u>reduce</u> the attractiveness of the area to <u>tourists</u>.

4) Local Brazilian <u>rubber tappers</u> who extract natural rubber from rubber trees have <u>lost</u> their <u>livelihoods</u> as trees have been cut down.

Soil Erosion

1) Brazil is losing up to <u>100 tonnes</u> of <u>topsoil</u> per hectare each year because of <u>soil erosion</u>. This may lead to <u>landslides</u> and <u>flooding</u> in the future.

2) With less tree canopy to intercept rainfall and fewer tree roots to absorb it, <u>more water</u> reaches the soil. This <u>reduces soil fertility</u> as <u>nutrients</u> in the soil are <u>washed away</u>.

3) Commercial and subsistence <u>farmers</u> are then forced to find <u>new areas</u> to farm, leading to further <u>deforestation</u>.

The Global Rate of Deforestation is Changing

1) The <u>global</u> rate of deforestation is very <u>high</u>. From 2007 to 2017, an average of <u>22 million hectares</u> of forest were lost each year. The rate varies, but it's generally <u>increasing</u>.

2) The amount of deforestation <u>varies</u> between countries. From 2001 to 2014, <u>Brazil</u> and <u>Indonesia</u> accounted for <u>almost half</u> of global deforestation.

3) Some countries are now working to <u>reduce</u> their deforestation rates, e.g. from 2004 to 2012, the rate of deforestation in <u>Brazil</u> decreased by about <u>80%</u>. This was because:

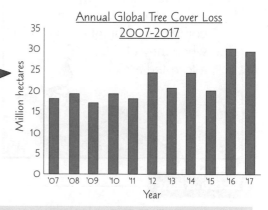
Annual Global Tree Cover Loss 2007-2017

- As part of the <u>Paris Agreement</u> (p.18), Brazil pledged to reduce its <u>carbon emissions</u> by <u>37%</u> by 2025.
- Increased <u>global awareness</u> about deforestation has <u>reduced</u> the <u>demand</u> for products from deforested areas, e.g. the UK supermarket Iceland stopped manufacturing palm oil products in 2018.

4) Efforts to decrease deforestation in Brazil include:

- Protecting over <u>44%</u> of the Amazon using funding from the World Bank, the WWF and other groups.
- The Brazilian government uses <u>satellite imagery</u> to prevent large-scale illegal logging.

5) However, rates of deforestation are <u>increasing</u> in some countries, e.g. Cambodia and Liberia.

EXAM QUESTION

If only we could order a few billion trees with next day delivery...

Ahh... the good ol' environmental and economic impacts. Boy do examiners love them...

1) Outline one possible economic impact of deforestation. [2]

Tropical Rainforests — Sustainable Management

It's not all doom and gloom for rainforests. In fact, this page is dedicated to the ways to <u>manage</u> them.

Tropical Rainforests are Very Valuable to People and the Environment

1) Many <u>products</u>, including rubber, coffee, chocolate and medicines, are <u>sourced</u> from the rainforest. If species become <u>extinct</u>, it's harder to discover new <u>medicines</u> and develop new products.

2) Sustainable development can offer long-term <u>economic benefits</u>, e.g. ecotourism.

3) Protecting the rainforests may <u>reduce</u> the <u>greenhouse effect</u> (p.16) by reducing CO_2 <u>emissions</u> (from burning, etc.), and allowing the trees to continue <u>absorbing</u> CO_2.

4) Some of the <u>impacts</u> of rainforest destruction, e.g. climate change, could affect <u>all countries</u>, not just the countries where deforestation is happening.

5) Rainforests also help <u>regulate</u> the <u>climate</u> and <u>water cycle</u> — without them the risks of drought and flooding in certain areas can increase.

Tropical Rainforests can be Sustainably Managed

Rainforests can be <u>managed</u> in a way that's <u>sustainable</u>, i.e. getting the resources we need today, without damaging the environment so that resources aren't available in the future. Here's how:

Replanting

1) This is when <u>new trees</u> are planted to <u>replace</u> the ones that are cut down.

2) It's important that the <u>types</u> of trees replanted match those that were cut down.

3) In some countries there are <u>laws</u> to make logging companies <u>replant</u> trees when they clear a forested area.

Selective Logging

1) Only <u>some</u> trees (e.g. old ones) are felled — <u>most</u> trees remain.

2) This is <u>less damaging</u> to the forest than clearing a whole area. If only a few trees are taken from an area the overall forest <u>structure</u> is <u>kept</u> — the canopy remains and the soil isn't exposed. This allows the forest to <u>regenerate</u>.

3) The least damaging forms are '<u>horse logging</u>' and '<u>helicopter logging</u>' — dragging felled trees out of the forest using horses or removing them with helicopters instead of huge trucks.

EXAMPLE: <u>Helicopter logging</u> is used in <u>Sarawak</u>, Malaysia.

Ecotourism

1) Ecotourism <u>minimises damage</u> to the <u>environment</u> and <u>benefits local people</u>.

2) Only a <u>small number</u> of visitors are allowed into an area at a time and rules are imposed to minimise environmental impacts. E.g. waste and litter are disposed of properly to prevent the contamination of land and water supplies.

3) Ecotourism provides a source of <u>income</u> for local people, e.g. they can act as guides and provide accommodation or transport. It can also raise <u>awareness</u> of <u>conservation issues</u> and bring in more money to help protect rainforests.

4) If local people are employed in tourism, they <u>don't</u> have to <u>log</u> or <u>farm</u> to make money, meaning <u>fewer trees</u> are <u>cut down</u>. If a country's economy <u>relies</u> on ecotourism, there's an <u>incentive</u> to conserve the environment.

EXAMPLE: Ecotourism has been very <u>successful</u> in <u>Costa Rica</u>. It is the largest source of income for the country and has led to <u>21%</u> of the country being <u>protected</u> from development.

Tropical Rainforests — Sustainable Management

A few more sustainable ways to manage rainforests...

Education

1) Educating the international community about the <u>impacts</u> of deforestation can encourage people to buy <u>products</u> from sustainable sources.

2) Local people might damage the forest (e.g. by logging illegally) to overcome their poverty, <u>without realising</u> the long-term effects of their actions.

3) Educating local people about the <u>impacts</u> of deforestation can help to reduce <u>damage</u> to rainforests.

4) Teaching local people about <u>alternative</u> ways to make <u>money</u> that don't damage the environment as much, means they won't be dependent on <u>unsustainable</u> options in order to make a living.

EXAMPLE: The <u>Rainforest Alliance</u> is teaching communities in <u>Guatemala</u> about <u>sustainable livelihoods</u>.

Conservation

1) Many countries have set up <u>national parks</u> and <u>nature reserves</u> within rainforests. In these areas damaging activities, e.g. logging, are <u>restricted</u>. However, a <u>lack</u> of <u>funds</u> can make it difficult to police the restrictions.

2) As a result, some countries have set up <u>funds</u> which <u>overseas governments</u> and businesses can <u>invest</u> in. The countries get the money in exchange for rainforest conservation.

3) The money can be used to <u>enforce restrictions</u> on damaging activities and to <u>promote sustainable</u> use of the rainforests.

EXAMPLE: In 2018, <u>Norway</u> paid <u>$70 million</u> into <u>Brazil's Amazon Fund</u> to be used for conservation.

Reducing Debt

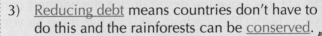

1) Many tropical rainforests are found in <u>lower income countries</u>, which often borrow money from wealthier countries or organisations (e.g. the World Bank).

2) This money must be paid back with interest, so poorer countries log, farm and mine in the rainforests to <u>make money</u> to <u>pay back</u> the debt.

3) <u>Reducing debt</u> means countries don't have to do this and the rainforests can be <u>conserved</u>.

4) Debt can be <u>cancelled</u> by countries or organisations, but there's <u>no guarantee</u> that the repayment money will be spent on <u>conservation</u>.

5) A better solution is a <u>conservation swap</u>, where part of a country's debt is paid off in <u>exchange</u> for a <u>guarantee</u> that the money will be spent on conservation.

EXAMPLE: In 2011, the <u>USA</u> reduced Indonesia's debt by <u>$29 million</u> in exchange for conserving their rainforests.

International Hardwood Agreements

1) Hardwood is a general term for wood from certain tree species, e.g. <u>mahogany</u> or <u>teak</u>. The wood tends to be dense and hard, so it's often used to make <u>furniture</u>.

2) <u>High demand</u> for hardwood from consumers in richer countries means that some tropical hardwood trees are becoming increasingly <u>rare</u> as more are cut down.

3) There are <u>international agreements</u> in place to try to prevent illegal logging, and to <u>promote</u> the use of hardwood from <u>sustainably managed</u> forests.

© Betastock / Alamy Stock Photo

EXAMPLE: The <u>Forest Stewardship Council</u>® (FSC®) mark <u>sustainably-sourced timber</u> with their <u>logo</u> so that consumers can choose products that don't contribute to unsustainable deforestation.

Sustainable management of revision — exam success now and forever...

Sustainability sounds complex but it's simple really — present needs shouldn't negatively impact future needs.

Hot Deserts

Hot deserts are, well... <u>hot</u> and also very <u>dry</u>. This affects the plants and animals that can live there.

Hot Deserts Are Found in Hot, Dry Climates

Climate

1) There's very <u>little rainfall</u> — less than 250 mm per year.
2) Rainfall <u>patterns vary</u> — it might rain once every few years.
3) <u>Temperatures</u> are <u>extreme</u> because of the lack of cloud cover — it can reach 45 °C in the day, then drop below 0 °C at night.

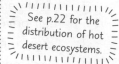
See p.22 for the distribution of hot desert ecosystems.

Soil

1) A lack of leaf fall limits the soil's <u>fertility</u>.
2) Little rainfall means the soil <u>dries out</u> often.
3) Soil is often <u>shallow</u> with a <u>gravelly</u> texture.

Plants

1) Due to the low rainfall, plant growth is <u>sparse</u> — the plants that do grow, such as thornbushes and <u>cacti</u>, don't need much water.
2) Plants are usually <u>short</u> (e.g. low shrubs or short woody trees) though cacti can grow fairly tall.
3) Many plants have <u>short life cycles</u>, growing quickly after rain.

© mauritius images GmbH / Alamy Stock Photo

Animals

1) Hot deserts contain animals <u>adapted</u> to the <u>harsh environment</u>.
2) Mammals tend to be <u>small</u> and <u>nocturnal</u>, e.g. kangaroo rats.
3) Most <u>birds leave</u> the desert during the harshest conditions but some birds, like roadrunners, can live there all year round.

© Arterra Picture Library / Alamy Stock Photo

People

1) Many people living in deserts grow a few <u>crops</u> near natural water sources, usually in the <u>desert fringes</u>.
2) Indigenous people are often <u>nomadic</u> — they keep travelling to find food and water for their livestock.

Hot Deserts are Fragile, Interdependent Ecosystems

1) The <u>biotic</u> (living) components of hot deserts (plants, animals and people) and the <u>abiotic</u> (non-living) components (climate, water, soils) are all <u>closely related</u> — many of them are dependent on each other.

- <u>Plants</u> take up nutrients from the <u>soil</u> and provide nutrients and water to the <u>animals</u> that eat them. In turn, animals spread <u>seeds</u> through their <u>dung</u>, helping the plants to reproduce.
- The <u>hot</u> and <u>dry</u> climate affects the soil in deserts. Soils are <u>salty</u> due to high evaporation rates, and relatively low in nutrients because there is little decomposition of dead plant material by fungi and bacteria. This means that plants <u>struggle</u> to grow.
- The sparse vegetation limits the amount of <u>food</u> available, so the desert can only support <u>low-density</u> populations of animals and people.

2) <u>Changes</u> to one component of the ecosystem can have knock-on effects on the <u>whole</u> ecosystem:

Allowing cattle to overgraze can cause <u>soil erosion</u>. With fewer plant roots <u>stabilising</u> the soil, the wind can <u>blow</u> fine sand particles into the atmosphere, forming dust clouds. These <u>reduce rainfall</u>, making deserts even <u>drier</u>. Without rainfall, water supplies can dry up and people, plants and livestock may <u>die</u>.

Hot deserts are the best — it's sticky toffee pudding for me every time...

Make sure you understand how changing one thing, like the soil, can affect the rest of the desert ecosystem.

Hot Deserts — Adaptations

Phew, it's getting hot in here. Plants and animals can only survive in the desert because of some nifty <u>adaptations</u>.

Plants and Animals Have Adapted to the Physical Conditions

Desert <u>plants</u> have adaptations to help them <u>cope</u> with the <u>hot</u>, <u>dry</u> conditions.

1) Plant <u>roots</u> are either extremely <u>long</u> to reach <u>deep water</u> supplies (e.g. mesquite roots can grow 50 m long), or they can spread out very <u>wide</u> near the <u>surface</u> to absorb as much water as possible when it rains (e.g. prickly pear roots).

2) Many plants, e.g. cacti, are <u>succulents</u>. They have large, <u>fleshy stems</u> for storing water and thick <u>waxy skin</u> to reduce <u>transpiration</u> (water loss from plants).

3) Some plants have <u>small leaves</u> or <u>spines</u> to <u>lower</u> their surface area and reduce transpiration. These spines can contain <u>toxins</u> to <u>protect</u> the plants from predators.

4) Some plants (e.g. brittlebush) <u>only germinate</u> after it rains — if it's too <u>dry</u> the seeds stay <u>dormant</u> (inactive). However, when they do grow, they grow <u>quickly</u> to make the most of the wet conditions.

Prickly pear

Desert <u>animals</u> are also adapted to cope with the <u>high temperatures</u> and <u>limited</u> supply of <u>water</u>.

1) <u>Nocturnal</u> animals <u>stay cool</u> by sleeping when temperatures are hottest. Many desert animals also have <u>long limbs</u> or <u>ears</u>, giving them a <u>larger surface area</u> to lose heat from (e.g. fennec foxes have large ears).

2) Lots of animals live in <u>underground burrows</u>, where temperatures are less <u>extreme</u>. For example, desert tortoises spend around 95% of their time underground.

3) Some bigger animals store <u>fat</u> that they <u>break down</u> into <u>water</u> when needed, e.g. camels' humps.

4) Some animals get water from their food (e.g. cactus mice get water from cactus fruits) and most desert animals minimise their <u>water loss</u> through sweat and <u>urine</u>, e.g. kangaroo rats don't sweat and have very concentrated urine.

Rude.

5) Adaptations to cope with the <u>sand</u> are common, e.g. camels use their <u>triple eyelids</u>, <u>long eyelashes</u> and ability to <u>close</u> their <u>nostrils</u> to keep sand out of their eyes and nose during sandstorms. They also have <u>large</u>, <u>flat feet</u> so they don't <u>sink</u> into the sand.

Biodiversity in Deserts is Threatened

1) Hot deserts have relatively <u>low biodiversity</u>. Small areas around <u>ephemeral</u> (temporary) ponds and rivers or along the <u>desert margins</u> have the highest levels of biodiversity, and contain a high proportion of species that are <u>endemic</u> (unique) to the desert.

2) Areas with <u>water</u> also have the highest density of <u>human populations</u>. People can threaten biodiversity by increasing <u>desertification</u> (see p.33) and by over-using or <u>contaminating</u> water supplies.

3) Development around the desert margins also means that <u>habitats</u> are being <u>divided</u> up by roads. This is <u>threatening</u> animals that <u>migrate</u> over large distances to find food and water, e.g. desert bighorn sheep.

4) <u>Global warming</u> is making hot deserts <u>hotter</u> and <u>drier</u>. This is forcing some species to <u>move</u> to cooler areas. However, species that are already at the <u>limits</u> of their environment don't have anywhere else to go, so are at risk of <u>decline</u> or <u>extinction</u>.

5) Low biodiversity and pressure from development and climate change mean that deserts contain many <u>biodiversity hotspots</u> — places where there are a high proportion of endemic species that are threatened with extinction.

I'm perfectly adapted to my environment — I can use the TV remote...

Well, you'll get your just deserts if you don't learn this page. It's not the trickiest one in the world after all. Think about the good ol' cacti — spiky and waxy with blobby stems. It's all about conserving water in the desert.

Hot Deserts — The Sahara

Right, slap on the sunblock and grab your raddest pair of shades — it's time to head out into a real desert...

There are *Lots of Development Opportunities* in the Sahara...

The Sahara is Earth's largest desert — it covers a USA-sized area, stretching across many north African countries. There are many opportunities for economic development in the Sahara including:

Mineral resources — Morocco is the world's third largest exporter of phosphate, which is used in fertilisers. There are also reserves of iron, copper, lead and silver.

Oil and gas — Algeria is a leader in oil extraction in the Sahara, with around 94% of its exports coming from the oil and gas industries.

Solar energy — Over 12 hours of bright sunlight every day is ideal for generating solar power. A 100 km² solar energy development in Tunisia will be launched between 2018 and 2025, and will supply enough electricity for more than 2.5 million homes.

Tourism — Tourism in the Sahara is small-scale, but many people visit the outskirts, e.g. Marrakesh, Morocco. Popular activities include sandboarding and cross-desert camel treks.

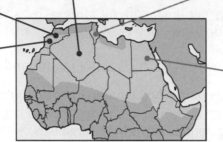

Farming — Water is essential for growing crops (e.g. cotton, corn and rice) so commercial agriculture is only possible with enough irrigation water. E.g. the Aswan Dam provides Egypt with water all year round.

...but there are also *Challenges to Development*

The harsh conditions mean that the Sahara's population is only about 2.5 million. Most people live in small fertile areas, where a water source (e.g. a well) can irrigate the ground to grow crops. Others are nomadic, never staying anywhere for long. Challenges to development include:

Extreme Temperatures

1) Daily temperatures can range from over 40 °C during the day to below freezing at night — exposure to these extreme temperatures can be dangerous.

2) The hot season is often too hot for tourists so employment in the tourism industry can be seasonal.

3) Physical work is difficult at high temperatures, so opportunities like farming and mining can be limited.

Limited Water Supply

1) The Sahara's annual rainfall is low and unpredictable (less than 70 mm in some places) and most rivers only flow for part of the year. Providing enough water for workers, industry and irrigation is challenging.

2) However, some desert resources are so valuable that expensive water pipes are built to help extract them.

3) Deep boreholes extract water stored under the Sahara without replenishing it — this isn't sustainable.

EXAMPLE: Since 1969, mining and agriculture have depleted Morocco's groundwater by 1.5 m a year.

Inaccessibility

1) Providing services, e.g. medical care, is difficult in isolated and remote communities.

2) Extensive pipelines have to be built to transport products, e.g. oil and gas, from remote areas.

3) The Sahara is huge with few roads, so people and materials travel long distances — often by air.

EXAMPLE: It takes 5 days by truck to transport salt from salt mines in Mali out of the desert.

Feelin' hot, hot, hot — and also pretty dry and inaccessible...

Whichever desert you've studied, make sure you have examples of the opportunities and challenges it offers.

Desertification

Deserts have their <u>problems</u> and desertification is a pretty big one. Luckily, there are ways to <u>manage</u> it.

Desertification is Caused by Human and Physical Factors

1) Desertification is the <u>degradation</u> of land, making it <u>drier</u> and <u>less productive</u>.
   A <u>third</u> of the world's land is at <u>risk</u> of desertification, particularly desert <u>margins</u>.

2) Desertification occurs when vegetation dies or is removed. <u>Exposed soil</u> is easily <u>removed</u>
   by wind or water as there are <u>no roots</u> to hold it together. <u>Nutrients</u> in the soil are <u>lost</u>,
   making it <u>unproductive</u>. Eventually the ground becomes sandy, dusty, stony or bare rock.

3) The main <u>causes</u> of desertification are:

Climate Change

1) <u>Rainfall</u> — climate change is expected to <u>reduce</u> rainfall
   in areas that are already <u>dry</u>. Less rain means <u>less water</u>
   is available for plant growth, so more plants <u>die</u>.

2) <u>Temperatures</u> — global temperatures are <u>increasing</u>.
   Higher temperatures cause <u>more</u> water to <u>evaporate</u> from
   the land. This makes soils <u>drier</u>, so plants struggle to grow.

Human Activities

1) <u>Removal of fuel wood</u> — many people in arid (dry) areas rely on <u>wood</u>
   as fuel for cooking. Removal of trees leaves the soil exposed.

2) <u>Overgrazing</u> — too many cattle or sheep eat plants <u>faster</u> than
   they can re-grow. <u>Trampling</u> by animals also erodes the soil.

3) <u>Over-cultivation</u> — if crops are planted in the same area continually, all the <u>nutrients</u>
   in the soil are <u>used up</u>. This means that plants can no longer be grown in those areas.

4) <u>Population growth</u> — more people put more <u>pressure</u> on the land, leading to even
   more <u>deforestation</u> (e.g. for firewood), more <u>overgrazing</u> and more <u>over-cultivation</u>.

The Risk of Desertification Can Be Reduced

There are lots of <u>different strategies</u> for reducing the risk of desertification, for example:

1) **WATER MANAGEMENT** — growing <u>crops</u> that <u>need</u> little water (e.g. millet, sorghum
   or olives) can reduce water use. Using <u>drip irrigation</u> on crops instead of surface
   irrigation means that the soil isn't eroded by lots of water being added all at once.

2) **TREE PLANTING** — trees can be planted to act as <u>windbreaks</u>, reducing <u>wind erosion</u>. Trees can
   also <u>stabilise</u> the sand and <u>prevent</u> desert from <u>encroaching</u> on farm land. Growing trees in <u>amongst</u>
   <u>crops</u> protects them and the soil by providing <u>shade</u>, reducing temperatures and evaporation rates.

3) **SOIL MANAGEMENT** — leaving areas of land to <u>rest</u> in between grazing or planting lets them
   <u>recover</u> their nutrients. <u>Rotating</u> crops that take different nutrients from the soil prevents the same
   nutrients from being continually removed. <u>Compost</u> can be used to add <u>extra</u> nutrients to the soil.

4) **APPROPRIATE TECHNOLOGY** — this involves using <u>cheap</u>, <u>sustainable</u> and <u>easily available</u>
   materials to build things that are easy for <u>local people</u> to maintain. For example, <u>sand fences</u>
   (barriers to trap windblown sand) or <u>terraces</u> can be constructed to <u>stabilise</u> the soil and reduce
   erosion. The rate of deforestation can also be reduced by using <u>solar cookers</u>, which use the <u>sun's</u>
   <u>energy</u> to heat food. They are <u>cheap</u> and <u>easy</u> to make, and don't require fuel wood to work.

EXAM QUESTION

Desertification — what happened when I tried stand-up comedy...

Time to see if you really know this page as well as (deep down inside) you know you should:

1) Explain how climate change can contribute to desertification.   *[4]*

Cold Environments — Polar and Tundra

Woolly hats at the ready — it's time for a foray into the ice cold world of <u>polar</u> and <u>tundra</u> environments...

Polar and Tundra Environments are Found in Cold Climates

Climate

1) Polar areas are very cold, normally <u>below freezing</u>. Winters tend to drop to -40 °C and can reach -90 °C.

2) Tundra areas are also cold. Warm months only reach a maximum of <u>10 °C</u>, while winters can plunge to <u>-50 °C</u>.

3) Precipitation is <u>low</u> — less than 100 mm a year in polar areas and less than 380 mm in tundra areas.

4) The <u>seasons</u> are well <u>defined</u> in both environments — cold summers and even colder winters.

Antarctica

Alaskan tundra

Soil

1) <u>Ice sheets</u> cover polar areas, so no soil is exposed.

2) Tundra soil is <u>thin</u>, <u>acidic</u> and not very <u>fertile</u>.

3) Beneath the thin soil is a layer of <u>permafrost</u> (frozen ground), holding trapped <u>greenhouse gases</u>.

© iStock.com / SeppFriedhuber

Plants

1) Polar areas have few plants — <u>lichens</u> and <u>mosses</u> grow on rocks, and <u>grasses</u> grow on the coast.

2) In tundra areas, hardy <u>shrubs</u> (e.g. bearberry), grasses, mosses and lichens are common. Small, <u>short</u> trees may grow in <u>warmer</u> areas.

Animals

1) There are relatively <u>few species</u> in these ecosystems.

2) Polar bears, penguins, whales and seals are found in <u>polar</u> areas.

3) Lemmings, wolves and reindeer live in <u>tundra</u> areas.

© Juniors Bildarchiv GmbH / Alamy Stock Photo

Lemming

People

1) Polar areas are mostly <u>uninhabited</u>, but the Arctic has some indigenous residents and a few scientists work in Antarctica.

2) Tundra areas are home to many <u>indigenous</u> people, as well as oil and gas <u>workers</u> in larger <u>towns</u>.

Cold Environments are Fragile, Interdependent Ecosystems

1) The <u>biotic</u> (living) components of cold environments (plants, animals, people) and the <u>abiotic</u> (non-living) components (climate, soils, permafrost) are <u>closely related</u> — many of them are dependent on each other:

- The cold climate causes plants to grow slowly and to decompose <u>slowly</u> when they die, so <u>plant cover</u> is <u>low</u>. This means that the soil is relatively low in <u>nutrients</u>, further limiting plant growth.

- <u>Herbivores</u> (e.g. reindeer) that rely on plants (e.g. mosses) to survive must <u>migrate</u> to areas where plants are able to grow. <u>Carnivores</u> (e.g. wolves) have to <u>follow</u> the herbivores.

- In <u>summer</u>, when the tundra has greater plant cover, the surface plants absorb <u>heat</u> from the sun, preventing the <u>permafrost</u> below from <u>thawing</u>. The permafrost provides <u>water</u> for plants.

2) <u>Changes</u> to one component of the ecosystem can have knock-on effects on the <u>whole</u> ecosystem:

If <u>humans</u> trample lots of plants, the soil is exposed to sunlight and warms up. This may thaw the permafrost, <u>saturating</u> soil and preventing plant growth. With fewer plants to eat, animals will struggle to find enough food to survive. Melting permafrost also releases <u>greenhouse gases</u>, which contribute to <u>global warming</u>.

Cold, acidic and full of gas — permafrost sounds like my Uncle Tony...

Icy you there... reading this page. Don't forget to take plenty of breaks — revising is easier when you're chilled.

Cold Environments — Adaptations

Cold environments are pretty tricky to survive in — even well-equipped polar explorers can get it wrong. Plants and animals have some nifty tricks to survive, which you can read about from your nice warm chair...

The Plants and Animals have Adapted to the Cold, Dry Climate

Plants in tundra environments have adapted to survive the extreme cold and strong winds. They must also endure the dry winter conditions when all moisture is frozen, and wet summer conditions when the top layer of soil thaws and the ground becomes boggy and waterlogged.

1) Most plants become dormant (inactive) to survive the cold, dark winters.

2) Plants are low-growing and round-shaped to provide protection from the wind.

3) Most plants have shallow roots because of the layer of permafrost beneath the soil layer.

4) Leaves are generally small to limit the amount of moisture lost through transpiration.

5) The warmer, wetter summer is very short, so most plants have adapted to have a growing season of just 50-60 days.

6) Many plants reproduce using underground runners or bulbs to cope with the cold and because the growing season is short.

Tundra vegetation

Animals in cold environments have also adapted to the cold, dry, snowy conditions:

1) Animals in cold environments tend to be well-insulated — they might have thick fur like polar bears or a layer of blubber like seals. This reduces the amount of energy they have to use to keep warm.

2) Some animals hibernate to conserve energy and survive the winter, e.g. Arctic ground squirrels hibernate for 7-8 months of the year and can survive even if their body temperature drops below freezing.

3) Animals that don't hibernate have adapted to survive on the limited food sources available, e.g. reindeer eat lichens during the winter.

4) Many birds migrate to warmer areas for the winter, e.g. Arctic terns live in the Arctic during the northern hemisphere summer, then fly to the Antarctic for the southern hemisphere summer.

5) Many animals grow white winter coats for camouflage — this helps predators to sneak up on their prey, and helps prey to hide in the snow, e.g. some weasels (also called ermine), Arctic foxes and Arctic hares.

An Arctic tern

An Arctic hare, camouflaged (and cute)

Cold Environments have Low Biodiversity

1) Cold environments have very low biodiversity (particularly Antarctica) — there are fewer species of plants and animals in cold environments than most other environments.

2) Low biodiversity means when the population of one species changes it can affect the population of dependent species — e.g. changes to the lemming population will affect the populations of their predators, e.g. Arctic foxes.

3) Global warming is causing some species to move towards the poles, where it is colder, in response to temperature rises in their natural habitat. Species already adapted to polar environments can't go anywhere colder, so are at risk of decline or extinction if climate change causes the polar areas to warm up too much.

Now I'm in my thirties, I'm finding more Arctic hairs every day...

I know it's tempting to hibernate until your exams are over, but a cooler idea (not sorry) is to do a smashing job of learning how plants and animals adapt to their conditions, and why biodiversity is low in cold environments.

Cold Environments — Alaska

Alaska is one example of a cold environment where the extreme climate creates challenges to development.

There are Development Opportunities in Alaska...

Alaska is a cold environment that's part of the USA. Northern Alaska is inside the Arctic circle. Opportunities for economic development include:

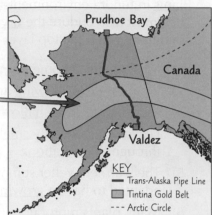

1) Energy — over half Alaska's income comes from the oil and gas industry. Most oil fields are around Prudhoe Bay, which is linked to Valdez by the Trans-Alaska oil pipeline so that oil can be shipped to customers.

2) Mineral resources — materials such as gold, silver, iron ore and copper are all mined in Alaska, particularly in the Tintina gold belt. In 2015, $154 million worth of gold was exported from Alaska.

3) Fishing — In 2016, Alaska's fishing industry had a value of $1.7 billion and employed almost 30 000 fishermen (e.g. of salmon, cod and crab).

4) Tourism — tourists are attracted by Alaska's scenic wilderness areas. Each year, around 2 million tourists visit Alaska, bringing in almost $2.5 billion and generating employment for about 39 000 people.

KEY
— Trans-Alaska Pipe Line
▨ Tintina Gold Belt
--- Arctic Circle

...but there are also Challenges to Development

1) Alaska's state population is one of the smallest in the US, despite being the largest state by area. Most people live on the state's southern and south-eastern coastline where it is warmer and less remote.

2) It's difficult to access resources and find a workforce in Alaska because of the extreme conditions, remote location and poor infrastructure. These factors make development very challenging:

Extreme Temperature

1) It's really cold — Prudhoe Bay's mean annual temperature is about −9 °C and extreme weather, such as snow and strong winds, is common. Exposure to extreme cold makes working outside dangerous, so opportunities for development are limited.

2) Daylight hours vary a lot — Barrow, north Alaska, is in darkness for up to 67 days in the winter, but in the summer it might see 80 warmer days of uninterrupted sunlight.

Inaccessibility

1) Alaska is a long way from the rest of the US. Some areas are extremely remote, and the mountainous terrain makes access difficult and expensive, limiting development.

2) In winter, the only way to get to some towns is via expensive air travel or dangerous ice roads. In summer, there are no roads to some towns because the ground is too soft.

3) The population of Alaska is small and scattered — people in small towns may be a long way from employment opportunities or services.

Buildings and Infrastructure

1) Providing buildings and infrastructure to cope with either soft or frozen ground and extreme weather is difficult and expensive.

2) Most construction work can only take place in summer, when the days are longer and temperatures are warmer.

3) The value of some resources means that people find ways to overcome the challenges, e.g. some parts of the Trans-Alaska oil pipeline are raised on stilts to prevent it melting the permafrost, which would make the ground unstable.

I tried a gold belt once — not my best look...

Cold environments can be challenging — it's what you get when you combine a beautiful, frozen wilderness with some jolly useful development opportunities. Now get learning. Examiners might ask you about this...

Cold Environments — Sustainable Management

Cold environments are <u>fragile</u> areas that need to be <u>sustainably managed</u> to protect them from damage.

Cold Environments are Valuable Wilderness Areas Worth Conserving

Large parts of cold environments are <u>wilderness areas</u> — wild, natural environments that are mostly <u>undeveloped</u>, <u>uninhabited</u> and <u>undisturbed</u>, e.g. Denali Park, Alaska.

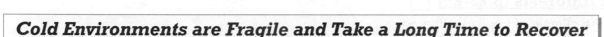

It is important to conserve wilderness areas in cold environments because:

1) They provide <u>habitats</u> for organisms that couldn't survive elsewhere.

2) Scientists can study <u>natural</u> environments including <u>landforms</u>, <u>plants</u> and <u>animals</u> that are relatively <u>unaffected</u> by people — this provides valuable knowledge about fragile ecosystems.

3) Studying natural ecosystems may help scientists to <u>replicate</u> the same conditions in managed ecosystems. This can help <u>preserve</u> rare <u>species</u> outside the protected areas.

Cold Environments are Fragile and Take a Long Time to Recover

Cold environments are extremely <u>fragile</u> — it can take <u>centuries</u> for them to return to their original state after human <u>interference</u>. This is because:

1) Plant growth is <u>slow</u> — if plants are <u>damaged</u> (e.g. by vehicle tyres), <u>regrowth</u> takes time.

2) Species are highly <u>specialised</u>, so find it difficult to <u>adapt</u> to change. E.g. polar bears are adapted to hunt on <u>ice</u> — their numbers are <u>decreasing</u> as sea ice <u>melts</u> earlier each year.

Strategies are Needed to Balance Economic Development with Conservation

International Agreements

1) Some cold environments are <u>protected</u> by <u>international agreements</u>, e.g. Antarctica.

2) The <u>1959 Antarctic Treaty</u>, signed by 12 nations, <u>limits visitors</u> to 100 per site, ensures peaceful non-military activities, prohibits nuclear activities and prevents cruise ships with over 500 passengers from stopping.

3) This <u>allows</u> tourism, but in a controlled way that <u>won't harm</u> the fragile ecosystem.

Conservation Groups

1) Conservation groups, e.g. Greenpeace and the WWF, <u>pressure</u> governments to <u>protect</u> cold environments.

2) This can lead to more <u>sustainable development</u> that doesn't damage at-risk areas.

Using Technology

1) Development can cause problems. E.g. heated buildings can melt <u>permafrost</u>, leading to <u>subsidence</u> which may cause buildings to <u>collapse</u> and pipes to <u>crack</u>.

2) However, modern construction methods can <u>minimise</u> environmental <u>impacts</u>, e.g. by building on <u>gravel beds</u> to prevent buildings <u>warming</u> the ground.

The Role of Governments

1) <u>Unregulated</u> development can <u>damage</u> the <u>environment</u>, e.g. <u>mining</u> can <u>pollute</u> water and <u>oil pipelines</u> can disrupt animal migration.

2) Governments can pass <u>laws</u>, such as the <u>1964 Wilderness Act</u>, to protect designated wilderness areas (e.g. much of Alaska) from development. This means that development has to take place <u>elsewhere</u>, reducing <u>conflict</u> over land use in wilderness areas.

EXAM QUESTION

No space for ice cream — a worrying development in my freezer...

Here's a lovely question to help you on your way to the next page:

1) Suggest one way that cold environments can be developed with conservation in mind. [2]

Revision Summary

What a world — I feel pretty alive right now, let me tell you. Now's the time to check you've got everything you need to know about the living world learnt, and I've got just the thing to help you — a page of summary questions. If you get stuck, all the answers are in this book — so go back and learn that bit again.

Remember that you only need to learn <u>one</u> out of Hot Deserts and Cold Environments for the exam.

Ecosystems (p.20-22) ☑

1) What is an ecosystem?
2) Give two abiotic features of ecosystems.
3) What is a producer?
4) Describe the role of decomposers in ecosystems.
5) Where are temperate deciduous forests found?
6) What type of ecosystem is nearly always found between the Tropics of Cancer and Capricorn?

Tropical Rainforests (p.23-29) ☐

7) Describe the climate of tropical rainforests.
8) What is biodiversity?
9) Give an example of an interdependent relationship in the tropical rainforest ecosystem.
10) Describe one way that humans are interfering with interdependent relationships in tropical rainforests.
11) Describe two adaptations of plants and two adaptations of animals in tropical rainforests.
12) Give six causes of deforestation in tropical rainforests.
13) a) Give an example of a tropical rainforest.
    b) Describe the environmental impacts of deforestation in that rainforest.
14) How is the global rate of deforestation changing?
15) Why is it important to protect tropical rainforests?
16) What is selective logging?
17) Explain how reducing debt can be used in the sustainable management of tropical rainforests.
18) How do international hardwood agreements help in the sustainable management of tropical rainforests?

Hot Deserts (p.30-33) ☑

19) Describe the climate in hot deserts.
20) What is the soil like in hot deserts?
21) Give two adaptations of plants to hot desert environments.
22) Give two adaptations of animals to hot desert environments.
23) Describe one issue related to biodiversity in hot deserts.
24) Describe how inaccessibility can make development challenging in hot desert environments.
25) Explain how tree planting can reduce the risk of desertification.
26) Give one strategy, other than tree planting, that can reduce the risk of desertification.

Cold Environments (p.34-37) ☑

27) Describe the climate of cold environments.
28) Name two differences between polar and tundra environments.
29) Give two adaptations of plants to cold environments.
30) Give two adaptations of animals to cold environments.
31) Describe one issue related to biodiversity in cold environments.
32) How can inaccessibility make development challenging in a cold environment?
33) Why are wilderness areas worth protecting?
34) Name two ways that economic development and conservation can be balanced in cold environments.

The UK Physical Landscape

Ah, the UK landscape. Majestic <u>mountains</u>, cracking <u>coasts</u> and raging <u>rivers</u> — I could go on all day...

The UK has large Upland and Lowland Areas, and Important Rivers

1) The UK's main <u>upland</u> areas (orange and red on the map below) tend to be in the <u>north</u> and <u>west</u> of the country. These areas (e.g. the Scottish Highlands and northern Wales) are formed of hard, <u>igneous</u> (e.g. granite) and <u>metamorphic</u> (e.g. slate and schist) rocks that are resistant to erosion.

2) The UK's main <u>lowland</u> areas (green on the map) to the <u>south</u> and <u>east</u>, are formed of softer, <u>sedimentary</u> rocks (e.g. chalk and clays) that erode more easily.

3) Most <u>cities</u> are in <u>lowland</u> areas and often on the UK's main <u>rivers</u> — such as London (on the Thames), Liverpool (on the Mersey) and Cardiff (on the Severn Estuary).

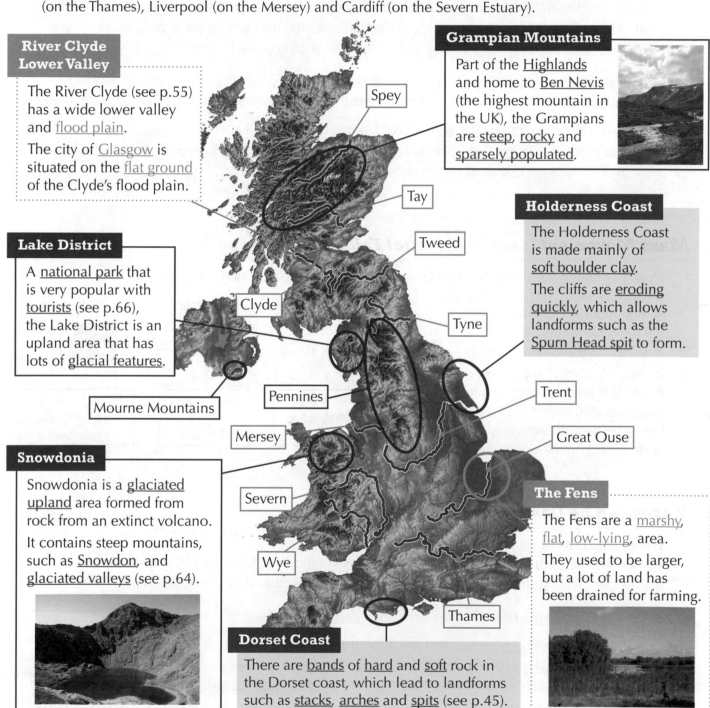

River Clyde Lower Valley

The River Clyde (see p.55) has a wide lower valley and <u>flood plain</u>.

The city of <u>Glasgow</u> is situated on the <u>flat ground</u> of the Clyde's flood plain.

Grampian Mountains

Part of the <u>Highlands</u> and home to <u>Ben Nevis</u> (the highest mountain in the UK), the Grampians are <u>steep</u>, <u>rocky</u> and <u>sparsely populated</u>.

Lake District

A <u>national park</u> that is very popular with <u>tourists</u> (see p.66), the Lake District is an upland area that has lots of <u>glacial features</u>.

Holderness Coast

The Holderness Coast is made mainly of <u>soft boulder clay</u>.

The cliffs are <u>eroding quickly</u>, which allows landforms such as the <u>Spurn Head spit</u> to form.

Snowdonia

Snowdonia is a <u>glaciated upland</u> area formed from rock from an extinct volcano.

It contains steep mountains, such as <u>Snowdon</u>, and <u>glaciated valleys</u> (see p.64).

The Fens

The Fens are a <u>marshy</u>, <u>flat</u>, <u>low-lying</u>, area.

They used to be larger, but a lot of land has been drained for farming.

Dorset Coast

There are <u>bands</u> of <u>hard</u> and <u>soft</u> rock in the Dorset coast, which lead to landforms such as <u>stacks</u>, <u>arches</u> and <u>spits</u> (see p.45).

Map labels: Spey, Tay, Tweed, Clyde, Tyne, Pennines, Mourne Mountains, Mersey, Severn, Wye, Trent, Great Ouse, Thames

I think you'll find the UK physical portrait is much easier to fit on a page...

This is a lovely little introduction to the rest of the UK physical landscapes section. You can actually revise it by looking through your holiday snaps or out the window on a long journey. Or by gazing at a lovely map...

Coastal Processes

Weathering is the breakdown of rocks in situ (where they are), and erosion is when rocks are broken down and carried away by something, e.g. by seawater. Poor coastal zone, I bet it's worn down.

Rock is Broken Down by Mechanical and Chemical Weathering

1) Mechanical weathering is the breakdown of rock without changing its chemical composition.
   One type of mechanical weathering that affects coasts is freeze-thaw weathering:

> 1) It happens when the temperature alternates above and below 0 °C (the freezing point of water).
> 2) Water enters rock that has cracks, e.g. granite.
> 3) When the water freezes it expands, which puts pressure on the rock.
> 4) When the water thaws it contracts, which releases the pressure on the rock.
> 5) Repeated freezing and thawing widens the cracks and causes the rock to break up.

2) Chemical weathering is the breakdown of rock by changing its chemical composition.
   Carbonation weathering is a type of chemical weathering that happens in warm and wet conditions:

> 1) Rainwater has carbon dioxide dissolved in it, which makes it a weak carbonic acid.
> 2) Carbonic acid reacts with rock that contains calcium carbonate, e.g. carboniferous limestone, so the rocks are dissolved by the rainwater.

Mass Movement is when Material Falls Down a Slope

1) Mass movement is the shifting of rocks and loose material down a slope, e.g. a cliff.
   It happens when the force of gravity acting on a slope is greater than the force supporting it.

2) It causes coasts to retreat rapidly.

3) It's more likely to happen when the material is full of water — water acts as a lubricant, and makes the material heavier.

4) When material shifts, it can create a scarp (a steep 'cut' in the side of the slope).

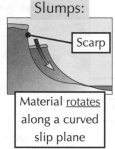

Slides:

Material shifts in a straight line along a slide plane

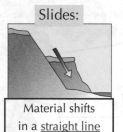

Slumps:

Scarp

Material rotates along a curved slip plane

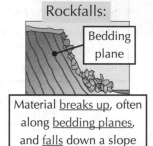

Rockfalls:

Bedding plane

Material breaks up, often along bedding planes, and falls down a slope

Waves can be Destructive or Constructive

There's more about processes of erosion and deposition on the next page.

1) When wind blows over the surface of the sea, it creates waves.
   The greater the fetch (the distance the wind blows over the sea), the more powerful the wave.

2) Storms can create storm surges — temporary sea level rises caused as strong winds push water onshore.

Some waves erode the coast — these are called destructive waves:

- They have a high frequency, and are high and steep.
- Their backwash (water moving down the beach) is more powerful than their swash (water moving up the beach), so material is removed.

Some waves deposit material — these are called constructive waves:

- Constructive waves have a low frequency, and are low and long.
- Their swash is more powerful than the backwash, so material is deposited.

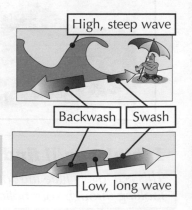

High, steep wave

Backwash   Swash

Low, long wave

Coastal Processes

Waves Wear Away the Coast Using Three Processes of Erosion

Erosion occurs when waves hit the shore:

1) Hydraulic power — waves crash against rock and compress the air in the cracks. This puts pressure on the rock. Repeated compression widens the cracks and causes bits of rock to break off.

2) Abrasion — eroded particles in the water scrape and rub against rock, removing small pieces.

3) Attrition — eroded particles in the water collide, break into smaller pieces and become more rounded.

Material is Transported Along the Coast by Longshore Drift

1) Waves follow the direction of the prevailing (most common) wind.

2) They usually hit the coast at an oblique angle (any angle that isn't a right angle).

3) The swash carries material up the beach, in the same direction as the waves.

4) The backwash then carries material down the beach at right angles, back towards the sea.

5) Over time, material zigzags along the coast.

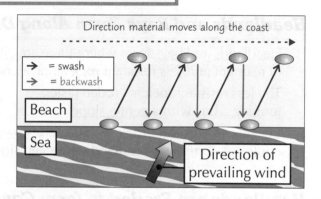

Direction material moves along the coast

→ = swash
→ = backwash

Beach

Sea

Direction of prevailing wind

There are Four Other Processes of Transportation

How material is transported depends on how powerful the movement of water is and the size of the particles:

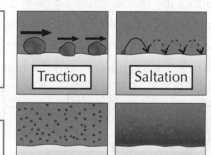

Traction — large particles like boulders are pushed along the sea bed by the force of the water.

Traction

Saltation

Saltation — pebble-sized particles are bounced along the sea bed by the force of the water.

Suspension — small particles like silt and clay are carried along in the water.

Suspension

Solution

Solution — soluble materials (e.g. limestone) dissolve in the water and are carried along.

Deposition is the Dropping of Material

1) Deposition occurs when water carrying sediment loses energy and slows down.

2) Coasts build up when the amount of deposition is greater than the amount of erosion.

3) The amount of material that's deposited on an area of coast is increased when:

- There's lots of erosion elsewhere on the coast (so more material is available).
- Lots of material is transported into the area.

4) Constructive waves drop more material than they remove — there's more deposition than erosion.

Depositing material on a beach? Sounds like littering to me.

To get a feel for how material moves along the coast, you could try drawing your own longshore drift diagram.

Unit 1C — Coastal Landscapes in the UK

Coastal Landforms

Don't let your concentration wash away just yet — have a read about some <u>erosional landforms</u> first...

Coastlines can be Concordant or Discordant

1) Rock type and <u>geological structure</u> influence the <u>erosional landforms</u> that develop on a coastline:
   - <u>Hard</u> rocks like granite take a long time to erode, while <u>softer</u> rocks like sandstone erode more quickly.
   - Rocks with lots of <u>joints</u> and <u>faults</u> (cracks and <u>weaknesses</u> in the rock) erode faster.
2) <u>Discordant coastlines</u> are made up of alternating bands of hard and soft rock at right angles to the coast.
3) On a <u>concordant coastline</u>, the alternating bands of hard and soft rock are <u>parallel</u> to the coast.

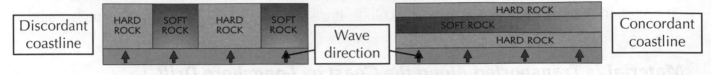

Headlands and Bays Form Along Discordant Coastlines

1) <u>Headlands</u> and <u>bays</u> form where there are <u>alternating bands</u> of resistant and less resistant rock along a coast.
2) The less resistant rock is eroded <u>faster</u>, forming a bay with a <u>gentle slope</u>.
3) Because the resistant rock erodes more <u>slowly</u>, it <u>juts</u> out, forming a headland with <u>steep sides</u>.

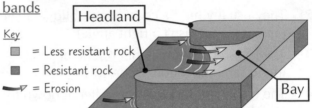

Key
 = Less resistant rock
 = Resistant rock
 = Erosion

Headlands are Eroded to form Caves, Arches and Stacks

1) The <u>resistant rock</u> that makes up headlands often has <u>weaknesses</u> like cracks.
2) <u>Waves</u> crash into the headlands and <u>enlarge</u> the cracks (mainly by <u>hydraulic power</u> and <u>abrasion</u>).
3) Repeated <u>erosion</u> and enlargement of the cracks causes a <u>cave</u> to form.
4) Continued erosion <u>deepens</u> the cave until it breaks through the headland to form an <u>arch</u>, e.g. Durdle Door.
5) Erosion continues to wear away the rock supporting the arch, until it eventually <u>collapses</u>.
6) This forms a <u>stack</u> — an isolated rock that's <u>separate</u> from the headland, e.g. Old Harry in Dorset.

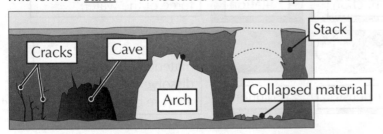

Durdle Door, Dorset

Waves Erode Cliffs to Form Wave-cut Platforms

1) Waves cause <u>most erosion</u> at the <u>foot</u> of a cliff, forming a <u>wave-cut notch</u> which is enlarged over time.
2) <u>Repeated erosion</u> causes the rock above the notch to become <u>unstable</u> and it eventually <u>collapses</u>.
3) The collapsed material is <u>washed away</u> and a new wave-cut notch starts to form.
4) After repeated collapses the cliff <u>retreats</u>, leaving a <u>wave-cut platform</u>, e.g. Southerndown, South Wales.

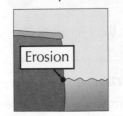
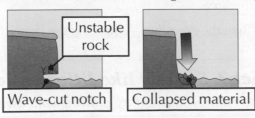
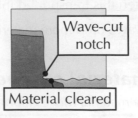
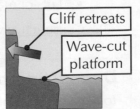

Coastal Landforms

Here are some more exciting landforms for you to learn about. This time it's all about deposition.
Unfortunately you're going to be slightly disappointed — sandcastles won't be in the exam.

Beaches are formed by Deposition

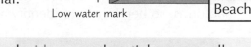

1) Beaches are found on coasts between the high and low water marks.
2) They're formed by constructive waves (see p.40) depositing material.
3) Sand and shingle beaches form in different ways:

- Sand beaches are created by low energy waves and are flat and wide — sand particles are small so the weak backwash can move them back down the beach, creating a long, gentle slope.
- Shingle beaches are created by high energy waves and are steep and narrow — sand particles are washed away but larger shingle is left behind. The shingle particles build up to create a steep slope.

Deposited Sediment also forms Spits, Bars and Sand Dunes

Spits

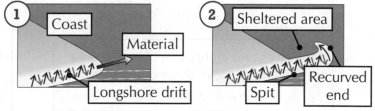

1) Spits form at sharp bends in the coastline, e.g. at a river mouth.
2) Longshore drift transports sand and shingle past the bend and deposits it in the sea.
3) Strong winds and waves can curve the end of the spit (forming a recurved end).
4) The area behind the spit is sheltered from waves, so material accumulates and plants are able to grow.
5) Over time, the sheltered area can become a mud flat or a salt marsh, e.g. Welwick Saltmarsh, Yorkshire.

Bars

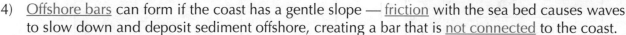

1) A bar forms when a spit joins two headlands together.
2) The bay between the headlands gets cut off from the sea.
3) This means a lagoon can form behind the bar.
4) Offshore bars can form if the coast has a gentle slope — friction with the sea bed causes waves to slow down and deposit sediment offshore, creating a bar that is not connected to the coast.

Sand Dunes

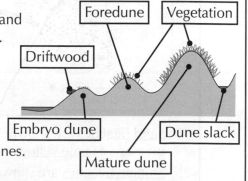

1) Sand dunes (e.g. Camber Sands, East Sussex) are formed when sand deposited by longshore drift is moved up the beach by the wind.
2) Obstacles (e.g. driftwood) cause wind speed to decrease so sand is deposited, forming small embryo dunes.
3) Embryo dunes are colonised by plants, e.g. Marram grass. The roots of the vegetation stabilise the sand, encouraging more sand to accumulate there. This forms foredunes and, eventually, mature dunes. New embryo dunes form in front of stabilised dunes.
4) Dune slacks (small pools) can form in hollows between dunes.

Depositional bars — they serve a delicious long beach iced tea...

Spits in geography have a very specific meaning. Don't get the wrong one and mess up your exam.

1) Explain how bars are formed. You may include a diagram in your answer. [2]

Identifying Coastal Landforms

I love <u>maps</u>, all geographers love maps. I can't get to sleep unless I've got one under my pillow. So I'm going to do you a favour and share my passion with you — check out these <u>coastal landforms</u>...

Identifying Landforms Caused by Erosion

You might be asked to <u>identify</u> coastal landforms on a <u>map</u> in the exam. The simplest thing they could ask is whether the map is showing erosional or depositional landforms, so here's how to identify a few <u>erosional landforms</u> to get you started:

Have a gander at pages 129-130 for more on reading maps.

Caves, Arches and Stacks

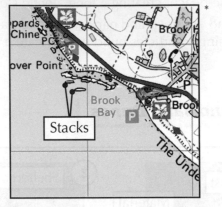

1) <u>Caves</u> and <u>arches</u> can't be seen on a map because of the rock above them.
2) <u>Stacks</u> look like <u>little blobs</u> in the sea.

Cliffs and Wave-cut Platforms

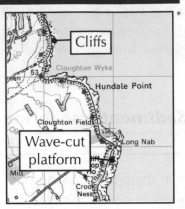

1) <u>Cliffs</u> (and other steep slopes) are shown on maps as little <u>black lines</u>.
2) <u>Wave-cut platforms</u> are shown as <u>bumpy edges</u> along the coast.

I don't need no map...

Identifying Landforms Caused by Deposition

Identifying <u>depositional landforms</u> is easy once you know that beaches are shown in yellow on maps. Here's how to identify a couple of depositional landforms:

Beaches

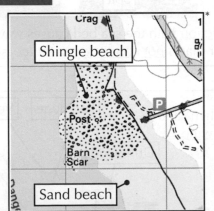

1) <u>Sand beaches</u> are shown on maps as <u>pale yellow</u>.
2) <u>Shingle beaches</u> are shown as white or yellow with <u>speckles</u>.

Spits

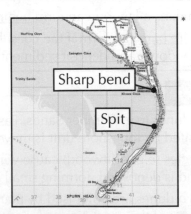

1) <u>Spits</u> are shown by a beach that carries on <u>out to sea</u>, but is still attached to the land at one end.
2) There might also be a <u>sharp bend</u> in the coast that caused it to form (see p.43).

Find the spit on the map — and then wipe it off...

There are some seriously easy marks up for grabs with map questions so make sure you learn this page. You could practise looking for landforms on any maps you can find, though you might struggle with the Tube map.

Coastal Landscape — Dorset

If coastal landforms are your thing (and let's face it, how could they not be), then the Dorset coast is paradise on Earth. It's got the lot — headlands, bays, arches, stacks, coves, lagoons...

The Dorset Coast has Examples of many Coastal Landforms

The Dorset coast is made from bands of hard rock (like limestone and chalk) and soft rock (like clay). The rocks have been eroded at different rates, giving headlands, bays and lots of other exciting landforms.

Durdle Door

Durdle Door is a great example of an arch. It formed on a concordant coastline (see page 42), after a band of limestone was mostly eroded. As the band of softer rock behind this eroded quickly, the remaining limestone formed a headland. Wave action opened up a crack in the side of the headland, which developed into an arch.

Lulworth Cove

Lulworth Cove is a small bay formed after a gap was eroded in a band of limestone. Behind the limestone is a band of clay, which has been eroded to form the bay. The same is now starting to happen at Stair Hole further west along the coast.

Key: ▢ Clay and sandstone ▢ Chalk ▢ Limestone ▢ Clay ▢ Mudstone

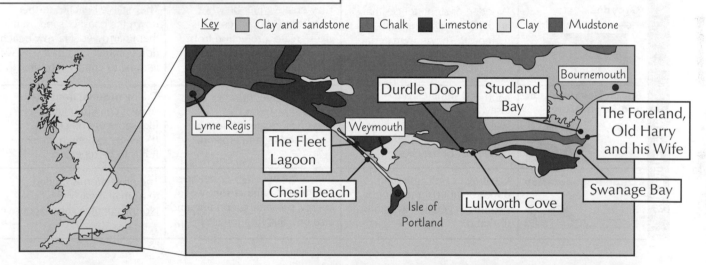

Chesil Beach

Chesil Beach is a tombolo (a type of bar) formed by longshore drift. It joins the Isle of Portland to the mainland. Behind Chesil Beach is a shallow lagoon called The Fleet Lagoon.

Swanage Bay, The Foreland and Studland Bay

Swanage Bay, Studland Bay and The Foreland all formed on a discordant coastline. The two bays formed in areas of soft rock (clay and sandstone). In between them, The Foreland is a headland made from a band of harder rock (chalk). The end of the headland has eroded to become a stack called Old Harry and a stump (a collapsed stack) called Old Harry's Wife.

I heard Chesil Beach was actually formed by some bored sculptors...

That's actually Old Harry's second wife. His first wife collapsed into the sea in 1896. It was sad, but she would've wanted him to move on. Before you move on, learn the names of the landforms of the Dorset coast.

Coastal Management Strategies

The aim of coastal management is to protect people and the environment from the impacts of erosion and flooding. Not all coastal areas can be managed though — the amount of money available is limited.

Coastal Defences Include Hard and Soft Engineering

Hard Engineering

Man-made structures built to control the flow of the sea and reduce flooding and erosion.

Soft Engineering

Schemes set up using knowledge of the sea and its processes to reduce the effects of flooding and erosion.

	Defence	What it is	Benefits	Costs
Hard Engineering	**Sea Wall**	A wall made out of a hard material like concrete that reflects waves back to sea.	It prevents erosion of the coast. It also acts as a barrier to prevent flooding.	It creates a strong backwash that erodes under the wall. Expensive to build and maintain.
	Gabions	A wall of wire cages filled with rocks, usually built at the foot of cliffs.	Gabions absorb wave energy and so reduce erosion. They're cheap and easy to build.	They're ugly to look at and the wire cages can corrode over time.
	Rock Armour	Boulders that are piled up along the coast. (It's also sometimes called rip-rap.)	It absorbs wave energy, reducing erosion and flooding. It's a fairly cheap defence.	Boulders can be moved around by strong waves, so they need to be replaced.
	Groynes ←— longshore drift	Wooden or stone fences that are built at right angles to the coast. They trap material transported by longshore drift.	They create wider beaches which slow the waves. This gives greater protection from flooding and erosion. They're a fairly cheap defence.	They starve beaches further down the coast of sand, making them narrower. Narrow beaches don't protect the coast very well, leading to greater erosion.
Soft Engineering	**Beach Nourishment and Reprofiling**	Sand and shingle from elsewhere (e.g. from the seabed) or from lower down the beach that's added to the upper part of beaches.	It creates wider beaches which slow the waves. This gives greater protection from flooding and erosion.	Taking material from the seabed can kill organisms like sponges and corals. It's a very expensive defence. It has to be repeated.
	Dune Regeneration	Creating or restoring sand dunes by nourishment, or by planting vegetation to stabilise the sand.	Dunes create a barrier between land and sea and absorb wave energy, preventing flooding and erosion. Stabilisation is cheap.	The protection is limited to a small area. Nourishment is very expensive.

Another Option is to just do Nothing — Managed Retreat

1) Managed retreat involves removing current defences and allowing the sea to flood the land behind.

2) Over time the land will become marshland, which then protects the land behind it from flooding and erosion.

3) It is a cheap and easy strategy, and it doesn't need maintaining. The marshland can also create new habitats for plants and animals.

4) However, it can cause conflicts, e.g. flooding farmland affects the livelihood of farmers and saltwater can have a negative effect on existing ecosystems.

5) Managed retreat was carried out at Alkborough Flats, Lincolnshire. A 20-metre-wide breach was created in the flood wall to allow water to flow inland. The area provides a habitat for many bird and fish species, and helps protect 400 000 homes from floods.

Breach in old defences

New marshland

Managed Retreat — "Going forward, we're going backwards..."

It seems like a lot to remember, but I promise you, it's really not that tough. Make sure you know at least a couple of benefits and costs for each hard and soft engineering strategy and you'll be a winner in the exam.

Coastal Management — Lyme Regis

Lyme Regis is a historic town in Dorset, southwest England. The coast there has been managed for many years.

The Cliffs of Lyme Regis need Protecting from Erosion

1) Powerful waves from the south west erode the sea cliffs, causing them to collapse. In May 2008, about 400m of cliff slipped between Lyme Regis and Charmouth.

2) Much of the town's eastern side is built along the edge of the cliffs, and many properties have been damaged by landslides, slumps and waves breaching the sea walls.

3) Around 1 km of the coastline at Lyme Regis is managed using hard engineering strategies because:

- Lyme Regis has a population of over 3600 people, and around 500 000 tourists visit each year.
- Around 900 m of the A3052 road, which links Lyme Regis to other towns along the coast, would have been lost within 50 years.
- The local economy depends on tourism (about £42 million was spent by tourists in 2015), but erosion of the coast could threaten the historic town centre and the tourism industry.

Parts of Lyme Regis are Protected by Sea Walls and Rock Armour

In the 1990s, West Dorset District Council began a scheme to provide long-term protection for the town:

1) Phase I (completed 1995) involved building new rock armour on the eastern end of the sea front.

2) Phase II (completed 2007) protected the front of the main town — the sand and shingle beaches were replenished and stabilised, existing rock armour was extended (Beacon Rocks) and realigned (North Wall Rockery), and drainage systems were improved (to reduce water build up and prevent landslides). It cost £26 million.

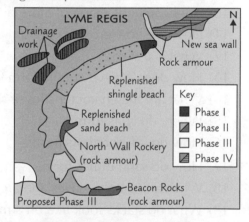

3) Phase III was meant to prevent landslides to the west of Lyme Regis, but was never carried out — it wasn't worth the high cost.

4) Phase IV (completed 2015) cost £19.5 million. It included 390 m of sea walls and rock armour, and protects roads into the town.

The Defences Protect Lyme Regis... but Have Still Caused Conflicts

The coastal management scheme was successful — the town of Lyme Regis is now much better protected. As well as the positive outcomes, the management strategy also resulted in some conflicts:

Positive Effects	Conflicts
It's thought the improved beaches have increased trade by up to 20% in some parts of the town.	Greater numbers of tourists mean that there's more traffic, litter and noise pollution.
The rock armour absorbs the energy of the powerful waves, protecting the harbour and the boats inside.	Important fossils have been found in the area, but the defences stop new fossils from being exposed.
People feel more secure buying property in Lyme Regis — the new defences have made it easier to insure houses against coastal erosion and landslides.	Some residents think it was very expensive for a relatively short-term solution, as the defences could need rebuilding in around 60 years' time.

Rock armour — more use protecting beaches than in jousting matches...

Managing coasts is a time-consuming business. The Lyme Regis scheme started more than 20 years ago and has only recently 'finished' (and it'll need ongoing work). And you thought that GCSEs took ages...

Revision Summary

So, you've coasted through another topic — that means it's time to find out just how much of this information has been deposited in your noggin. Have a go at the questions below. If you're finding it tough, just look back at the pages in the topic and then have another go. You'll be ready to move on when you can answer all of these questions without breaking into a sweat.

Remember, you only need to learn two from Coastal, River and Glacial Landscapes in the UK, so if you're not a coasts sort of a person, you don't need to answer these question — you can go straight onto rivers instead.

Coastal Processes (p. 40-41) ☑

1) How does freeze-thaw weathering break up rock?
2) Describe a process of chemical weathering.
3) What are the three types of mass movement?
4) Give the characteristics of destructive waves.
5) What are the characteristics of constructive waves?
6) What are the three types of erosion caused by waves? Explain how they work.
7) How does longshore drift transport sediment along a coast?
8) Apart from longshore drift, what are the four other processes of transport?
9) a) When does deposition occur?
    b) Give two reasons why the amount of material that is deposited might increase.

Coastal Landforms (p. 42-45) ☑

10) Are headlands made of more or less resistant rock?
11) Describe how erosion can turn a crack in a cliff into a cave.
12) What is a stack?
13) How does a wave-cut platform form?
14) What are the characteristics of shingle beaches?
15) Where do spits form?
16) How do offshore bars form?
17) How do sand dunes form?
18) Why can't cracks, caves and arches be seen on a map?
19) What do stacks look like on a map?
20) How are cliffs shown on a map?
21) On maps, what do speckles on top of yellow shading tell you?
22) a) Name a coastal area which has erosional and depositional landforms.
    b) Name one erosional landform in that area.
    c) Name one depositional landform in that area.

Coastal Management (p. 46-47) ☑

23) Describe the difference between hard engineering and soft engineering coastal management strategies.
24) What is a disadvantage of using sea walls as a coastal defence?
25) What are gabions?
26) What is rock armour?
27) a) Name two soft engineering strategies.
    b) Give one benefit of each strategy.
28) What is managed retreat?
29) a) For a named coastline, explain why coastal management is needed.
    b) Give three examples of conflicts caused by coastal management along this coastline.

The River Valley

You're probably best off going to the loo before you start this topic. It's all about <u>flowing water</u>...

A River's Long Profile and Cross Profile Vary Over its Course

1) The <u>path</u> of a river as it flows <u>downhill</u> is called its <u>course</u>.

2) Rivers have a steep <u>upper</u> course (nearer the source), a gently sloping <u>middle</u> course and an almost flat <u>lower</u> course (nearer the mouth).

3) The <u>long profile</u> of a river shows you how the <u>gradient</u> changes.

4) Rivers form <u>channels</u> and <u>valleys</u> as they flow downhill.

5) They <u>erode</u> the landscape and <u>transport</u> eroded <u>material</u> to somewhere further along the course, where it's <u>deposited</u>.

6) The <u>shape</u> of the valley and channel <u>changes</u> along the river depending on whether erosion or deposition is the dominant process.

7) The <u>cross profile</u> shows you what a <u>cross-section</u> of the river looks like.

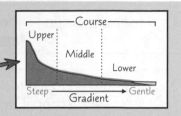

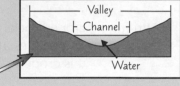

Course	Gradient	Valley and channel shape	Cross profile
Upper	<u>Steep</u>	<u>V-shaped</u> valley, steep sides. <u>Narrow</u>, <u>shallow</u> channel.	
Middle	<u>Medium</u>	<u>Gently sloping</u> valley sides. <u>Wider</u>, <u>deeper</u> channel.	
Lower	<u>Gentle</u>	Very <u>wide</u>, almost <u>flat</u> valley. Very <u>wide</u>, <u>deep</u> channel.	

Upland area, e.g. mountains

Source

Upper

Middle

Lower

Mouth

Body of water, e.g. the sea or a lake

Vertical and Lateral Erosion Change the Cross Profile of a River

Erosion can be <u>vertical</u> or <u>lateral</u> — both types happen at the <u>same time</u>, but one is usually <u>dominant</u> at <u>different points</u> along the river:

There's more on the processes of erosion on the next page.

Vertical erosion

This <u>deepens</u> the river valley and channel, making it <u>V-shaped</u>. It's dominant in the <u>upper</u> course of the river. High <u>turbulence</u> causes the rough, angular particles to be <u>scraped</u> along the river bed, causing intense <u>downwards</u> erosion.

Lateral erosion

This <u>widens</u> the river valley and channel during the formation of <u>meanders</u> (see page 52). It's dominant in the <u>middle</u> and <u>lower</u> courses of the river.

Don't show me that cross profile — just go with the flow...

Sit back, close your eyes and imagine gently babbling brooks. Then you'd best get on with learning this page. Make sure you can describe a river's long profile as well as its cross profile at different points along its course.

Erosion, Transportation and Deposition

Rivers <u>scrape</u> and <u>smash</u> rocks up, <u>push</u> them about, then <u>dump</u> them when they've had enough...

There are Four Processes of Erosion

1) <u>Hydraulic action</u> — The <u>force</u> of the river water colliding with rocks <u>breaks</u> rock particles away from the river channel.

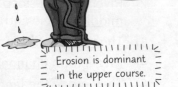

I'm taking hydraulic action against this revision.

Erosion is dominant in the upper course.

2) <u>Abrasion</u> — Eroded rocks <u>picked up</u> by the river <u>scrape</u> and <u>rub</u> against the channel, wearing it away. Most erosion happens by abrasion.

3) <u>Attrition</u> — Eroded rocks <u>picked up</u> by the river <u>crash</u> into each other and <u>break</u> into smaller fragments. Their edges also get <u>rounded</u> off as they rub together. The further material travels, the more it is eroded — attrition causes particle <u>size</u> to <u>decrease</u> from a river's source to its mouth.

4) <u>Solution</u> — River water <u>dissolves</u> some types of rock, e.g. chalk and limestone.

The faster a river's flowing, the more erosion happens.

Transportation is the Movement of Eroded Material

How material is transported depends on the <u>velocity</u> of the <u>water</u>, and the <u>size</u> of the <u>particles</u>:

Traction
<u>Large</u> particles like boulders are <u>pushed</u> along the <u>river bed</u> by the force of the water.

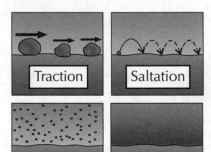

Traction | Saltation

Suspension | Solution

Saltation
<u>Pebble-sized</u> particles are <u>bounced</u> along the <u>river bed</u> by the force of the water.

Solution
<u>Soluble</u> materials (e.g. limestone) <u>dissolve</u> in the water and are <u>carried</u> along.

Suspension
<u>Small</u> particles like silt and clay are <u>carried</u> along by the water.

Deposition is When a River Drops Eroded Material

1) Deposition is when a river <u>drops</u> the <u>material</u> it's transporting.

2) It occurs when a river <u>loses velocity</u> and <u>energy</u>.
There are a few <u>reasons</u> why rivers slow down and deposit material:

- The <u>volume</u> of water <u>falls</u>.
- The amount of eroded <u>material increases</u>.
- The water is <u>shallower</u>, e.g. on the inside of a bend.
- The river reaches its <u>mouth</u>.

Deposition is dominant in the lower course.

3) <u>Particle size</u> affects <u>how far</u> material is <u>transported</u>, and therefore where in a river's course it's <u>deposited</u> — smaller particles are transported further and deposited closer to the river's mouth.

I can't bear the suspension — just go ahead and dump me...

There are lots of very similar names to remember here — try not to confuse saltation, solution and suspension. And yes, confusingly, solution is both a process of erosion and transportation. Now saltate on to the next page...

River Landforms — Erosion

If you don't know anything about <u>waterfalls</u> then you haven't been watching enough shampoo adverts. Now's your chance to find out all about them and other landforms created by erosion.

Waterfalls and Gorges are Found in the Upper Course of a River

1) Waterfalls form where a river flows over an area of <u>hard rock</u> <u>followed</u> by an area of <u>softer rock</u>.

2) The softer rock is <u>eroded</u> (by hydraulic action and abrasion) more than the hard rock, creating a '<u>step</u>' in the river.

3) As water flows over the step it erodes more and more of the softer rock.

4) A <u>steep drop</u> is eventually created, which is called a <u>waterfall</u>. E.g. High Force waterfall on the River Tees, County Durham.

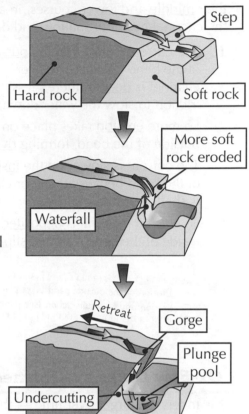

5) The hard rock is eventually <u>undercut</u> by erosion. It becomes unsupported and <u>collapses</u>.

6) The collapsed rocks are <u>swirled</u> around at the foot of the waterfall where they erode the softer rock by abrasion (see previous page). This creates a deep <u>plunge pool</u>.

7) Over time, more undercutting causes more collapses. The waterfall <u>retreats</u>, leaving behind a steep-sided <u>gorge</u>.

You might be asked about 'fluvial' landforms — don't panic, it's just another word for 'river'.

Interlocking Spurs are Nothing to do with Cowboys

1) In the <u>upper</u> course of a river most of the erosion is <u>vertically</u> downwards. This creates <u>steep-sided</u>, <u>V-shaped</u> valleys.

2) The rivers <u>lack</u> the <u>power</u> to erode <u>laterally</u> (sideways), so they have to <u>wind around</u> the high hillsides that stick out into their paths on either side.

3) The hillsides that interlock with each other (like a zip if you were looking from above) as the river winds around them are called <u>interlocking spurs</u>.

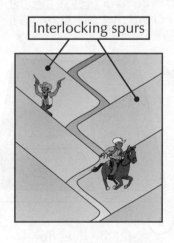
Interlocking spurs

Interlocking spurs along a river in Ashes Hollow, Shropshire

Some river landforms are beautiful — others are gorge-ous...

Step over the hard rock and plunge into the pool — that's how I remember how waterfalls are formed. Geography examiners love river landforms (they're a bit weird like that) so make sure you learn how they form.

River Landforms — Meanders

When a river's <u>eroding</u> and <u>depositing</u> material, <u>meanders</u> and <u>ox-bow lakes</u> can form.

Meanders are Formed by Erosion and Deposition

Rivers develop large <u>bends</u> called <u>meanders</u> in their <u>middle</u> and <u>lower</u> courses, in areas where the channel has both shallow and deep sections:

1) The current is <u>faster</u> on the <u>outside</u> of the bend because the river channel is <u>deeper</u> (there's less friction to slow the water down).

2) So more <u>erosion</u> takes place on the outside of the bend, forming <u>river cliffs</u>.

3) The current is <u>slower</u> on the <u>inside</u> of the bend because the river channel is <u>shallower</u> (there's more friction).

4) So eroded material is <u>deposited</u> on the inside of the bend, forming <u>slip-off slopes</u>.

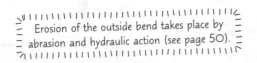

The line of deepest water and fastest flow in a river channel is called the thalweg.

Erosion of the outside bend takes place by abrasion and hydraulic action (see page 50).

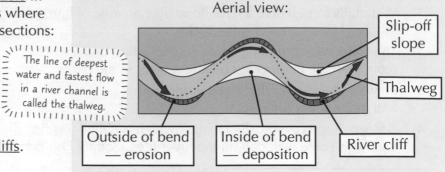

Aerial view:

Slip-off slope

Thalweg

Outside of bend — erosion

Inside of bend — deposition

River cliff

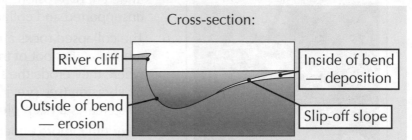

Cross-section:

River cliff

Outside of bend — erosion

Inside of bend — deposition

Slip-off slope

Ox-Bow Lakes are Formed from Meanders

Meanders get <u>larger over time</u> — they can eventually turn into an ox-bow lake:

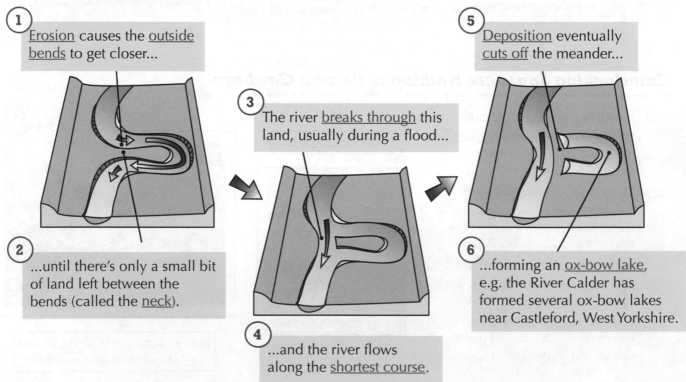

1) <u>Erosion</u> causes the <u>outside bends</u> to get closer...

2) ...until there's only a small bit of land left between the bends (called the <u>neck</u>).

3) The river <u>breaks through</u> this land, usually during a flood...

4) ...and the river flows along the <u>shortest course</u>.

5) <u>Deposition</u> eventually <u>cuts off</u> the meander...

6) ...forming an <u>ox-bow lake</u>, e.g. the River Calder has formed several ox-bow lakes near Castleford, West Yorkshire.

Fun fact — 'meanders' is a rubbish anagram of 'dreamers'...

Don't be afraid to draw diagrams of river landforms in the exam — examiners love them and they can make your answer clearer. Oh, and bonus CGP grammar tip: say "Her and me" or "She and I", not "Me and 'er"...

River Landforms — Deposition

When <u>rivers dump material</u> they don't do it by text message — they make attractive <u>landforms</u> instead.

Flood Plains are Flat Areas of Land that Flood

1) The flood plain is the <u>wide valley floor</u> on either side of a river which occasionally floods.

2) When rivers flood, the water slows down, loses energy and <u>deposits</u> the <u>material</u> that it's <u>transporting</u>. This <u>builds up</u> the flood plain.

3) Meanders <u>widen</u> as they <u>migrate</u> (move) across floodplains <u>laterally</u>.

4) Over time, meanders also migrate <u>downstream</u>.

5) The <u>deposition</u> that happens on the <u>slip-off slopes</u> of meanders also builds up the flood plain.

Flood plain, Afon Glaslyn, Snowdonia, Wales

© PearlBucknall / Alamy Stock Photo

All these landforms are found in the lower course of a river.

Levees are Natural Embankments

1) Levees are <u>natural embankments</u> (raised banks) along the <u>edges</u> of a river <u>channel</u>.

2) During a flood, eroded material is deposited over the <u>whole</u> flood plain.

3) The <u>heaviest</u> material is <u>deposited closest</u> to the river <u>channel</u>, because it gets dropped first when the river slows down and loses energy.

4) Over time, the deposited material <u>builds up</u>, creating <u>levees</u> along the edges of the channel. E.g. along the River Trent in Nottinghamshire.

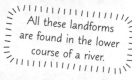

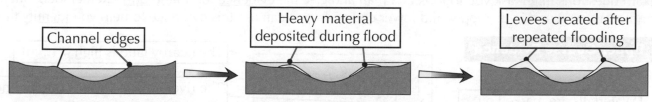

Channel edges

Heavy material deposited during flood

Levees created after repeated flooding

Estuaries are Tidal Areas Where the River Meets the Sea

1) <u>Estuaries</u> are found at river <u>mouths</u>. The land is close to <u>sea level</u> and the river valley is at its <u>widest</u>.

2) The water here is <u>tidal</u> — the river level rises and falls each day.

3) When the water <u>floods</u> over the <u>banks</u> of the river, it carries silt and sand onto the valley floor.

4) As the <u>tide</u> reaches its <u>highest</u> point, the water moves slowly and has little energy, so it <u>deposits sediment</u>.

5) Over time, more mud <u>builds up</u>, creating large <u>mudflats</u>, e.g. the Severn Estuary, Gloucestershire.

6) At <u>low tide</u>, the wide, muddy banks are <u>exposed</u>.

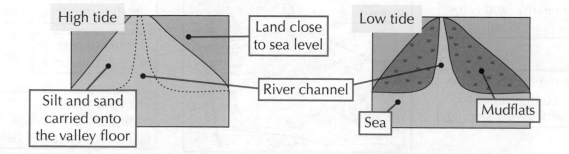

High tide

Land close to sea level

Silt and sand carried onto the valley floor

River channel

Low tide

Sea

Mudflats

EXAM QUESTION

Oh, I just love a levee — it must be my cheery deposition...

Last few landforms to learn, honest. These ones are all about water slowing down and dropping stuff.

1) Describe the process of formation of river flood plains.   *[3]*

Identifying River Landforms

You need to be able to spot river <u>features</u> on <u>maps</u>, or some of the exam questions will be a wee bit tricky...

Contour Lines Tell you the Direction a River Flows

Contour lines are the <u>orange lines</u> drawn all over maps. They tell you about:

- The <u>height</u> of the land (in metres) by the numbers marked on them.
- The <u>steepness</u> of the land by how <u>close</u> together they are (closer lines means a steeper the slope).

It sounds obvious, but rivers only flow <u>downhill</u>. Unless gravity's gone screwy, a river <u>flows</u> from <u>higher</u> contour lines to <u>lower</u> ones. Have a look at this map of Cawfell Beck in the Lake District (Cumbria):

Take a peek at pages 129-130 for more on reading OS® maps.

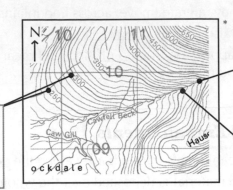

1 The height values get <u>smaller</u> towards the <u>west</u> (left), so west is <u>downhill</u>.

2 Cawfell Beck flows from <u>east</u> to <u>west</u>.

3 A <u>V-shape</u> is formed where the contour lines <u>cross</u> the <u>river</u>. This <u>points uphill</u> to where the river came from.

Maps contain Evidence for River Landforms

Exam questions might ask you to look at a <u>map</u> and give the <u>evidence</u> for a <u>landform</u>. Remember, different landforms are found in the upper and lower course — you can use this evidence to help you <u>identify</u> them:

Upper Course Evidence

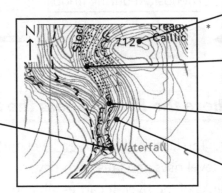

<u>Waterfalls</u> are marked on maps, but the symbol for a <u>cliff</u> (black, blocky lines) and the <u>close contour lines</u> are evidence for an upper-course waterfall.

The nearby land is <u>high</u> (712 m).

The river <u>crosses</u> lots of <u>contour lines</u> in a short distance — it's <u>steep</u>.

The river's <u>narrow</u> (a <u>thin</u> blue line).

The <u>contour lines</u> are very <u>close</u> together and the valley floor is narrow — the river is in a <u>steep-sided</u>, <u>V-shaped</u> valley.

Lower Course Evidence

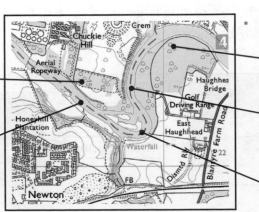

The nearby land is <u>low</u> (less than 15 m).

The river <u>doesn't cross</u> any <u>contour lines</u> so it's very <u>gently sloping</u>.

The river meanders across a large <u>flat</u> area (no contours), which is the <u>flood plain</u>.

The river's <u>wide</u> (a <u>thick</u> blue line).

The river has large <u>meanders</u>. An <u>ox-bow lake</u> may be formed here.

My contours are largely a result of too much chocolate...

It's important to understand maps, so read this page, find a map and explain it to anyone who will listen.

River Landscape — River Clyde

EXAMPLE

You can see many of the <u>landforms</u> of <u>erosion</u> and <u>deposition</u> from pages 51-53 along the River Clyde.

The River Clyde Flows Through Scotland

1) The River Clyde is about <u>160 km</u> long.

2) Its source is in the <u>Southern Uplands</u> of Scotland, and it <u>flows north-west</u> through Motherwell and Glasgow.

3) The River Clyde's <u>mouth</u> is an estuary on the <u>west coast</u> of Scotland.

4) You need to know the major <u>landforms</u> that can form in river valleys. Some examples from the valley of the River Clyde are below.

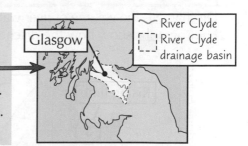

Glasgow

∿ River Clyde
⬚ River Clyde drainage basin

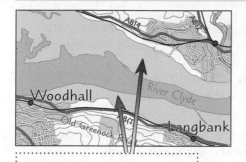

The River Clyde's flood plain

The river's <u>estuary</u> is about 34 km west of Glasgow. It is about <u>3 km wide</u>. These areas next to the river channel show the <u>mudflats</u>, which are exposed at low tide.

Glasgow is built on the <u>flood plain</u> of the River Clyde. The land is about <u>5 m</u> above sea level on either side of the river.

There's also a <u>gorge</u> along this part of the river, formed by the waterfalls <u>retreating</u>.

The river <u>meanders</u> between Motherwell and Glasgow.

The Falls of Clyde are four <u>waterfalls</u> near Lanark. The highest fall is <u>Corra Linn</u> — it's about <u>27 m high</u>.

There are <u>interlocking spurs</u> at Crawford. The spurs are between 300 and 500 m high.

Corra Linn

There's a meander in the New Lanark area that may form an <u>ox-bow lake</u> over time.

The many falls of Clyde — he has two left feet, the poor fellow...

Rivers with river landforms — who would've thought. Check you know what they look like before moving on.

River Discharge and Flooding

We've not really talked much about the actual <u>water</u> in a river. Well, all that's about to change — hooray.

River Discharge is the Volume of Water Flowing in a River

<u>Discharge</u> is the <u>volume</u> of river water flowing <u>per second</u>, measured in <u>cumecs</u> — cubic metres per second (m^3/s).
<u>Hydrographs</u> show how the discharge at a certain point in a river changes over time in relation to rainfall:

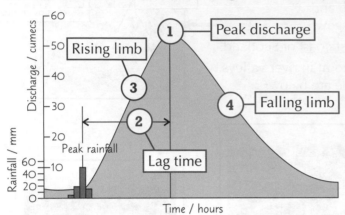

① <u>Peak discharge</u>: The <u>highest discharge</u> in the period of time you're looking at.

② <u>Lag time</u>: The <u>delay</u> between peak rainfall and peak discharge.

③ <u>Rising limb</u>: The <u>increase</u> in river discharge as rainwater flows into the river.

④ <u>Falling limb</u>: The <u>decrease</u> in river discharge as the river returns to its normal level.

Lag time occurs because most rainwater <u>doesn't land directly</u> in the river <u>channel</u>. It flows quickly overland
(<u>surface runoff</u>), or soaks into the ground (<u>infiltration</u>) and then flows slowly underground to the channel.

Physical and Human Factors Affect Flood Risk

Flooding occurs when a river's level <u>rises</u> so much that it <u>spills</u> over its banks. There are several factors
that <u>shorten</u> the <u>lag time</u>, so the peak discharge is higher and <u>flooding</u> is more likely to occur:

Heavy Rainfall

Heavy rainfall means that water <u>arrives too quickly</u> to infiltrate, so there's a lot of surface runoff, which increases discharge.

Geology (rock type)

Clay soils and some rocks, e.g. granite and shale, are <u>impermeable</u> (i.e. they don't allow infiltration), so runoff is increased.

Prolonged Rainfall

Prolonged rainfall can <u>saturate</u> the soil. Any further rainfall can't infiltrate, increasing runoff into river channels.

Relief (changes in land height)

If a river is in a <u>steep-sided valley</u>, water will reach the river channel quicker because it can <u>flow faster</u> down the steep slopes — this rapidly increases discharge.

Changing the <u>land use</u>, e.g. by <u>building</u> on it or <u>removing trees</u>, can also increase the flood risk.

Land use

1) Buildings are often made from <u>impermeable materials</u> (e.g. concrete) and surrounded by roads made from impermeable <u>surfaces</u> (e.g. tarmac), increasing surface runoff. Man-made <u>drains</u> then quickly transport runoff to rivers, increasing discharge.

2) Trees <u>intercept</u> rainwater on their leaves, which then <u>evaporates</u>. Trees also take up and <u>store</u> water from the ground. This means that cutting down trees increases the volume of water that enters the river channel.

Revision lag time — the time between starting and getting bored...

Hydrographs look scary, but they're not too bad — just read until the knowledge infiltrates your brain.
1) Describe how changing land use can increase the risk of flooding. [4]

Hard vs Soft Engineering

Floods can be <u>devastating</u>, but there are a number of <u>different strategies</u> to stop them or lessen the blow.

Engineering can Reduce the Risk of Flooding or its Effects

There are <u>two</u> types of <u>strategy</u> to deal with <u>flooding</u>:

- <u>Hard engineering</u> — <u>man-made</u> structures built to <u>control</u> the flow of rivers and <u>reduce flooding</u>.

- <u>Soft engineering</u> — <u>schemes</u> set up using <u>knowledge</u> of a river and its processes to <u>reduce the effects</u> of flooding.

There's <u>debate</u> about which strategies are <u>best</u>, so you'll need to know the <u>benefits</u> and <u>costs</u> of a few of them. Here's a lovely big table for you to enjoy:

	Method	What it is	Benefits	Disadvantages
HARD ENGINEERING	**Dams and reservoirs**	Dams are <u>barriers</u> built across the rivers, usually in the upper course. A reservoir (<u>artificial lake</u>) is formed behind the dam.	Reservoirs <u>store water</u> (e.g. after heavy rain), control water flow and prevent floods downstream. They can also be used to generate <u>hydroelectric power</u> (HEP).	Dams are very <u>expensive</u> to build. Creating a reservoir can <u>flood</u> existing settlements. Material is <u>deposited</u> in the reservoir, not along the river's course, so <u>farmland</u> downstream can become <u>less fertile</u>.
	Channel straightening	<u>Meanders</u> are <u>removed</u> by building straighter, artificial channels.	<u>Water leaves</u> the area more <u>quickly</u> rather than building up, so flood risk is lower.	<u>Flooding</u> may happen <u>downstream</u> instead. Faster-moving water may cause more <u>erosion</u> downstream.
	Embankments	<u>Raised walls</u> are built along river <u>banks</u>.	The river can hold more water, so floods are less frequent.	They're quite <u>expensive</u>, and there's a <u>risk</u> of <u>severe flooding</u> if the water rises above the level of the embankments or if they break.
	Flood relief channels	Channels are built to <u>divert water</u> around built-up areas or to divert excess water if the river level gets too high.	<u>Gates</u> on the channels mean that the release of <u>water</u> can be <u>controlled</u>, reducing flood risk.	There will be <u>increased discharge</u> where the <u>relief channel</u> rejoins the <u>river</u> (or joins another river), which could cause flooding in that area.
SOFT ENGINEERING	**Flood warnings and preparation**	The Environment Agency issues <u>flood warnings</u> through various media (e.g. TV, radio, internet). <u>Buildings</u> are <u>modified</u> to minimise flood damage. Residents can prepare <u>sandbags</u> and <u>flood boards</u> prior to floods.	Warnings give people <u>time</u> to move possessions upstairs, put sandbags in place or <u>evacuate</u>. This reduces the <u>impact</u> of flooding.	Warnings <u>don't prevent</u> floods. People may not have access to the warnings. Modifying buildings is <u>expensive</u>. Preparation doesn't guarantee safety from a flood and it could give people a <u>false sense of security</u>.
	Flood plain zoning	<u>Restrictions</u> prevent building on parts of a flood plain that are likely to be affected by a flood.	Flood <u>risk</u> is reduced — <u>fewer impermeable surfaces</u> are created (e.g. roads). The <u>impact</u> of flooding is also reduced — there are no buildings to damage.	The <u>expansion</u> of an urban area is <u>limited</u> if there aren't any other suitable building sites. It <u>can't help</u> in areas with <u>existing buildings</u>.
	Planting trees	<u>Planting trees</u> in the river valley increases the <u>interception</u> of rainwater (and <u>lag time</u>).	Discharge and flood risk decrease. Vegetation <u>reduces soil erosion</u> in the valley and provides <u>habitats</u> for wildlife.	<u>Less</u> land is available for <u>farming</u>.
	River restoration	Making the river more <u>natural</u>, e.g. by removing man-made levees, so that the flood plain can <u>flood</u> naturally.	Discharge is reduced, so there's less risk of flooding downstream. <u>Little maintenance</u> is needed and there are better <u>habitats</u> for wildlife.	<u>Local flood risk</u> can <u>increase</u>, especially if nothing is done to prevent major flooding.

Flood your mind — with knowledge of flood defence schemes...

See — that table was both lovely and big. It might look like a lot of stuff to learn, but it's not too difficult at all.

Unit 1C — River Landscapes in the UK

Flood Management — Oxford

That's right — another real life <u>UK example</u> for you to dive into. What's more, this one makes a real splash.

Severe Flooding Showed the Need for Flood Defences in Oxford

Oxford, 2007

1) Oxford is situated at the <u>confluence</u> of the <u>River Thames</u> (to the west) and the <u>River Cherwell</u> (to the east). The Cherwell is a <u>tributary</u> of the Thames — the two rivers join just south of the city centre.

2) Its proximity to these <u>river channels</u> means the city is at risk of flooding during periods of heavy rain. In 2007, river discharge increased rapidly, causing <u>flash floods</u>.

Flash floods are floods that happen quickly, often due to a short burst of heavy rain.

3) The intense <u>flooding</u> of Oxford in July <u>2007</u> meant that over <u>250 homes</u> had to be <u>evacuated</u> in the Botley area and the A420 road was flooded for about 100 metres. A later flood in January <u>2014</u> caused trains to be cancelled and drains to overflow.

4) These floods <u>restricted</u> people's <u>access</u> to work and services, as well as <u>damaging</u> the local <u>economy</u> by preventing tourists visiting Oxford's historic centre.

A Flood Management Scheme is Being Put in Place

In 2014, planning began on the <u>Oxford Flood Alleviation Scheme</u>. It will span <u>5 km</u> and includes both <u>hard</u> and <u>soft</u> engineering <u>strategies</u>:

The scheme will <u>divert</u> water away from more densely <u>populated areas</u> and protect the city centre by:

- Increasing water storage in the floodplain and in an existing <u>bypass channel</u> southwest of Oxford — <u>400 000 m^3</u> of earth will be dug up to <u>increase capacity</u>.

- Planting <u>20 000 trees</u> and shrubs around the excavated area to slow runoff and <u>decrease peak discharge</u>.

- Reusing excavated material to <u>build</u> new <u>flood walls</u> and <u>embankments</u> to protect areas that remain at risk.

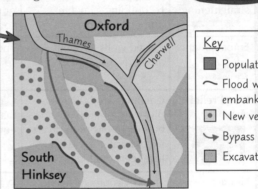

Oxford

Thames

Cherwell

South Hinksey

Key
- ■ Populated areas
- ～ Flood walls & embankments
- ⊡ New vegetation
- ↘ Bypass channel
- ▨ Excavated area

Work on the scheme is expected to start in <u>2019</u> and finish by <u>2023</u>.

The Scheme has Social, Economic and Environmental Issues

Social Issues

1) Compulsory Purchase Orders (<u>CPOs</u>) were sent to <u>landowners</u> whose land was needed to widen the floodplain. Some people did not want to sell their land.

2) Construction may <u>disrupt</u> residents' lives, e.g. because of noise <u>pollution</u> and large vehicles blocking roads.

3) The scheme will <u>improve</u> public <u>footpaths</u>, providing more opportunities for <u>recreation</u>.

4) Residents will feel more <u>confident</u> that their homes won't flood.

Economic Issues

1) The scheme is expected to cost over <u>£120 million</u> in total, and not all of the funding has been secured yet.

2) Over 1000 <u>homes</u> and <u>businesses</u> will be better <u>protected</u>, so there's less risk of expensive damage to property, loss of stock and rising insurance costs.

Environmental Issues

1) Over <u>2000 trees</u> and 2 hectares of <u>rare grassland</u> will be <u>removed</u>. They will be replanted, but it may take a while for vegetation to grow back.

2) The scheme will create over 20 hectares of new riverside <u>habitats</u>, improving the area's <u>biodiversity</u>.

Flash flooding — sometimes brought on by the stress of exams...

That's about it for rivers, folks. Learn the details of a flood management scheme and you'll be home and dry...

Revision Summary

Wat-er load of fun that was. Now it's time to see how much information your brain has soaked up. I think you'll be surprised — I reckon about 16 litres of knowledge has been taken in. Have a go at the questions below and then go back over the topic to check your answers. If something's not quite right, pore over the page again. Once you can answer everything correctly you're ready to sail away, sail away, sail away... to the next topic.

If Rivers is not one of the options that you've chosen, do a little celebratory dance, then move directly onto some lovely revision of Glacial Landscapes.

River Valley Profiles and Processes (p.49-50) ☑

1) What does a river's long profile show?
2) Describe the cross profile of a river's lower course.
3) Name the part of the river course where vertical erosion is dominant.
4) What's the difference between abrasion and attrition?
5) Name two processes of transportation.
6) When does deposition occur?

Features of Erosion and Deposition (p. 51-53) ☑

7) Where do waterfalls form?
8) How is a gorge formed?
9) What are interlocking spurs?
10) a) Where is the current fastest on a meander?
    b) What feature of a meander is formed where the flow is fastest?
11) Name the landform created when a meander is cut off by deposition.
12) What is a flood plain?
13) Where are estuaries found?
14) Outline the main features of a river estuary.

Evidence for River Landforms (p.54-55) ☑

15) What do the contour lines on a map show?
16) Give two pieces of map evidence for a waterfall.
17) Give two pieces of map evidence for a river's lower course.
18) Suggest what you might look for to identify an estuary on a map.
19) What features would you expect to see in a photo of a flood plain?
20) List the main landforms of a named river landscape.

Flooding and Flood Defences (p.56-58) ☑

21) What is river discharge?
22) What is lag time?
23) Describe two physical factors that can cause floods.
24) Explain how cutting down trees can increase flooding.
25) Define hard engineering.
26) Define soft engineering.
27) Describe how channel straightening reduces the risk of a flood.
28) Describe the disadvantages of flood warnings.
29) Describe the advantages of river restoration.
30) a) Using a named example of a flood management scheme, explain why the scheme was needed.
    b) Give two features of the scheme and explain how they reduce the flood risk.
    c) Describe the social issues caused by the scheme.

Glacial Processes

Glaciers are masses of ice that fill valleys and hollows. As they slowly make their way downhill, they erode the landscape and drop all sorts of stuff behind them as they go. It's a good thing they're pretty...

Glaciers Erode the Landscape as They Move

1) The weight of the ice in glaciers makes them move downhill.

2) Some glaciers have a thin layer of meltwater which accumulates beneath the ice and acts as a lubricant, helping the glacier to move by a process called basal sliding.

3) As they advance, glaciers erode the landscape in two ways:

> Abrasion — bits of rock stuck in the ice grind against the rock below the glacier, wearing it away.

> Plucking — meltwater at the base, back or sides of a glacier freezes onto rock. As the glacier moves forward it pulls out pieces of rock.

4) At the top end of the glacier the ice doesn't move in a straight line — it moves in a circular motion called rotational slip. This can erode hollows in the landscape and deepen them into bowl shapes.

5) The rock above glaciers is also broken down by freeze-thaw weathering. This is where water gets into cracks in rocks. The water freezes and expands, putting pressure on the rock. The ice then thaws, releasing the pressure. If this process is repeated it can weaken rock, leaving it more vulnerable to erosion.

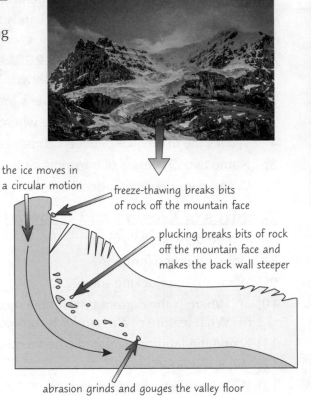

the ice moves in a circular motion

freeze-thawing breaks bits of rock off the mountain face

plucking breaks bits of rock off the mountain face and makes the back wall steeper

abrasion grinds and gouges the valley floor

Glaciers Transport and Deposit Material Called Till

1) Glaciers can move material (such as sand, clay and rocks) over very large distances — this is called transportation. The unsorted mixture of material is called till.

2) Transported material is frozen in the glacier, carried on its surface or pushed in front of it. When glaciers push loose material ahead of them, it's called bulldozing.

3) If a glacier is overloaded with material, or when the ice melts, the material is deposited on the valley floor, forming landforms such as moraines and drumlins (see p.62).

4) Most glacial deposits aren't sorted by size and weight — rocks of all shapes and sizes are mixed up together.

5) However, fine material such as sand and gravel can get washed away from the front of the glacier by small meltwater streams. The streams sort the material by size and deposit it in layers (called outwash) in front of the glacier.

Glacial valley

Plucking and abrasion — beauty treatments glacier style...

Just thinking about this section is making me feel chilly. To stay warm, make sure you memorise (or should I say memor-ice) the differences between plucking, abrasion and freeze-thaw weathering. Then shiver on over to...

Glacial Landforms

If you've ever been to an <u>upland</u> area in the UK, chances are the <u>landscape</u> will have been considerably affected by <u>ice</u>. This page covers some of the <u>landforms</u> that you could've unknowingly passed by.

Much of the UK Used to be Covered in Ice

1) There have been lots of <u>glacial periods</u> (ice ages) over the last <u>2.6 million years</u>.

2) During some glacial periods, parts of the <u>UK</u> were covered by a massive <u>ice sheet</u>.

3) This map shows the <u>maximum extent</u> of ice cover during the last glacial period, <u>20 000 years ago</u>.

4) Ice covered most of <u>Scotland</u>, <u>Ireland</u> and <u>Wales</u> and came as far south as the <u>Bristol Channel</u> in England.

5) The <u>erosion</u>, <u>transport</u> and <u>deposition</u> of material by ice has been very important in <u>shaping</u> the landscape of the UK.

Approximate maximum extent of ice during the last glacial period.

There's more on glacial periods on page 15.

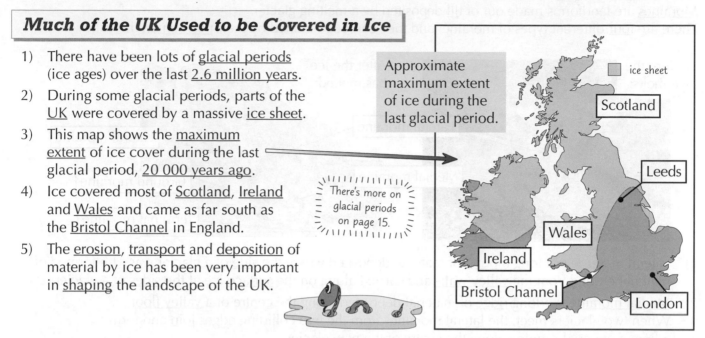

ice sheet

Scotland

Leeds

Wales

Ireland

Bristol Channel

London

Glacial Erosion Produces a Range of Landforms

An <u>arête</u> is a <u>narrow</u>, <u>steep-sided</u> ridge formed when two glaciers flow in <u>parallel</u> valleys. The glaciers erode the <u>sides</u> of the valleys, <u>sharpening</u> the ridge between them and giving it a <u>jagged</u> profile. **EXAMPLE:** Striding Edge, Lake District.

A <u>pyramidal peak</u> is a <u>pointed</u> mountain peak with at least <u>three</u> sides. It's formed when <u>three or more</u> back-to-back glaciers erode a mountain. **EXAMPLE:** Snowdon, Snowdonia.

<u>Corries</u> (also called cirques) begin as <u>hollows</u> containing a small glacier. As <u>rotational slip</u> takes place, the hollow is eroded into a <u>steep-sided</u>, <u>armchair</u> shape with a lip at the <u>bottom</u> end. When the ice melts, it can leave a small circular lake called a <u>tarn</u>. **EXAMPLE:** Red Tarn, Lake District

<u>Truncated spurs</u> are <u>cliff-like</u> edges on the valley side formed when <u>ridges</u> of land (<u>spurs</u>) that <u>stick out</u> into the main valley are <u>cut off</u> as the glacier moves past.

<u>Hanging valleys</u> are valleys formed by small <u>tributary glaciers</u> that flow into a main glacier. The glacial <u>trough</u> of the larger glacier is eroded much more <u>deeply</u>, so when all of the glaciers <u>melt</u> the tributary glacier's valleys are left at a <u>higher</u> level.

<u>Ribbon lakes</u> are <u>long</u>, <u>thin</u> lakes that form <u>after</u> a glacier retreats. They form in <u>hollows</u> where <u>softer</u> rock was eroded <u>more</u> than the surrounding <u>hard</u> rock. **EXAMPLE:** Windermere, Lake District.

<u>Glacial troughs</u> are <u>steep-sided</u> valleys with <u>flat floors</u>. They start off as a <u>V-shaped</u> river valley but change to a <u>U-shape</u> as the glacier <u>erodes</u> the sides and floor, making it <u>deeper</u> and <u>wider</u>. **EXAMPLE:** Nant Ffrancon, Snowdonia.

Glacial Landforms

Glaciers Deposit Material as Different Types of Moraine

<u>Moraines</u> are landforms made out of <u>till</u> deposited by a melting glacier.
There are <u>four</u> different types of moraine, and they can be identified by their <u>position</u> on the valley floor:

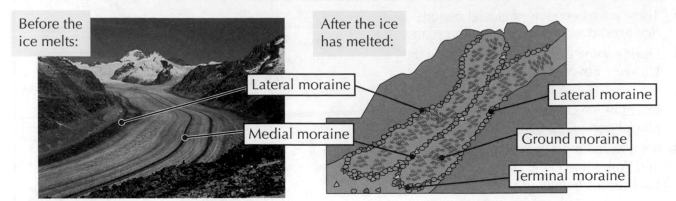

Before the ice melts:

After the ice has melted:

Lateral moraine

Medial moraine

Lateral moraine

Ground moraine

Terminal moraine

1) <u>Lateral</u> moraine is a long <u>mound</u> of material deposited where the <u>side</u> of a glacier was. It's formed of material eroded from the <u>valley walls</u> and carried along on the <u>surface</u> ice at the <u>sides</u> of a glacier.

2) <u>Medial moraine</u> is a long <u>ridge</u> of material deposited along the <u>centre</u> of a <u>valley floor</u>. When two glaciers <u>meet</u>, the <u>lateral</u> moraines from the two colliding edges <u>join</u> and form a line of material running along the <u>centre</u> of the new glacier.

3) <u>Terminal moraine</u> builds up at the <u>snout</u> of a glacier — it marks the furthest point reached by the ice. Material that's <u>abraded</u> and <u>plucked</u> from the valley floor is <u>transported</u> at the <u>front</u> of glaciers, and then deposited as <u>semicircular mounds</u> when the ice <u>retreats</u>.

4) <u>Ground moraine</u> is eroded material that was dragged along the <u>base</u> of a glacier. It is deposited over a <u>wide area</u> on the <u>valley floor</u> when the ice melts.

Material can also be Deposited as Drumlins and Erratics

Drumlins

1) Drumlins are <u>elongated hills</u> thought to be formed when overloaded or melting glaciers deposit material. This material builds up over time, forming hills beneath the glaciers.

2) Continuing ice flow over these hills shapes them — they're round, blunt and steep at the <u>upstream</u> end, and tapered, pointed and gently sloping at the <u>downstream</u> end. The largest ones can be over <u>1000 m long</u>, <u>500 m wide</u> and <u>50 m high</u>, e.g. in Wisconsin, USA.

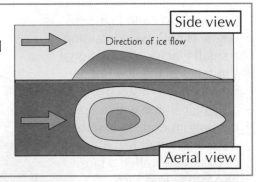

Side view

Direction of ice flow

Aerial view

Erratics

1) Erratics are <u>rocks</u> that have been <u>picked up</u> by a glacier, carried along and <u>dropped</u> in an area that has a completely <u>different</u> rock type.

2) Erratics often look <u>out of place</u>, e.g. a large boulder on its own.

Glencoe, Scotland

An erratic erratic

The glacial weather forecast — cold, with mor-raine on the way...

Check you know the differences between the four different types of moraine — try sketching the diagram. If you remember everything on this page you'll be laughing in the exam. Or at least sniggering quietly.

Identifying Glacial Landforms

In the exam you might be asked to spot <u>glacial landforms</u> on an <u>OS®ᵐᵃᵖ</u>. I swear it's not as scary as it sounds.

Use Contour Lines to Spot Pyramidal Peaks, Corries and Arêtes on a Map

<u>Contour lines</u> are the <u>orange</u> lines drawn all over maps. They tell you about the <u>height</u> of the land by the <u>numbers</u> marked on them, and the <u>steepness</u> of the land by how <u>close together</u> the lines are (the closer they are, the steeper the slope). Here's how to spot <u>pyramidal peaks</u>, <u>arêtes</u> and <u>corries</u> on a map:

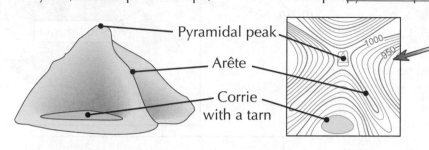

Pyramidal peak

Arête

Corrie with a tarn

This is the sort of thing you're looking for on a <u>map</u>.

But on a <u>real map</u>, like this one of Snowdon in Wales, it's not as blindingly obvious.

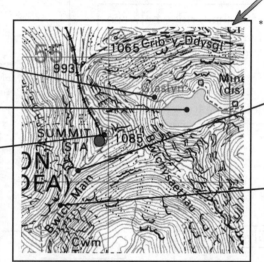

<u>Corries</u> have <u>tightly packed</u> contours in a <u>U-shape</u> around them.

Some corries have a <u>tarn</u> in them.

A pyramidal peak has <u>tightly packed</u> contour lines that <u>curve away</u> from a <u>central high point</u>. If you find this you'll find the <u>arêtes</u> and <u>corries</u> around it.

<u>Arêtes</u> are quite hard to see. Look for a really <u>thin</u> hill with <u>tightly packed</u>, <u>parallel</u> contours on either side.

Arêtes often have <u>corries</u> or <u>tarns</u> on either side, and <u>footpaths</u> on them with names like 'Something <u>Edge</u>', e.g. 'Striding Edge'.

You can also use Maps to Spot Glacial Troughs and Ribbon Lakes

You might be asked to spot a <u>glacial trough</u> or a <u>ribbon lake</u> on a map extract. This map of <u>Nant Ffrancon</u> (a glacial trough) and <u>Llyn Ogwen</u> (a ribbon lake) in Wales shows the classic things to look out for:

Glacial troughs are <u>flat valleys</u> with very <u>steep sides</u>. There are <u>no</u> contour lines on the <u>bottom</u> of the valley but they're <u>tightly packed</u> on the <u>sides</u>.

Look for a <u>wide</u>, <u>straight</u> valley in a <u>mountainous</u> area with a <u>river</u> that looks <u>too small</u> to have formed the valley.

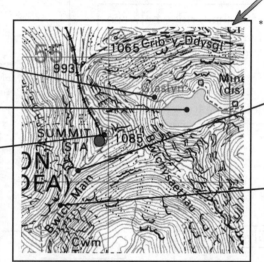

Many glacial troughs have <u>ribbon lakes</u> in them. Look for a <u>flat valley</u> with <u>steep sides</u> surrounding a <u>long</u>, <u>straight lake</u>.

Llyn Ogwen

Some corries have tarns, others have drama and hotpots...

There's lots of potential here for easy marks in the exam, just study the map carefully and say what you see. Make sure you refer to the map in your answer though — there's more about using maps on pages 129-130.

Glacial Landscape — Snowdonia

Snowdonia is a great place to look for glacial landforms. It may not be covered in ice now, but it's sure seen a lot of ice in the past. Here's a lovely example of some of the landforms that are found there.

Snowdonia is a Glacial Landscape in North Wales

1) Snowdonia is an area in north Wales. It has been repeatedly covered by ice during glacial periods (see page 15).

2) The upland areas of Snowdonia (e.g. the Glyders — mountains north-east of Snowdon) show many landforms from pages 61-62.

3) Here are some of the glacial features that are found in the Glyders and their surrounding area:

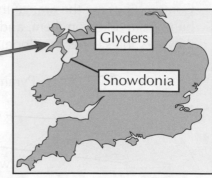

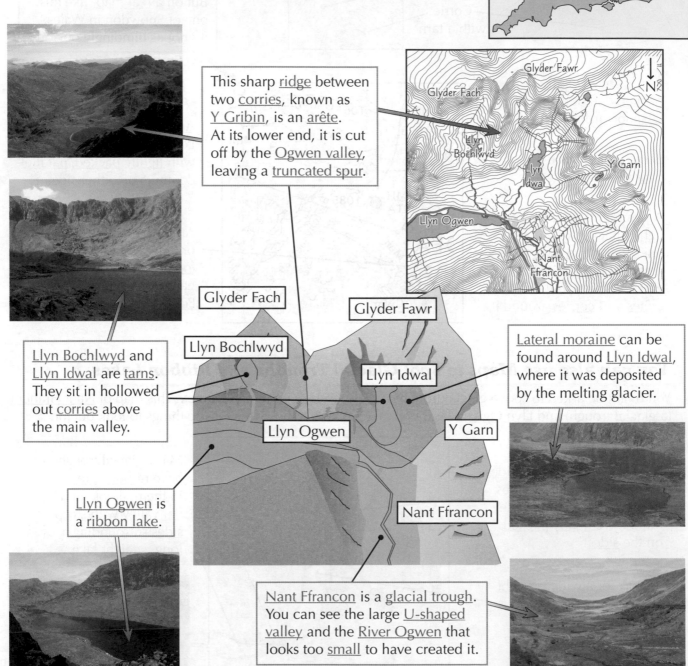

This sharp ridge between two corries, known as Y Gribin, is an arête. At its lower end, it is cut off by the Ogwen valley, leaving a truncated spur.

Glyder Fach

Glyder Fawr

Llyn Bochlwyd

Llyn Idwal

Lateral moraine can be found around Llyn Idwal, where it was deposited by the melting glacier.

Llyn Bochlwyd and Llyn Idwal are tarns. They sit in hollowed out corries above the main valley.

Llyn Ogwen

Y Garn

Llyn Ogwen is a ribbon lake.

Nant Ffrancon

Nant Ffrancon is a glacial trough. You can see the large U-shaped valley and the River Ogwen that looks too small to have created it.

Update to the glacial weather forecast — it's snowd-on-ia mountains...

If you don't know your U-shaped valleys from your truncated spurs by the end of all this lot, I suggest you go back and look at the pretty pictures again. Looking back at the landforms on pages 61-62 might help too.

Land Use in Glacial Landscapes

People use glaciated areas in loads of different ways. Unfortunately, these different activities create conflicts.

Glaciated Areas have Many Economic Uses

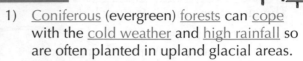

Farming

1) Sheep farming is common in upland glacial areas because the steep slopes and poor soils make it unsuitable for most other farming.

2) Crops can grow at lower altitudes, e.g. grass grown on the valley floor is used to make hay for cattle.

Forestry

1) Coniferous (evergreen) forests can cope with the cold weather and high rainfall so are often planted in upland glacial areas.

2) These trees can be easily used for building materials, paper and furniture.

Quarrying

1) Glacial erosion has left lots of rock exposed, making it easy to access.

2) Glacial landscapes are often quarried for slate, granite, and limestone to use for construction.

Tourism

1) Glaciated areas have dramatic landscapes, making them attractive tourist hotspots.

2) There are lots of activities to do, e.g. hiking, climbing, boating, cycling and skiing.

Land Use Causes Conflict in Glacial Landscapes

1) Upland glacial areas attract different groups, e.g. farmers, tourists, and logging and quarrying industries.

2) Unfortunately, these different groups often come into conflict over land use. For example:

Tourists can disrupt farming by damaging property, scaring sheep, leaving gates open and trampling crops — so some farmers may try to block footpaths.

Local residents may object to the noise of a quarry and the frequent passing of large trucks transporting quarried stone. Quarries can also be eyesores, so fewer tourists come and spend money.

3) Development also comes into conflict with conservation in glacial areas — conservationists want to preserve the environment, but development is needed to provide employment, roads and facilities. This is a common conflict in many of the UK's glacial landscapes, including in and around Snowdonia:

* It can be beneficial to develop glacial landscapes because tourism and farming provide many jobs and contribute enormously to the UK economy — Wales' three national parks made £500 million from tourism in 2018.

© Dave Ellison / Alamy Stock Photo

* These areas can also provide renewable energy (e.g. the proposed Glyn Rhonwy hydroelectric power station) which helps combat climate change.

* However, some conservationists argue that developments and construction sites destroy habitats and deter tourists, e.g. they oppose the Glyn Rhonwy hydroelectric power station.

* Farming developments can also damage the environment — grazing sheep remove vegetation, preventing the landscape from returning to its natural, forested state.

* Coniferous plantations don't support as many species as mixed forests — many conservationists would prefer more natural habitats. Chopping down trees for timber can also damage habitats.

* Conservationists may think that developing infrastructure to support tourism (e.g. the visitor centre at Snowdon's summit) is unnecessary — tourists often visit glacial areas for their natural appeal.

* Despite this, developing roads and infrastructure to improve access benefits many people (not just tourists), as rural glacial landscapes often have narrow roads that are tricky to navigate.

There is also conflict between revision and a social life...

So much conflict — it seems that whatever you do, someone won't like it. Learning this page will probably conflict with your desire to go and watch TV, but it's got to be done. So, find your notebook and get cracking.

Tourism in Glacial Areas — Lake District

Glacial landscapes in the UK are extremely attractive to tourists — I mean, what's not to like about the sharp edge of an arête or the abrupt halt of a truncated spur. Anyhow, popularity comes at a price...

The Lake District Attracts Millions of Tourists

The Lake District National Park, Cumbria, gets almost 19.2 million visitors a year. The attractions for visitors include:

1) Beautiful scenery — large lakes (e.g. Windermere) and mountains (e.g. Scafell Pike).

2) Cultural attractions — e.g. the Wordsworth Museum and Beatrix Potter's house.

3) Activities — e.g. water sports, bird watching, fishing, rock-climbing, hiking and mountain biking.

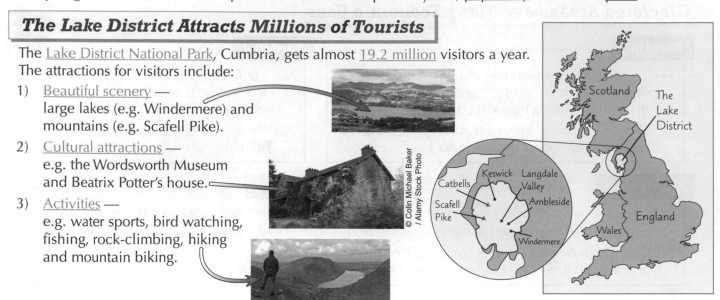

© Colin Michael Baker / Alamy Stock Photo

Tourism is Having Big Impacts on the Area

Environmental Impacts

1) Catbells is a popular mountain for walkers, but the large number of people using the main footpath from Keswick has led to severe erosion.

2) Tourists park on grass verges in Langdale Valley, damaging vegetation.

3) Noise, erosion and water pollution is caused by boats and water sports on Windermere lake.

4) However, tourist's money can be reinvested in the environment, e.g. from 2015-2016, the 'Visit Give Protect' scheme raised £19 000 for the Fix the Fells project to repair eroded footpaths.

Catbells

Economic Impacts

1) Tourism employed over 18 000 people in 2017 and made almost £1.5 billion. This supports local businesses, but the work tends to be seasonal and low-paid.

2) The average price of a house in the National Park is over £350 000 (due to holiday homes etc.) but the average local household income is only £20 000, so many local people may not be able to afford to stay living in the area.

FOR SALE
CGP Homes
£350 000

Social Impacts

1) It's estimated that 83% of visitors to the park arrive by car. Traffic is heavy on the roads linking the National Park with the motorway, especially at the end of the day when day trippers are going home.

2) Businesses in many villages cater for tourists rather than locals — in Ambleside roughly 40% are cafés, restaurants, hotels etc. and 10% sell outdoor clothing. Prices of everyday goods are high and local residents often travel to Kendal to buy their food and clothes.

3) Almost 25% of properties in the National Park are second homes or holiday homes. This means fewer people live in the National Park all year, so bus services are limited, some primary schools in Langdale Valley have closed, and many local doctors are underfunded because they have too few local patients.

Ambleside

© Washington Imaging / Alamy Stock Photo

Tourism in Glacial Areas — Lake District

Management Strategies are Reducing the Negative Impacts of Tourism

In the Lake District, several <u>strategies</u> have been put in place to tackle <u>problems</u> caused by tourism:

1 Traffic and Parking

1) People are <u>encouraged</u> to use bikes, buses, boats and trains, e.g. by providing <u>discounts</u>.
2) <u>Public transport</u> is <u>increased</u> in the tourist season, e.g. more buses run.
3) <u>Road networks</u> have been <u>improved</u>, e.g. better on-street parking has eased traffic flow around Bowness.

EXAMPLE: <u>Ambleside</u> has <u>Controlled Parking Zones</u> in the town centre where people can park for free for <u>1 hour</u>. This encourages a <u>high turnover</u> of parking spaces. The <u>GoLakes Travel programme</u> also aims to <u>reduce</u> cars, e.g. by introducing 'bike & ride' buses.

2 Footpath Erosion

1) Paths have been <u>resurfaced</u> using <u>hard-wearing</u> materials like rocks, plastic mesh or stone slabs.
2) Visitors are encouraged to use <u>alternative</u> routes by <u>signposts</u> and <u>fencing</u>.
3) <u>Reseeding vegetation</u> can reduce the <u>visual</u> impact of erosion.

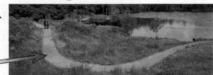

EXAMPLE: At <u>Tarn Hows</u>, severely eroded paths have been <u>reseeded</u>, and the main <u>route</u> has been <u>gravelled</u> to protect it.

© PURPLE MARBLES CUMBRIA / Alamy Stock Photo

3 Littering

1) <u>Signs</u> are put up to <u>remind</u> people to take their <u>rubbish</u> home.
2) <u>Covered</u> bins are provided at the most <u>popular</u> sites.
3) <u>Volunteers</u> in the local community <u>collect</u> any litter that's left.

Litter is rubbish!

EXAMPLE: The charity, <u>Friends of the Lake District</u>, set up the <u>Great Cumbrian Litter Pick</u> in <u>2018</u>, which encourages people of all ages across the county to crack down on <u>litter</u>.

4 Water and Noise Pollution

<u>Speed limits</u> and <u>zoning schemes</u> (where water sports are only allowed in certain areas) have been set up to help <u>cope</u> with the <u>noise</u>, <u>erosion</u> and <u>pollution</u> from water sports.

EXAMPLE: Windermere has a <u>10 knot speed limit</u> for boats, falling to <u>6 knots</u> in some zones.

5 House Prices

<u>Affordable housing</u> and <u>local occupancy schemes</u> (where people must fit certain <u>criteria</u> before buying a particular house) help locals to stay in the area and <u>prevent</u> people buying <u>second</u> or <u>holiday homes</u>.

EXAMPLE: A <u>£10 million</u> project was approved in 2016 to turn the derelict <u>Backbarrow Ironworks</u> into a housing development. The plan includes <u>five</u> affordable houses, to be completed by <u>2019</u>.

EXAM QUESTION

Amphibious cars — surely the answer to traffic issues in the Lakes...

Make sure you know some strategies used to cope with tourism's impacts on a glacial landscape.

1) Explain how tourism has had economic impacts on a named glaciated area. [4]

Revision Summary

Time to whip off your hat and scarf and warm up with some revision questions. The bad news is that if you don't know the answers you're going to have to dip back into the icy depths of this topic. Once you're confident of all the answers I recommend that you indulge in some kind of recreational activity. Don't disappear for too long though, there's plenty more revision where this topic came from.

You only have to study two from Coasts, Rivers and Glacial Landscapes, so if this is not one of you chosen themes, you are released from the grip of winter to go frolic in pastures new — turn over to Urban Issues.

Glacial Processes (p.60) ☑

1) Describe two ways that ice erodes the landscape.
2) What is rotational slip?
3) Explain what freeze-thaw weathering is.
4) What is bulldozing?
5) Describe the formation of outwash.

Glacial Landforms (p.61-62) ☑

6) Describe the maximum extent of ice in the UK during the last glacial period.
7) What is a corrie?
8) How does a pyramidal peak form?
9) Give an example of a pyramidal peak.
10) Explain how a hanging valley forms.
11) What is a glacial trough?
12) Give one difference between lateral and ground moraine.
13) Where is medial moraine deposited?
14) Describe the formation of terminal moraine.
15) Describe what a drumlin looks like.
16) What is an erratic?

Identifying Glacial Landforms (p.63-64) ☑

17) How would you identify a pyramidal peak on a map?
18) How would you identify an arête on a map?
19) Describe what a glacial trough looks like on a map.
20) What does a ribbon lake look like on a map?
21) a) Give an example of a glaciated upland area in the UK.
    b) Name some of its major features of erosion.
22) How would you identify a corrie in a photograph?
23) Give an example of a glacial trough.
24) Describe what an arête looks like.

Land Use in Glacial Landscapes (p.65-67) ☑

25) What type of farming might take place in a glacial landscape?
26) Other than farming, name three economic uses for glacial landscapes.
27) Give two examples of conflicts that might be caused by quarrying in glacial landscapes.
28) Describe two other conflicts over land use that might occur in glacial landscapes.
29) Explain why tourists are attracted to one glacial area you have studied.
30) Describe the environmental impacts of tourism on a named glaciated upland area.
31) Using a named example, describe the social impacts of tourism on a glaciated area.
32) Give two strategies that might be used to manage the social impacts of tourism.
33) For a named upland area, describe one way that environmental impacts of tourism have been managed.

Urbanisation

Urban areas (towns and cities) are popular places to be and getting ever more so. You need to know why...

Urbanisation is Happening Fastest in Poorer Countries

1) Urbanisation is the growth in the proportion of people living in urban areas.
2) Around 55% of the world lives in urban areas and this is constantly increasing.
3) The rate of urbanisation differs between richer and poorer countries:

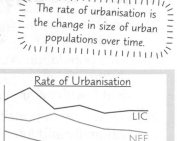

The rate of urbanisation is the change in size of urban populations over time.

- Higher Income Countries (HICs) are more economically developed, e.g. the UK and Japan. Most HICs have already experienced urbanisation, so around 80% of the population live in urban areas. Many people in HICs leave urban areas for less crowded, rural areas, so the rate of urbanisation is low — usually under 1%.
- Lower Income Countries (LICs) are less economically developed, e.g. Ethiopia and Afghanistan. Only around 30% of the population currently live in urban areas, but most LICs have high rates of urbanisation — up to 6%.
- Newly Emerging Economies (NEEs) are countries where economic development is increasing rapidly, e.g. Brazil and China. Their urban population is around 50%, though for countries experiencing rapid urban growth this figure can be much higher. Their rate of urbanisation is typically around 2%.

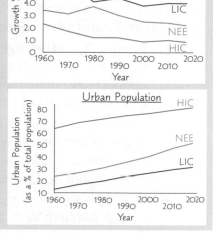

Urbanisation is Caused by Rural-Urban Migration and Natural Increase

1) Rural-urban migration is the movement of people from the countryside to cities.
2) The rate of rural-urban migration is affected by a combination of push factors (which encourage people to leave an area) and pull factors (which encourage people to move to an area).

Push factors

- Natural disasters can damage property and farmland, which is costly. Rural areas can find it harder to recover as they tend to have fewer resources.
- Mechanised agricultural equipment needs fewer workers, so there are fewer jobs.
- Desertification makes land unproductive (see p.33), so people can't support themselves. Farmers' income is unstable as it depends on good harvests.

Pull factors

- There are more jobs in urban areas that are often better paid.
- There's access to better healthcare and educational opportunities.
- Other family members might have already moved to an urban area.
- People think they will have a better quality of life.

3) Urbanisation is also caused by natural increase, which is when birth rate exceeds death rate. As more people are being born than are dying, the population grows.
4) It's normally young people that move to cities to find work. These migrants then have children, increasing the proportion of the population living in urban areas. Access to better healthcare in urban areas also increases life expectancy, preventing the decline of urban populations.

High rates of urbanisation are leading to the growth of megacities (urban areas with more than 10 million residents, e.g. Mumbai, India). As of 2018, there are 33 megacities, and 27 of them are located in LICs and NEEs. By 2030, the number of megacities is expected to have increased to 43.

Zip wires and bouncy pavements — that would be a mega city...

1) Suggest two reasons for the rapid rate of urban growth in some NEEs. [2]

Urban Growth — Lagos

The lure of the city lights can be strong, but many dreams have been crushed by the <u>challenges</u> of <u>urban growth</u>. I'm not trying to be cruel, it's just that the streets aren't always paved with gold...

Lagos is the Biggest City in Africa

1) Lagos is a city in <u>Nigeria</u> — Nigeria is an <u>NEE</u> and has the <u>highest GDP</u> of any country in Africa. The city's population is estimated to be over <u>14 million</u>. It's one of the <u>fastest-growing</u> urban areas in the world, with an annual growth rate of <u>3.2%</u>.

2) Lagos is an important city regionally, nationally and internationally:

   - <u>Regionally</u> — The large <u>migrant</u> population increases <u>cultural diversity</u>. It is also very well connected to other major towns, making it an important centre for regional <u>trade</u>.

   - <u>Nationally</u> — Lagos is home to <u>80%</u> of Nigeria's industry, as well as many global companies. Lagos was also the <u>capital</u> of Nigeria until <u>Abuja</u> became capital in <u>1991</u>.

   - <u>Internationally</u> — Lagos is the main <u>financial centre</u> for the whole of West Africa and the 5th largest economy on the continent. The international port and airport are important for <u>global trade</u>.

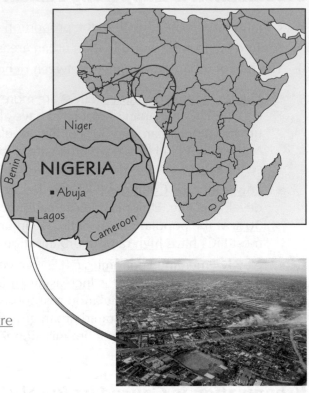

Many Factors have Caused Lagos to Grow Rapidly

1) The British <u>colonised</u> Lagos in the 1860s, making it a centre for <u>trade</u> and attracting many <u>merchants</u>.

2) Many <u>ex-slaves</u> returned home to Lagos in the 1800s (e.g. from Brazil) as slavery was <u>abolished</u>.

3) When Lagos gained <u>independence</u> in 1960, there was rapid <u>economic development</u> as Nigeria's resources (e.g. <u>oil</u>) were no longer controlled by the British.

4) The government then financed lots of <u>construction</u> projects, e.g. oil refineries, sea ports and factories, creating many jobs and causing rapid <u>urbanisation</u>.

5) Lagos' <u>recent</u> growth has been caused by <u>natural increase</u> and <u>migration</u>:

- <u>Natural increase</u> — Nigeria's birth rate is roughly <u>35.2 births</u> per 1000 people, compared to a death rate of around <u>9.6</u>, so the population is rapidly increasing.

  The world's average birth rate is around 19 births per 1000 people, and the average death rate is 7.6.

- <u>Migration</u> — an estimated 1200 immigrants enter Lagos every day, either from neighbouring countries (e.g. Chad and Niger) or from <u>rural areas</u> in northern Nigeria. Much of this <u>rural-urban migration</u> is due to ethnic and religious <u>conflict</u> and high levels of <u>poverty</u> elsewhere in Nigeria and Africa. Many people expect a better <u>quality of life</u> in Lagos.

Urban Growth — Lagos

CASE STUDY

Lagos Provides Social and Economic Opportunities...

Social Opportunities

Lagos has better access to <u>services</u> and <u>resources</u> than rural Nigeria:

1) There are more <u>healthcare</u> centres, hospitals and a better range of <u>medicines</u> in Lagos.

2) Almost <u>90%</u> of Nigerian children in urban areas attend <u>primary school</u> — only around 60% in rural areas attend school. The state Lagos is in has almost <u>20 000</u> schools.

3) Lagos has better access to <u>electricity</u> than much of Nigeria — the city uses about <u>40%</u> of the country's electricity supply. Many people can <u>light</u> their homes and <u>cook</u> more easily.

4) <u>Water treatment plants</u> provide <u>safe water</u> that is piped directly to some areas of the city.

Economic Opportunities

Incomes can be four times higher in Lagos than in rural Nigeria, so many people migrate in search of <u>better paid jobs</u>.

1) <u>Rapid growth</u> means that there are lots of <u>construction</u> jobs, e.g. building the new commercial centre, <u>Eko Atlantic</u>.

2) Lagos is home to many of the country's <u>banks</u>, <u>government</u> departments and <u>manufacturing</u> industries. There are also two major <u>ports</u> and a growing <u>fishing</u> industry.

3) Lagos also has a thriving <u>film</u> and <u>music</u> industry — 'Nollywood' films are very popular.

... But Rapid Growth has Led to Many Problems

Lagos' <u>population density</u> has rapidly increased to around <u>20 000 people per km²</u>, creating <u>challenges</u>:

Slums and Squatter Settlements

Slum in Lagos
© iStock.com / peeterv

1) House construction can't keep up with Lagos' population growth, increasing house prices and making them <u>too costly</u> for many people. As a result, <u>66%</u> of people in Lagos live in illegal settlements (<u>slums</u>).

2) Houses in slums are often flimsy wooden huts. As they are built <u>illegally</u>, people face <u>eviction</u> if slums are <u>demolished</u> to clean up the city.

Access to Clean Water, Sanitation and Energy

1) <u>Water</u> — Only about <u>40%</u> of the city is connected to the state water supply. Water is in such short supply that people pay hugely <u>inflated prices</u> to get water from <u>informal sellers</u>.

2) <u>Sanitation</u> — Up to <u>15</u> households can share a toilet, and waste often goes straight into local <u>water sources</u>. Contaminated water can cause <u>health problems</u>, e.g. cholera.

3) <u>Energy</u> — Lagos doesn't have enough <u>electricity</u> to power the whole city at once, so neighbourhoods take it in turns. Some people get electricity from <u>illegal connections</u>, but these often cut out.

Access to Health and Education

1) There aren't enough <u>healthcare facilities</u> for everyone and many people <u>can't afford</u> treatment.

2) There aren't enough <u>schools</u> for the growing population (e.g. there is only <u>one primary school</u> in the Makoko slum) and many families can't <u>afford</u> to send their children to school.

Unemployment and Crime

1) There aren't enough formal jobs for the <u>growing population</u> — people have to find other ways to make money, e.g. by <u>scavenging</u> items to sell from rubbish dumps.

2) About <u>60%</u> of the population work in <u>informal</u> jobs without any <u>legal protection</u>. E.g. street sellers' stalls may be <u>bulldozed</u> to make way for <u>new developments</u>.

3) There are high levels of crime — many slums, e.g. Makoko, are <u>patrolled</u> by gangs called '<u>area boys</u>' who <u>commit crimes</u> and <u>police</u> the slum themselves.

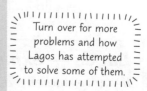
Turn over for more problems and how Lagos has attempted to solve some of them.

Unit 2A — Urban Issues and Challenges

Urban Growth — Lagos

CASE STUDY

Environmental Issues

1) The huge population produces over <u>9000 tonnes</u> of <u>waste</u> a day. Only about <u>40% of rubbish</u> is officially collected and there are <u>large rubbish dumps</u>, e.g. Olusosun, which contain <u>toxic waste</u>.

2) <u>Waste disposal</u> and <u>emissions</u> from factories are not regulated or controlled, leading to <u>water</u> and <u>air pollution</u>.

3) <u>Traffic congestion</u> is really bad — many workers face <u>2-hour</u> commutes in rush hours, known as the 'go slow'. <u>Limited public transport</u> and poor links to the city centre worsen this problem. The severe congestion leads to further air pollution.

Congestion in Lagos

Urban Planning Schemes Aim To Improve Quality of Life in Lagos

EXAMPLE

1) The <u>poorest</u> people in urban areas are often the <u>worst affected</u> by urban growth problems.

2) <u>Urban planning schemes</u> can <u>reduce</u> the impact these problems have on people.

3) In <u>2013</u>, the <u>Makoko Floating School</u> prototype was built by <u>NLÉ Works</u> to give some of the poorest children in Lagos access to <u>free education</u>.

4) The scheme aimed to increase Makoko's <u>development</u> and <u>improve</u> the quality of life of its residents:

Social Benefits

Makoko Floating School
© dpa picture alliance / Alamy Stock Photo

- Up to <u>100</u> students could be educated for <u>free</u> — this meant that they didn't need to work or scavenge to pay school fees.

- The school was built by unskilled <u>local workers</u> — the skills they learnt equipped them to build and repair their own <u>homes</u>.

- The school was also used for local community <u>meetings</u> and <u>activities</u>, increasing Makoko's <u>community spirit</u>.

Economic Benefits

- Education improved local children's <u>job prospects</u>.

- The school provided jobs for local <u>teachers</u>.

- The school's success encouraged the government to launch its '<u>Makoko / Iwaya Regeneration Plan</u>'. This aims to develop the slum further, e.g. by building <u>homes</u> and a <u>biogas plant</u> to produce cooking gas for local people.

Environmental Benefits

- The school was built using <u>locally sourced</u> materials, including 250 floating barrels. This meant that its construction didn't <u>harm</u> the local environment and repairs would be easy.

- The school's <u>buoyancy</u> allowed it to adjust to different water levels, and <u>protect</u> children from floods.

- The school ran on <u>solar power</u> so its energy needs were met in a <u>sustainable</u> way.

- The school collected <u>rainwater</u> to meet its water needs — this meant that it didn't use resources that the local community relied on.

5) Unfortunately, the original floating school <u>collapsed</u> after a storm in 2016, but Makoko's residents vowed to <u>rebuild</u> it. The school's <u>architect</u> unveiled plans for a new, <u>stronger</u> version of the school later in 2016.

Lagos — expanding faster than my waistline at a buffet...

If you've studied a different example of urban growth and planning and you'd rather write about that one, then no problem — just make sure you have enough information to cover the key points from these past few pages.

UK Cities

Cities don't just spring up in any old place — most of them are where they are for a <u>reason</u>. If you know your <u>physical landscapes</u> of the UK (see page 39), the urban areas should slot nicely into place.

Most Cities are in Lowland Areas with Good Access to Natural Resources

The <u>population distribution</u> of the UK is very <u>uneven</u>. The <u>relief</u> (change in the height of the land) affects where most people live. Many of the <u>major</u> cities have developed into <u>conurbations</u> — towns that have merged to form <u>continuous</u> urban areas. These areas have the <u>highest</u> population density:

<u>Upland</u> regions such as the north of Scotland are <u>sparsely-populated</u> — they are difficult to farm and have few natural resources.

<u>Mineral wealth</u> (especially of coal and iron ore) has often led to <u>rapid</u> population growth because this was where <u>industries</u> developed. Many of the UK's cities developed on major coalfields, e.g. Newcastle and Leeds.

Many <u>coastal</u> areas have attracted human settlement — especially where there are <u>sheltered bays</u> and <u>river estuaries</u> suitable for building <u>harbours</u>. Key <u>ports</u> (e.g. Liverpool and Cardiff) have grown into major cities.

Most urban areas developed in <u>lowland</u> areas (e.g. Birmingham) — they are <u>easier</u> to build on and the climate is <u>milder</u> than upland areas.

Glasgow
Edinburgh
Belfast
Newcastle
Leeds
Manchester
Birmingham
Liverpool
London
Cardiff

Population density
(100s per km²)

- 23.7+
- 3.3 – 23.7
- 0 – 3.3

<u>London</u> is the UK's biggest city — it has around <u>9 million people</u>, which is <u>about 16%</u> of the UK's <u>total</u> population. It is the national <u>capital</u> and has many <u>industries</u> (e.g. it is a global financial centre).

Cities Have Different Zones

GEOGRAPHY SKILLS

Most UK cities have <u>four</u> distinct <u>zones</u>. Here's how to spot them on a <u>map</u>:

The <u>Central Business District</u> (CBD) is usually in the <u>middle</u> of a city. Most amenities and services are found here. The CBD is often surrounded by a <u>ring road</u>.

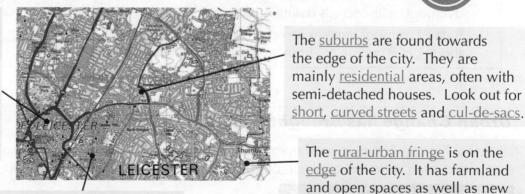

The <u>suburbs</u> are found towards the edge of the city. They are mainly <u>residential</u> areas, often with semi-detached houses. Look out for <u>short</u>, <u>curved streets</u> and <u>cul-de-sacs</u>.

The <u>rural-urban fringe</u> is on the <u>edge</u> of the city. It has farmland and open spaces as well as new housing developments and large retail and business parks. A mixture of <u>white space</u> and built-up areas show this on a map.

The <u>inner city</u> area often has a <u>mix</u> of land uses — mainly <u>residential</u> but with some <u>businesses</u> and <u>recreational</u> parks. Lots of short, <u>parallel</u> roads often show areas of terraced housing in the inner city.

The school zone is the one I usually try to avoid...

If you think anywhere south of Manchester is basically London, it's probably a good idea to take a long, hard look at the map at the top of this page. Urban zones will come in useful over the next few pages too.

Unit 2A — Urban Issues and Challenges

Change in UK Cities — Liverpool

CASE STUDY

Right, it's time for me to stop blabbing on about UK urban areas in general and put some meat on the bones. Liverpool is a classic example of how changes in a city provide both opportunities and challenges.

Liverpool is a Port City in North West England

Liverpool's Liver Building

1) Liverpool developed on the River Mersey estuary — its location allows it to export both goods and culture, making it a gateway between the UK and the rest of the world.

2) Liverpool is an internationally significant city — it's a UNESCO World Heritage Site, the World Capital City of Pop, and a European Capital of Culture. Almost 840 000 foreign tourists visited Liverpool in 2017, contributing £358 million to the UK's economy.

3) Liverpool also plays a vital role for people in the UK. It is the second biggest city in the North West, and contributes a great deal to the UK's manufacturing industry — 3000 companies employ over 50 000 local people and generate £3.2 billion for the economy.

Migration Has Influenced Liverpool's Growth and Character

Two types of migration have greatly influenced the character of Liverpool:

The accents of different groups of immigrants may have contributed to Liverpool's distinctive 'Scouse' accent.

1 National Migration

1) Welsh migrants arrived in Liverpool in the late 1700s and early 1800s, attracted by its developing industry and work on the canals and railways. By 1813, almost 10% of the population was Welsh.

2) National migration rates increased again when famine struck Ireland in 1845. Around 2 million Irish migrants arrived in Liverpool in a single decade and by 1850, over 20% of Liverpool's population was Irish.

3) About 75% of Liverpudlians have some Irish ancestry.

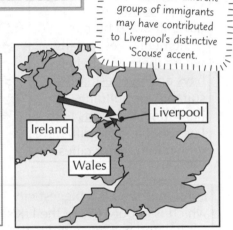

2 International Migration

1) Ships from around the world have been arriving in Liverpool since its port was built in 1715.

2) Liverpool is home to Europe's first ever Chinatown, dating back to the 19th century.

3) The UK's oldest Black African community is also found in Liverpool, with records dating back to at least 1730.

4) Today, Liverpool remains an ethnically diverse city — about 1 in 8 people are from an ethnic minority background.

Urban Change has Brought Opportunities to Liverpool...

Liverpool has slowly transitioned from a busy port and manufacturing centre to a modern tourist destination and centre for creative industries. This change has led to many opportunities:

Environmental Opportunities

1) Urban greening — the decline of industry left many areas of Liverpool run down and open spaces as wasteland. Planners are trying to develop and preserve open spaces such as public parks and gardens. Liverpool ONE, a large shopping and leisure complex, includes a five-acre park (called Chavasse Park) in the city centre.

2) Cycle and pedestrian routes — to encourage people to get out of their cars and reduce greenhouse gas emissions, green spaces are being made more accessible.

Change in UK Cities — Liverpool

Social and Economic Opportunities

1) Cultural mixing — ethnic diversity has brought a range of foods, festivals and cultural experiences to the city, attracting lots of people, e.g. Liverpool's Chinatown has a thriving Chinese community and is a popular tourist destination.

2) Recreation and entertainment — the Albert Dock has been restored and developed to include many shops, restaurants and museums (e.g. the Beatles Story). The Echo Arena sport and concert venue was built on a brownfield site at Kings Dock. £1 billion was spent regenerating the city centre to create Liverpool ONE.

3) Employment — the tourism and service sectors offer a combined total of 160 000 jobs. Development of the 'Baltic Triangle' area turned derelict factories and warehouses into spaces for creative industries, such as film-making and digital design. Some traditional industry also remains, e.g. a car manufacturing plant at Halewood, and Liverpool2 (a container port which opened in 2016).

4) Integrated transport systems — Merseytravel operates the city's bus, train and ferry networks. Prepaid cards can be used across all networks, making it easier to get around the city and encouraging public transport use.

...but also Challenges

Environmental Challenges

1) Dereliction — as wealthier people left the inner city, buildings were abandoned. Derelict buildings were vandalised and many areas, e.g. Toxteth, became run down.

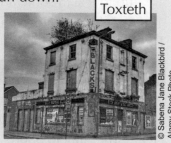
Toxteth

2) Building on brownfield and greenfield sites — as a city grows and more people move to the suburbs, pressure to build on greenfield sites increases. This destroys natural habitats. Liverpool City Council have to consider the environmental impact of proposed building works, e.g. in 2016 they rejected a plan to build 160 new homes on greenfield land. Building on brownfield sites is better for the environment but the land needs clearing and decontaminating first. Many developments in Liverpool have used brownfield sites, including Kings Dock and Jurys Inn.

3) Waste disposal — as the city's population increases, more people are producing waste but there is less space to store it. A new waste and recycling centre in Old Swan was opened in December 2015.

Social and Economic Challenges

1) Urban deprivation — industrial decline in the 20th century left Liverpool's inner city very deprived. Anfield and Toxteth are among the most deprived areas in England.

2) Housing inequality — regeneration in some parts of the city has increased inequality. Wealthier areas have better access to housing, education and healthcare. Old housing is being cleared and replaced with modern housing, but it's often too expensive for former residents, forcing them to leave.

3) Education and employment inequality — many children in deprived areas leave school without basic qualifications, leading to low incomes and high unemployment. Youth unemployment in Anfield is 8.5% compared to the 2.8% national average.

4) Unhealthy lifestyles — unhealthy behaviour, e.g. drinking, smoking and having a poor diet, is more common in deprived areas such as Knowsley, where the life expectancy for women is 15 years lower than the neighbouring (and wealthier) area of St. Helens.

Turn over for another problem that Liverpool faces — urban sprawl.

Change in UK Cities — Liverpool

CASE STUDY

Urban Sprawl Puts Pressure on the Rural-Urban Fringe

Urban sprawl is the unplanned growth of urban areas into the surrounding countryside. The rural-urban fringe is an area of transition where urban and rural land uses mix.

1) As Liverpool has grown, it has sprawled, merging with surrounding urban areas to create the Merseyside conurbation. This has affected the rural-urban fringe:

- Large housing estates, e.g. Croxteth Park, have been built on rural greenfield land, destroying open spaces and ecosystems.

- Out-of-town developments, e.g. Knowsley Business Park, take advantage of cheaper but still accessible land outside the city. However, rural land is lost when they are built, and they can cause pollution and congestion, as people often travel to them by car.

☐ Merseyside conurbation

2) Commuter settlements, e.g. Aughton, are places in the rural-urban fringe where the majority of the population leaves the town each day to work elsewhere. These settlements can cause challenges:

- New housing developments can affect a rural settlement's character and harm the environment.

- Demand for houses increases house prices, so some local residents can't afford to stay in the area.

- Businesses in commuter settlements may suffer, as the majority of the population are absent a lot of the time and may spend their money where they work rather than where they live.

- Large numbers of commuters can increase pollution, traffic congestion and parking problems.

The Anfield Project Aims To Regenerate Liverpool

EXAMPLE

Regeneration is the redevelopment of an urban area to improve the physical environment and quality of life for residents. Anfield was one of the most deprived areas in England:

- Many homes were substandard or derelict — those that were vacant for more than 5 years were being sold for just £1 (on the condition that they were fully renovated).

- The area had many economic and social problems including high unemployment (up to 9% in some areas), criminal activity and vandalism.

© Paul Thompson Images / Alamy Stock Photo

The Anfield Project is an urban regeneration project in Liverpool. Liverpool City Council, Liverpool Football Club and the Your Housing Group have pledged to invest £260 million to regenerate Anfield.

Social and Economic Features

1) Over £36 million has already been spent in Anfield and Rockfield — over 300 derelict houses have been refurbished, and there are plans for 600 new homes.

2) The Anfield Sports and Community Centre has been refurbished and a new health centre and school have opened.

3) A new high street has been planned, including a £10 million hotel. Existing businesses have been given the opportunity to stay, and local independent businesses are being encouraged to move in.

Artist's impression of Anfield Regeneration

© ken biggs / Alamy Stock Photo

Environmental Features

1) Stanley Park has seen major improvements — the footpath has been improved, dead trees have been replaced and the nearby car park has been resurfaced.

2) A £4.5 million environmental scheme started in 2017, aiming to narrow roads to create wider, tree-lined pavements and a pedestrian-friendly area.

My brain needs regenerating — it's been left derelict for so long...

Right, lots of stuff here... Make sure you know both the opportunities and challenges that urban change has created in the UK area you've studied. Then brush up on a regeneration project that tackled these challenges.

Sustainable Urban Living

Cripes, it's the 's' word again — it wouldn't be a geography topic without it though. This time it's about sustainable cities. Before starting, please put your eyelids in the open position and turn off your snoring...

Urban Areas Need to Become More Sustainable

1) Sustainable living means living in a way that lets people meet their needs now, without reducing the ability of people to meet their needs in the future.

2) Basically, it means living in a way that doesn't irreversibly damage the environment or use up resources faster than they can be replaced.

3) Big cities need so many resources that it's unlikely they'll ever be truly sustainable. But things can be done to make a city (and the way people live there) more sustainable.

Cities can Conserve Water and Energy

1) Water and energy are vital resources in cities, but they're rarely managed sustainably.

2) Conservation schemes can make the use of these resources more sustainable.

It's called energy conservation, ma'am...

Water Conservation Schemes

1) Only as much water should be taken from the environment as can be naturally replaced.

2) Water conservation schemes reduce the amount of water used. For example, by:

- collecting rainwater for use on gardens or for flushing toilets.
- installing toilets that flush less water.
- installing water meters so that people have to pay for the water that they use.
- encouraging people to use less water, e.g. by turning off taps when not in use.

EXAMPLE: In Curitiba in Brazil, the government has introduced various policies to promote sustainable water use, including the installation of water meters in homes and hosepipe bans. The city also has separate systems for non-drinking water, so less drinking water is used. These schemes have successfully reduced Curitiba's water consumption — it is around half that of other Latin American cities.

Energy Conservation Schemes

1) Burning fossil fuels to generate power isn't sustainable because they'll run out. They also contribute to climate change by producing greenhouse gases (see p.16).

2) Energy conservation schemes reduce the use of fossil fuels. For example, by:

- promoting renewable energy (e.g. wind or solar) over coal or gas fired power stations.
- encouraging people to make their homes more energy efficient, e.g. governments can let homeowners who generate electricity from renewable sources (e.g. solar panels) sell excess energy to the national grid.
- making sure that all new homes meet minimum energy efficiency requirements.
- encouraging people to reduce car use, e.g. by using public transport.

EXAMPLE: In 2009, Curitiba renovated its 'Green Line' transport system — it now includes dedicated bus lanes for biofuel buses. There is also a scheme to replace all of the city's street lights with energy-efficient bulbs, and the city gets 84% of its energy from renewable hydroelectric power. These schemes have been successful — Curitiba's CO_2 emissions from electricity are about 65% less than other Latin American cities.

Curitiba, Brazil

© Andre Seale / Alamy Stock Photo

Sustainable Urban Living

Creating Green Spaces Also Helps a City to Become Sustainable

1) Cities can be noisy, dirty, busy and hot — they are unsustainable because people find them unpleasant and stressful. Creating green space within urban areas ensures that they remain places where people want to live and work. This is because:

- they provide naturally cooler areas where people can relax in very hot weather.
- they encourage people to exercise more and to use alternative transport, e.g. bikes. This makes people healthier and less stressed.
- they make people feel happier by providing a break from the noise and bustle of the city.

2) Green spaces also have environmental benefits. For example, they reduce:

- air pollution by creating pockets of clean air.
- the risk of flooding by reducing surface runoff when it rains.

EXAMPLE: In 2007, Curitiba launched a government scheme that encouraged landowners to preserve green areas, limiting urban sprawl. People who created parks were exempt from local and federal taxes. There are now 28 parks in the city, including the 1.4 million m² Barigui Park, which is designed to absorb flood waters so unsightly flood defences are not needed.

Barigui Park, Curitiba

Cities Produce a Lot of Waste Which Needs to be Recycled

1) More recycling means fewer resources are used, e.g. metal cans can be melted down and used to make more cans.

2) Less waste is produced, which reduces the amount that goes to landfill.

3) Landfill is unsustainable as it wastes resources that could be recycled, and eventually there'll be nowhere left to bury the waste. Decomposing landfill also releases greenhouse gases.

4) Waste recycling schemes include:

- kerbside collections of recyclable materials.
- building recycling facilities to deal with larger items, e.g. fridges.
- websites, e.g. Freecycle™ and Freegle, where items are offered for free so they can be used by others instead of being thrown away.

If present trends continue, there will be 12 billion tonnes of plastic in landfill by 2050.

Free to a good home

EXAMPLE: Curitiba is one of only eight cities in the world which collects 100% of its waste, of which 70% is recycled. To further encourage recycling, the government launched 'The Green Exchange Programme' in 1989 — residents receive 1 kg of food or bus tickets for every 4 kg of recyclable waste collected. This scheme has led to the collection of 6800 tonnes of waste each year.

© Marion Kaplan / Alamy Stock Photo

Energy conservation — sloths have nailed it...

Examiners have been known to go mad for a bit of sustainability so if you don't learn this, you'll be throwing marks away. Get your head round everything, then have a crack at this question:

1) Explain two ways that urban areas can be made more sustainable. [4]

Traffic Management

Cities have so many cars that <u>traffic congestion</u> is a massive <u>problem</u>. Seems like we're going nowhere...

Traffic Congestion is a Big Problem for Urban Areas

Traffic congestion from cars and lorries causes <u>problems</u> in urban areas:

- <u>Environmental</u> problems — lots of traffic increases <u>air pollution</u>, and the release of <u>greenhouse gases</u> contributes to <u>climate change</u> (see page 16).
- <u>Economic</u> problems — congestion can make people <u>late</u> for work and <u>delay</u> deliveries, causing companies to <u>lose money</u>.
- <u>Social</u> problems — there is a higher chance of <u>accidents</u>. Congestion also causes <u>frustration</u> for drivers, <u>health issues</u> for pedestrians and cyclists (who breathe in polluted air) and can <u>delay</u> emergency vehicles.

Using Public Transport Reduces Traffic Congestion

Urban transport strategies encourage people to use <u>public transport</u> instead of travelling by car. Many of these strategies have been used in <u>London</u>:

1) The <u>Docklands Light Railway</u> is an automatic train system that connects <u>east London</u> to the <u>city centre</u>. It operates mostly on tracks <u>above</u> street level, though parts are <u>underground</u>. It is used by around <u>120 million</u> people each year.

2) London's <u>Underground</u> system takes <u>3 million people</u> off the roads every day. A new underground line, <u>Crossrail</u>, is being built <u>east</u> to <u>west</u> across the city — it will <u>increase</u> rail capacity in central London by <u>10%</u> when it's completed in Autumn 2019.

3) <u>Self-service bicycles</u> are available to hire, and are <u>cheaper</u> than other forms of public transport. <u>Bike lanes</u> and special bike <u>signals</u> at junctions can improve cyclists' <u>safety</u>.

4) Electronic 'Oyster Cards' allow people to travel on most of London's public transport networks without buying <u>separate</u> tickets. They can be automatically <u>topped up</u> and are <u>swiped</u> on <u>entry</u> and <u>exit</u> from stations and buses, making them <u>quick</u> and <u>easy</u> to use.

Docklands Light Railway, Canary Wharf

© Mark Bourdillon / Alamy Stock Photo

Traffic Flow Can Also be Managed

Traffic congestion can also be reduced by managing the <u>flow</u> of traffic through the city. For example:

1) <u>Ring roads</u> and <u>pedestrianised</u> shopping streets keep traffic away from the city centre, making it <u>safer</u> and <u>less polluted</u>, and preventing <u>congestion</u> on narrow city centre roads.

2) <u>Bus priority lanes</u> stop buses being held up in traffic, making them more <u>attractive</u> than driving.

3) <u>Parking restrictions</u> make sure parked cars don't <u>block</u> traffic flow on narrow roads. '<u>Urban clearways</u>' are major roads along which <u>stopping</u> or <u>parking</u> is very <u>limited</u>.

4) <u>Congestion charging</u> discourages drivers from entering the city centre at peak times. A scheme in <u>Durham</u> cut the number of cars entering the historic city centre by <u>85%</u>.

EXAMPLE: Curitiba's <u>Bus Rapid Transit</u> (BRT) system uses a series of dedicated <u>bus lanes</u> to ensure that bus journeys are quick. Over <u>700 000</u> passengers use the buses each day, and Curitiba's carbon emissions are <u>25% lower</u> per capita than the average Brazilian city. The city centre's main shopping area is also <u>pedestrianised</u>, further encouraging people to leave their cars at home.

Traffic jams — a sticky problem, and they're spreading...

Something for you to think over next time you're stuck in traffic. Basically, try to get as many people as possible to ditch their cars for public transport, then just cleverly manage the flow of the traffic that's left. Easy, no?

Revision Summary

Well, that was a whole load of fun. I bet you're dying to go and tell someone about all the opportunities and challenges in urban areas now — but if you can hold it in just a little bit longer, have a go at these questions to check you really know your megacities from your commuter settlements. Once you can answer them standing on your head, feel free to go and share the joy with as many people you like. Although you should probably crack on with the next section instead.

Urban Growth (p.69-72) ☐

1) What is urbanisation?
2) Describe the urbanisation trend in HICs.
3) In what type of country is urbanisation taking place most rapidly?
4) Give three push factors that lead to rural-urban migration.
5) Define pull factors and give two examples.
6) Give one factor, other than migration, that causes urbanisation.
7) What is a megacity?
8) Using a named example, describe two causes of urban growth.
9) a) Using a case study of a city in an LIC or NEE, describe the economic opportunities created by urban growth.
   b) Describe the environmental challenges that have been caused by rapid urban growth in that city.
10) a) Give a named example of an urban planning scheme in an LIC or NEE.
    b) Explain how it has improved the quality of life for the urban poor.

Change in UK Cities (p.73-76) ☑

11) Describe the distribution of population in the UK.
12) Why are most cities in the UK found in lowland areas?
13) Name the four different city zones.
14) Describe the location of a named UK city.
15) Explain the importance of a named UK city.
16) a) Explain how migration has influenced the character of a named UK city.
    b) Describe the economic opportunities that urban change has created in that city.
    c) Describe two challenges that urban change has created in that city.
17) What is urban sprawl?
18) Describe two ways that development is putting pressure on the rural-urban fringe.
19) What is a commuter settlement?
20) Using a named example, describe the problems that can occur in commuter settlements.
21) a) Explain why regeneration was needed in a named urban area of the UK.
    b) Describe the main features of an urban regeneration project in that area.

Urban Sustainability (p.77-79) ☑

22) What does sustainable urban living mean?
23) Describe how water conservation schemes can help make a city more sustainable.
24) Describe two energy conservation schemes that can be used to make a city more sustainable.
25) Explain the importance of green space for sustainable living in urban environments.
26) Describe how waste recycling can help make cities more sustainable.
27) Give two economic problems caused by traffic congestion in urban areas.
28) Describe two different ways that public transport can be used to reduce traffic congestion in urban areas.
29) Give three strategies for managing traffic flow in urban areas, and explain how they work.

Measuring Development

This topic is a little <u>tricky</u> — but take a deep breath and believe in yourself and you'll be just <u>fine</u>.

Development is when a Country is Improving

1) Development is the <u>progress</u> in <u>economic growth</u>, use of <u>technology</u> and improving <u>welfare</u> that a country has made. When a country develops it basically gets <u>better</u> for the people living there — their quality of life <u>improves</u> (e.g. their wealth, health and safety).

2) The <u>level</u> of development is <u>different</u> in different countries, e.g. France is more developed than Ethiopia. The difference in development between more and less developed countries is called the <u>global development gap</u>.

I make this development about 25 m.

There are Loads of Measures of Development...

1) Development is pretty <u>hard</u> to measure because it includes so many things. But you can <u>compare</u> the development of different countries using '<u>measures of development</u>'.

2) Some measures look at a country's level of <u>economic</u> development, while others look at <u>social</u> factors that provide information about people's quality of life.

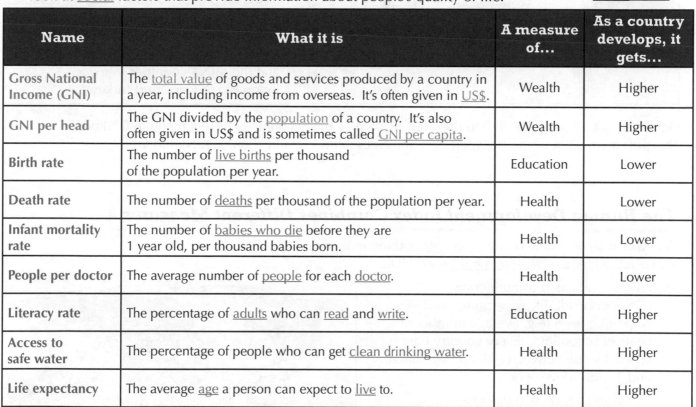

Name	What it is	A measure of...	As a country develops, it gets...
Gross National Income (GNI)	The <u>total value</u> of goods and services produced by a country in a year, including income from overseas. It's often given in <u>US$</u>.	Wealth	Higher
GNI per head	The GNI divided by the <u>population</u> of a country. It's also often given in US$ and is sometimes called <u>GNI per capita</u>.	Wealth	Higher
Birth rate	The number of <u>live births</u> per thousand of the population per year.	Education	Lower
Death rate	The number of <u>deaths</u> per thousand of the population per year.	Health	Lower
Infant mortality rate	The number of <u>babies who die</u> before they are 1 year old, per thousand babies born.	Health	Lower
People per doctor	The average number of <u>people</u> for each <u>doctor</u>.	Health	Lower
Literacy rate	The percentage of <u>adults</u> who can <u>read</u> and <u>write</u>.	Education	Higher
Access to safe water	The percentage of people who can get <u>clean drinking water</u>.	Health	Higher
Life expectancy	The average <u>age</u> a person can expect to <u>live</u> to.	Health	Higher

...But all these Measures have Limitations

1) GNI per head can be <u>misleading</u> when used on its own because it is an <u>average</u> — variations within the country don't show up.

   EXAMPLE: the GNI per person in <u>Qatar</u> is as high as some HICs, but Qatar actually has a <u>small</u> number of extremely <u>wealthy</u> people and a <u>lot</u> of relatively <u>poor</u> people.

Measures of development aren't always accurate either — e.g. GNI usually misses out informal employment, which can account for a large proportion of national income.

2) <u>Social</u> indicators can also be misleading if they are used on their <u>own</u> because, as a country develops, some aspects develop <u>before</u> others. So it might seem like a country is more developed than it actually is.

   EXAMPLE: <u>Cuba</u> has a <u>low birth rate</u>, which suggests that it is <u>more developed</u>, but a relatively <u>high death rate</u>, which suggests that it is <u>less developed</u>.

Measuring Development

Countries are often Classified Based on How Wealthy they are

Despite the problems with using one measure of development on its own, the most <u>common</u> way of classifying a country's level of development is by looking at its <u>wealth</u>.

When you write about countries at different levels of development, use the terms HIC, LIC and NEE.

Higher Income Countries (HICs)

HICs are the <u>wealthiest</u> countries in the world, where the GNI per head is <u>high</u>.
EXAMPLES: UK, USA, Canada, France.

Lower Income Countries (LICs)

LICs are the <u>poorest</u> countries in the world, where the GNI per head is very <u>low</u>.
EXAMPLES: Afghanistan, Somalia and Uganda.

Newly Emerging Economies (NEEs)

A country's wealth doesn't stay the <u>same</u>. Some countries (NEEs) are rapidly getting <u>richer</u> as their economy <u>moves</u> from being based on primary industry (e.g. agriculture) to secondary industry (manufacturing).
EXAMPLES: the <u>BRICS</u> (Brazil, Russia, India, China and South Africa) and the <u>MINT</u> countries (Mexico, Indonesia, Nigeria and Turkey).

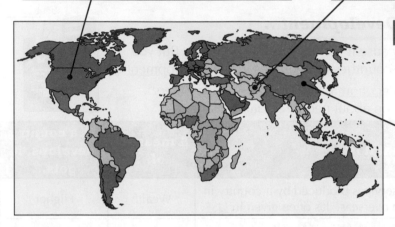

However, not all countries fit into this classification — many countries have a <u>medium</u> GNI per head. This puts them somewhere <u>between</u> LICs and NEEs in the classification, e.g. Namibia.

The Human Development Index Combines Different Measures

One way to <u>avoid</u> some of the <u>problems</u> of using individual measures is to use the <u>Human Development Index</u> (HDI).

1) HDI is calculated using <u>income</u> (GNI per head), <u>life expectancy</u> and <u>education level</u> (e.g. average number of years of schooling). Every country has an HDI value between <u>0</u> (least developed) and <u>1</u> (most developed).

2) The <u>combination</u> of measures means that a country's HDI value tells you about both the country's level of <u>economic development</u> and the <u>quality of life</u> for people who live there.

3) The classification of countries by HDI mostly looks <u>similar</u> to GNI per head, but there are some <u>differences</u> — e.g. <u>Nigeria</u> is an NEE according to its wealth, but it has a low HDI.

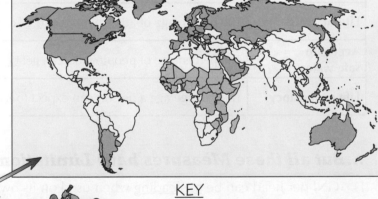

KEY
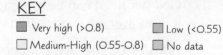
■ Very high (>0.8)   ■ Low (<0.55)
□ Medium-High (0.55-0.8)   ■ No data

You NEEd to get these pages LICked...
...or you might have a HICcup in your exam. Once you know them, have a go at this question:
1) Describe one limitation of using a single social indicator as a measure of development. [2]

Development and the DTM

Forget catwalk models, it's time for something much more exciting — a classic <u>population model</u>...

Development is Linked to the Demographic Transition Model

1) The <u>Demographic Transition Model</u> (DTM) shows how <u>birth rates</u> and <u>death rates</u> affect <u>population growth</u>.

2) When the birth rate is <u>higher</u> than the death rate, the population <u>grows</u> — this is called <u>natural increase</u>. It's called <u>natural decrease</u> when the death rate is higher than the birth rate.

3) Birth rates and death rates <u>differ</u> from country to country, depending on level of <u>development</u>. They also change <u>within</u> a country over time as it <u>develops</u>.

GEOGRAPHY SKILLS

Population pyramids show the population of a country by age. The number of men and women goes on the horizontal axis and their age groups go on the vertical axis (see p.133).

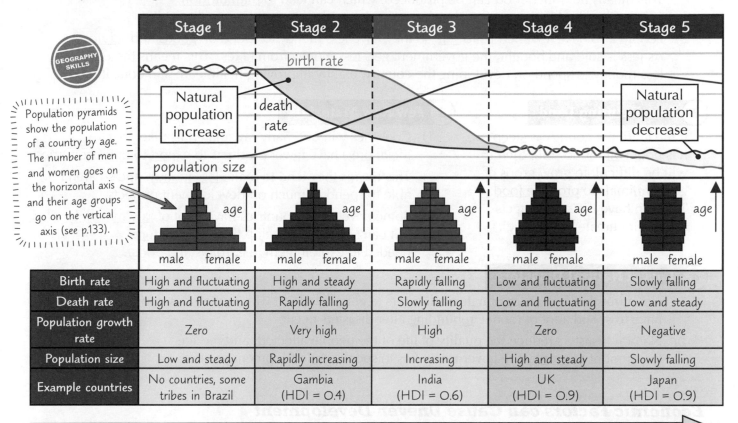

	Stage 1	Stage 2	Stage 3	Stage 4	Stage 5
Birth rate	High and fluctuating	High and steady	Rapidly falling	Low and fluctuating	Slowly falling
Death rate	High and fluctuating	Rapidly falling	Slowly falling	Low and fluctuating	Low and steady
Population growth rate	Zero	Very high	High	Zero	Negative
Population size	Low and steady	Rapidly increasing	Increasing	High and steady	Slowly falling
Example countries	No countries, some tribes in Brazil	Gambia (HDI = 0.4)	India (HDI = 0.6)	UK (HDI = 0.9)	Japan (HDI = 0.9)

DEVELOPMENT →

<u>Stage 1</u> is the <u>least developed</u> — very few places are at stage 1 now.

The birth rate is <u>high</u> because there's no use of <u>contraception</u>. People also have lots of children because <u>infant mortality</u> rates are <u>high</u>.

The death rate is high due to <u>poor healthcare</u> or <u>famine</u>, and life expectancy is low.

<u>Stage 2</u> is <u>not very developed</u> — many <u>LICs</u> are in stage 2.

The birth rate is high — the economy is based on <u>agriculture</u>, so people have lots of children to work on farms.

Better <u>healthcare</u> increases life expectancy, so death rates fall.

<u>Stage 3</u> is more <u>developed</u> — most <u>NEEs</u> are at stage 3.

The birth rate falls rapidly as the use of <u>contraception</u> increases and more women work instead of having children. The economy changes from farming to <u>manufacturing</u>, so fewer children are needed to work on farms.

Improved <u>healthcare</u> means that the death rate falls and life expectancy increases.

<u>Stages 4</u> and <u>5</u> are the <u>most developed</u> — most <u>HICs</u> are at one of these stages.

Birth rates are low — people expect a <u>high standard of living</u>, and may have dependent <u>elderly relatives</u>, so there is less money available for having children.

<u>Healthcare</u> is good, so the death rate is low and life expectancy is high.

So HDI and GNI for HICs and LICs link to the stages of the DTM, right...

I'd say that's TMA — too many acronyms. Still, the DTM is a useful thing to know, so make sure you learn it.

Uneven Development

Zzzzzz... oh, sorry, I nodded off for a minute there. You need to know the reasons why there are global inequalities — i.e. why countries differ in how developed they are. There are a fair few, but you'll be OK...

Physical Factors can Affect How Developed a Country is

A country is more likely to be less developed if it has:

1 A Poor Climate

1) Some countries have a really hot, really cold or really dry climate where not much will grow. This means not much food can be produced, which can lead to malnutrition, e.g. in Chad and Ethiopia. People who are malnourished have a low quality of life.

2) People also have fewer crops to sell, so they have less money to spend on goods and services. As less is sold and bought, the government gets less money from taxes. This means there's less money to spend on developing the country, e.g. by improving healthcare and education.

2 Poor Farming Land

If the land in a country is steep or has poor soil (or no soil), then it will be difficult to grow crops or graze animals to produce food. This can have the same effects as a poor climate (see above).

3 Few Raw Materials

1) Countries without many raw materials (like coal, oil or metal ores) have fewer products to export to other countries.

2) This means they tend to make less money, and so aren't able to spend as much on development projects.

3) Some developing countries have a lot of raw materials, but can't afford to develop the infrastructure needed to exploit them (e.g. roads and ports).

4 Lots of Natural Disasters

1) Countries that have a lot of natural disasters (e.g. Bangladesh, which often has floods) have to spend a lot of money rebuilding after disasters occur.

2) Natural disasters reduce the quality of life of the people affected, and reduce the amount of money the government has to spend on development projects.

Economic Factors can Cause Uneven Development

A country is more likely to be at a lower level of development if it has:

Poor Trade Links

1) Trade is the exchange of goods and services between countries.

2) World trade patterns (who trades with whom) influence a country's economy and so affect its level of development.

3) If a country has poor trade links (it trades a small amount with only a few countries) it won't make a lot of money, so there'll be less to spend on development.

Lots of Debt

1) Very poor countries borrow money from other countries and international organisations, e.g. to help cope with the aftermath of a natural disaster.

2) This money has to be paid back (sometimes with interest), so there's less for development.

An Economy Based On Primary Products

1) Countries that mostly export primary products (raw materials like timber and metal) tend to be less developed than countries that export manufactured goods. This is because primary products are sold for less profit than manufactured goods.

2) The prices of primary products also fluctuate — sometimes the price falls below the cost of production. For example, in 2018, the price of cocoa dropped below the cost of production in Ghana, and many farmers had to rely on subsidies from the government. Wealthy countries can also force down the prices of the raw materials they buy from poorer countries.

Uneven Development

There are also Historical Causes of Uneven Development

Colonisation

1) Countries that were <u>colonised</u> (ruled by another country) are often at a <u>lower</u> development level when they gain independence than they would be if they hadn't been colonised.

2) European countries colonised many countries in <u>Asia</u>, <u>Africa</u>, <u>Australasia</u> and the <u>Americas</u> between the 16th and 20th centuries. The colonisers removed <u>raw materials</u> and sold back <u>manufactured goods</u>. This meant that <u>profits</u> went to the <u>colonisers</u> rather than the colonised countries, increasing inequality. Colonisation also prevented the colonised countries from developing their own <u>industries</u>.

Conflict

1) <u>War</u>, especially <u>civil war</u>, can slow or reduce development, even after the war is over.

2) Money is spent on <u>arms</u> and on training soldiers instead of development, people are killed and damage is done to <u>infrastructure</u> and property. Important <u>services</u> such as healthcare and education are <u>disrupted</u>, which can lead to an increase in <u>infant mortality</u> rates and a decline in <u>literacy</u> rates.

3) For example, in 2008 <u>Syria</u> had an HDI value of 0.65. In 2016, after five years of war, this had <u>dropped</u> to 0.54.

Uneven Development has Consequences

Uneven development leads to differences in <u>wealth</u> and <u>health</u>, and has caused large flows of <u>international migration</u>.

Wealth

1) People in more developed countries have a <u>higher income</u> than those in less developed countries — e.g. GNI per head in the UK is over 40 times higher than in Chad.

2) Uneven development can also lead to big inequalities in wealth <u>within</u> countries, e.g. in 2017, the richest 10% of Kenya's population earned, on average, 23 times more than the poorest 10%.

3) Wealth can impact people's <u>standard of living</u> — the wealthy can afford goods and services that make their lives more <u>comfortable</u> and <u>convenient</u>, e.g. <u>cars</u>.

Health

1) Healthcare in more developed countries is usually <u>better</u> than in less developed countries.

2) People in HICs live longer — e.g. the UK's <u>life expectancy</u> is 81, but in Chad it's only 53.

3) <u>Infant mortality</u> is much higher in less developed countries — e.g. it's 73 per 1000 births in Chad, compared to 3.7 per 1000 births in the UK.

4) In LICs and NEEs, the lack of <u>adequate healthcare</u> can mean that people die from <u>diseases</u> that could be <u>easily treated</u> in HICs — e.g. in 2016, <u>diarrhoea</u> is estimated to have killed over 1.4 million people in South Asia and sub-Saharan Africa.

International Migration

1) Many people from LICs and NEEs move to HICs to escape <u>conflict</u> or to <u>improve</u> their quality of life.

2) For example, over 130 000 people move from Mexico (an NEE) to the USA (an HIC) legally each year (and thousands more enter illegally) in search of <u>better paid jobs</u> and a <u>higher quality of life</u>.

3) Migrant <u>workers</u> contribute to the economies of the <u>HICs</u> they move to instead of the <u>LICs</u> they leave, which further <u>increases</u> the <u>development gap</u>.

Diarrhoea — not always a laughing matter...

1) Giving one example of each, explain how physical, historical and economic factors can affect a country's level of development. [6]

Reducing the Global Development Gap

Reducing the global development gap is a <u>massive</u> task — but there are quite a few ways to go about it...

There are *Lots of Strategies* that can *Reduce the Development Gap*

Investment

1) <u>Foreign-direct investment</u> (FDI) is when people or companies in one country buy <u>property</u> or invest in <u>infrastructure</u> in another.

2) FDI leads to <u>better access</u> to finance, technology and expertise, as well as improved <u>infrastructure</u> and <u>industry</u>, and an increase in <u>services</u>.

3) E.g. between 1987 and 2018, <u>Vietnam</u> received FDI worth more than <u>US $182 billion</u>, which helped to develop many industries, such as motorbike manufacturing and telecommunications.

Aid

1) <u>Money</u> or <u>resources</u> (e.g. food, medicine) are given to a country by a charity or foreign government.

2) The money is used for <u>development projects</u>, e.g. for constructing schools, building dams and wells and providing farming knowledge and equipment. For example, in 2018-2019, the <u>UK</u> provided over <u>£180 million</u> in aid to <u>South Sudan</u>, funding 17 projects that included improving access to water, healthcare and education.

3) Aid can definitely help, but sometimes it is wasted by <u>corrupt governments</u>. Or once the money runs out, projects can stop working if there isn't enough <u>local knowledge</u> and <u>support</u>.

Fair Trade

1) The fair trade movement is all about <u>farmers</u> in LICs getting a <u>fair price</u> for the goods they produce, e.g. coffee and bananas, allowing them to provide for their families.

2) <u>Companies</u> who want to sell products labelled as 'fair trade' have to <u>pay producers</u> a fair price.

3) Buyers pay extra on top of that so that farmers receive a <u>premium</u> to help develop their local area. E.g. in 2016, Fairtrade <u>tea</u> farmers in <u>Malawi</u> used some of their premium to expand their local hospital, build a new school and install a pipeline for clean water.

4) But there are problems — in some cases, only a <u>tiny proportion</u> of the extra money reaches the producers, while the rest boosts retailers' <u>profits</u>.

Using Intermediate Technology

1) Intermediate technology includes tools, machines and systems that improve quality of life but are also <u>simple</u> to use, <u>affordable</u> to buy or build and <u>cheap</u> to maintain.

2) E.g. <u>solar-powered</u> LED <u>lightbulbs</u> are used in parts of <u>Nepal</u> where the only other lighting options are polluting and dangerous kerosene lamps or wood fires. This allows people to work, and children to study after dark. As a result, <u>skills</u>, <u>incomes</u> and industrial <u>output</u> can increase.

Microfinance Loans

1) Microfinance is when <u>small loans</u> are given to people in LICs who may not be able to get loans from banks. This enables them to start their own businesses and become financially <u>independent</u>.

2) For example, in the Amhara region of <u>Ethiopia</u>, people who joined a microfinance organisation benefited from <u>higher incomes</u> and were able to invest in more <u>livestock</u>.

3) Although microfinance works for some people, it can also cause problems by encouraging people to get into <u>debt</u>. It's also not clear that it can reduce poverty on a <u>large scale</u>.

Reducing the Global Development Gap

Industrial Development

In countries with a very low level of development, agriculture makes up a large portion of the economy. Developing industry boosts GNI and development, as productivity, skills and infrastructure are improved.

Debt Relief

1) Debt relief is when some or all of a country's debt is cancelled, or interest rates are lowered, meaning the country has more money to spend on development.

2) For example, Zambia had $4 billion of debt cancelled in 2005. In 2006, the country had enough money to start a free healthcare scheme for millions of people living in rural areas.

Tourism is Helping Kenya to Increase its Development — EXAMPLE

1) Kenya is a lower income country in East Africa.
   It attracts tourists because of its culture, safari wildlife, warm climate and unspoilt scenery. Kenya's government is trying to boost tourism to increase development. For example:

   • Visa fees for adults were cut by 50% in 2009 to make it cheaper to visit the country. They were also scrapped for children under 16 to encourage more families to visit.

   • Landing fees at airports on the Kenyan coast have been dropped for charter airlines.

2) Tourism increased from 0.9 million visitors in 1995 to 1.4 million in 2017.

Benefits

1) Tourism now directly contributes nearly 4% of Kenya's GDP — money that can be spent on development and improving quality of life. Since 2000, Kenya's score on the Human Development Index has increased from 0.45 to 0.59.

2) Over 1.1 million people are directly or indirectly employed by the tourism industry — that's 9% of all employment in Kenya.

3) Businesses and Kenya's government have invested in transport infrastructure to encourage more tourists to visit, which can also benefit local people. E.g. the new Madaraka Express railway links Kenya's capital, Nairobi, to the coast. This has created jobs, halved the journey time and made it cheaper for people to travel.

4) The 24 national parks charge entry fees to tourists. This money is used to maintain the national parks — this helps to protect the environment and wildlife, so tourists keep visiting.

Negatives

1) Only a small proportion of the money earned goes to locals. The rest goes to big companies, often based in HICs, so it doesn't help to close the development gap.

2) Some Maasai communities have been forced off their land to create national parks and game reserves for tourists.

3) Tourist vehicles damage the environment by destroying vegetation and disturbing animals.

4) In recent years, tourist numbers have fluctuated — especially following terrorist attacks in Kenya. This means that tourism isn't a reliable source of jobs and income.

EXAM QUESTION

Over a million visitors — Kenya believe it?

Make sure you know the main strategies for reducing the development gap, then try this question.

1) Explain how increased tourism can help an LIC or NEE reduce the development gap. [4]

Economic Development in India

India is an NEE with a huge population and lots of potential. Its level of development is middling, but increasing.

India is a Newly Emerging Economy in Southern Asia

1) India is a rapidly developing NEE. It has the second largest population in the world (around 1.3 billion) and is still growing.

2) India has the biggest population and economy in South Asia, so it plays a major role in trade and politics in the region. India's position in the Indian Ocean has also allowed it to establish trade links with south east Asia and the Middle East.

3) India is increasingly important globally — it exports services (e.g. IT support) and manufactured goods (e.g. medicines) across the world, and it's a member of the World Trade Organisation and the G20 (a group of 20 of the world's largest economies).

4) Development in India is happening in a unique political, social, cultural and environmental context:

> • **Political** — India was a British colony until 1947, but now has a democratically elected government.
>
> • **Social** — India has a medium level of development (HDI = 0.64). There are large inequalities — some people are very wealthy, but the majority are poor, and over 20% of the population live in poverty. Education is improving, but the adult literacy rate is still less than 75%.
>
> • **Cultural** — India has a rich and diverse culture. It has over 22 officially recognised languages and is home to followers of many major religions, including Hinduism and Islam. It's also renowned for its production of 'Bollywood' films, which are exported worldwide, and for its distinctive music and dancing styles, e.g. Bhangra.
>
> • **Environmental** — India has a varied landscape, including the Himalayas in the  north, the Thar Desert in the north west, and large areas of forest. The floodplains of several major rivers, such as the Ganges and the Indus, provide fertile farmland. India also has a long coastline — this makes it an attractive tourist destination and has allowed the development of ports, such as Mumbai, increasing trade.

India's Rapid Development means its Industrial Structure is Changing

Gross Domestic Product (GDP) measures a country's wealth.

1) Primary industry (e.g. agriculture) employs 42% of the working population, but is becoming a smaller part of India's economy. It makes up only 15% of GDP.

2) Secondary industry (manufacturing) has grown rapidly. In 1999 it only employed 16% of the workforce, whereas by 2018 it employed 24% of the workforce.

> • The growth of manufacturing industries has stimulated economic development in India by providing people with reliable jobs (compared to seasonal agricultural work).
>
> • Employment can lead to a positive cycle of economic growth, as workers spend their income in local shops and other businesses. These businesses pay taxes, allowing the government to spend more on development, e.g. education and infrastructure, which attracts more industry to the area.
>
> • E.g. in Hyderabad, the government has constructed new business districts and townships to attract industry. In 2018, the city had one of the fastest growing economies in the world.

3) Tertiary (service) and quaternary (knowledge) industries have become a much larger part of the economy, employing 34% of the workforce. Lots of this is due to growth in IT firms (especially in the city of Bengaluru) and in supplying services for foreign companies, such as customer service centres. Tertiary and quaternary industries contribute the most to India's GDP — 62%.

4) India's manufacturing and service industries are still growing quickly, so they're likely to make up a higher proportion of GDP and employ a bigger percentage of the workforce in the future.

Economic Development in India

CASE STUDY

Lots of Transnational Corporations Operate in India

1) <u>Transnational corporations</u> (TNCs) are companies that operate in <u>more than one country</u>.

2) TNC <u>factories</u> are usually located in <u>lower income</u> countries because labour is cheaper, and there are fewer environmental and labour regulations, which means they make more <u>profit</u>.

3) TNC <u>offices</u> and <u>headquarters</u> are usually located in <u>higher income</u> countries because there are more people with <u>administrative</u> skills (because education is better).

4) Many TNCs operate in India, including <u>Unilever</u> — one of the world's biggest food and consumer goods manufacturers. Hindustan Unilever Limited is its Indian division.

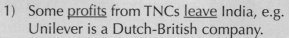

5) TNCs have both <u>advantages</u> and <u>disadvantages</u> for India:

Advantages

1) TNCs provide <u>employment</u> — Unilever employs over <u>16 000</u> people in India.

2) TNCs have to pay <u>tax</u> of about 40% of their income to the Indian government. Hindustan Unilever has annual sales of over <u>$5 billion</u>, so its taxes make a significant contribution to the government's income.

3) Some TNCs run programs to increase <u>development</u> in India. E.g. Unilever's <u>Project Shakti</u> helps poor women in rural areas become entrepreneurs by providing loans and products for them to sell. There are now about <u>75 000 women</u> in the scheme. Unilever has also worked with charities to improve sanitation for over <u>140 million</u> people in India.

Disadvantages

1) Some <u>profits</u> from TNCs <u>leave</u> India, e.g. Unilever is a Dutch-British company.

2) TNCs may <u>close</u> operations in LICs and NEEs, causing <u>job losses</u>. TNCs may also decide to <u>relocate</u> factories to a different area of the country to take advantage of local government incentives (e.g. tax breaks), so jobs can be <u>unreliable</u>.

3) TNCs can cause <u>environmental</u> problems, e.g. factories can contribute to air and water <u>pollution</u> or <u>deplete</u> water supplies.

4) Some TNCs, e.g. <u>fashion brands</u> whose clothes are manufactured in India, have been criticised because their employees receive <u>low pay</u> and have <u>poor working conditions</u>.

India's Relationship with the Wider World is Changing

India is playing a <u>larger role</u> in <u>regional</u> and <u>global politics</u> and <u>trade</u> as it develops:

Political relationships

1) <u>Pakistan</u> and <u>China</u> both disagree with India over who owns some of the land on the <u>border</u>. This has led to <u>tension</u> between the three countries and increased the risk of <u>conflict</u>.

2) India has built relationships with <u>other nations</u> in the region, e.g. by developing the <u>Act East</u> policy to increase its influence in southeast Asia and provide <u>security</u> for the region.

3) India is also working with its neighbours to build the <u>TAPI pipeline</u> to carry natural gas from Turkmenistan, through Afghanistan and Pakistan to India.

Trading relationships

1) <u>Trade</u> is <u>increasingly</u> important to India's <u>economy</u>. The government <u>limit</u> imports and exports, but since <u>1991</u>, they have <u>reduced barriers</u> to trade by reducing <u>tariffs</u> (mostly taxes on imported goods) and forming free trade agreements, such as the <u>Asia-Pacific Trade Agreement</u> with Bangladesh, China, South Korea and Sri Lanka.

2) <u>TNCs</u> account for a large proportion of global trade, so as more foreign companies start up in India (and Indian TNCs start up elsewhere), India's <u>trade increases</u>. In 2014, over <u>3000</u> foreign companies were operating in India. Between 2005 and 2015, <u>foreign direct investment</u> in India increased from US $7.3 billion to US $44 billion.

© Gilitukha / iStock Editorial / Getty Images Plus

Economic Development in India

India Receives Different Types of Aid

India receives <u>different types</u> of aid from <u>individual countries</u> and <u>international organisations</u>:

Type of aid	How it works	Impacts
Short-term	Money and supplies are given to help countries cope with <u>emergencies</u>.	It helps people survive <u>disasters</u>, but doesn't help <u>long-term recovery</u>. **EXAMPLE:** In 2010, <u>floods</u> affected over 1.7 million people in northern India. <u>UNICEF</u> provided emergency supplies, including <u>water purifying tablets</u> and <u>mosquito nets</u>.
Long-term	Money is invested in <u>longer-term</u> projects to help countries become more <u>developed</u>.	It can help India's long-term <u>development</u>, e.g. by improving <u>infrastructure</u> or <u>education</u>. However, India has had problems with corrupt officials <u>misusing</u> aid. **EXAMPLE:** Until 2015, the UK sent <u>£200 million</u> a year to India to <u>improve</u> education, healthcare and sanitation in the poorest areas.
Top-down	An <u>organisation</u> or the <u>government</u> <u>decides</u> how aid should be used.	Projects can improve the country's <u>economy</u>, but may not help the <u>poorest</u> people or be <u>supported</u> by local people. **EXAMPLE:** The <u>Sardar Sarovar dam</u> in Gujarat provides water for drinking and irrigation and generates hydro-electric power, but its construction <u>displaced</u> over 300 000 people.
Bottom-up	Money or supplies are given <u>directly</u> to <u>local communities</u> so they can decide how to use aid themselves.	Projects provide help where it is needed most, so they can improve <u>health</u>, <u>skills</u> and <u>income</u> in poor communities. **EXAMPLE:** The Self-Employed Women's Association (SEWA) has trained local women to <u>maintain</u> and <u>repair</u> water pumps in Gujarat, increasing their <u>skills</u> and improving <u>water supply</u>.

Economic Development has Impacts on Quality of Life and the Environment

As India has developed, there have been <u>positive</u> and <u>negative</u> effects for people and the environment:

Quality of Life

1) There are more <u>jobs</u>, and daily <u>wages</u> have <u>increased</u> by about 42 Rupees since 2010. People have more money to improve their life, e.g. by securing access to clean water.

2) Between 1990 and 2008, access to <u>clean water</u> increased from 68% of the population to 88%. Since 2000, HDI has increased from 0.49 to 0.64.

3) However, some jobs in industry, e.g. coal mining, can be <u>dangerous</u> or have poor working conditions, which can <u>reduce</u> workers' quality of life.

Environment

1) India's <u>energy consumption</u> has increased with economic development. Fossil fuels like coal and oil are the most readily available and affordable fuels, but release lots of <u>pollution</u> and <u>greenhouse gases</u>. The capital, Delhi, has the worst air pollution in the world.

2) Demand for resources can lead to the destruction of <u>habitats</u>, e.g. <u>coal mining</u> in Maharashtra has damaged the habitats of <u>Bengal tigers</u>.

3) Increased income from economic development means people can afford to <u>protect</u> the environment rather than <u>exploiting</u> it <u>unsustainably</u>. For example, since 1990, India's forest cover has stopped decreasing and started to grow.

Ohdia — I can't think of a decent gag for these pages...

Don't worry if you've studied a different country — you can learn that one instead, or use this one. Just make sure you know about the changes development is bringing, its impacts, and the pros and cons of TNCs and aid.

Economic Development in the UK

Changes in the economy of the UK are affecting <u>employment patterns</u> and <u>regional growth</u>.

The UK's Economy is Changing from Manufacturing to Services

The UK's economy used to be based on <u>manufacturing</u>. However, since the 1960s, manufacturing has declined, and <u>tertiary</u> and <u>quaternary</u> industries have grown. In 2017, these industries employed <u>83%</u> of the UK's workforce — and this proportion is <u>increasing</u>. Important industries include:

1) **Services** — e.g. <u>retail</u> and entertainment. Retail employs about <u>4 million</u> people in the UK.
2) **Information technology** — over <u>670 000</u> people work in IT, for companies like IBM® and Microsoft®.
3) **Finance** — the UK, and especially the <u>City of London</u>, is home to many global financial institutions. Some, like HSBC, have their global headquarters in the UK.
4) **Research** — research and development (R&D) is increasing in the UK, making use of the UK's <u>skilled</u> university graduates. In 2016, over <u>£33 billion</u> was spent on R&D in the UK.

Science and Business Parks

<u>Quaternary</u> industries are increasingly found in <u>science parks</u> or <u>business parks</u>. These are often:

1) On the outskirts of <u>cities</u> near to housing and good <u>transport links</u>, e.g. motorways and airports.
2) Near <u>universities</u> so that research businesses in science parks can work with university <u>researchers</u>.

The number of science and business parks has grown because:

- There is a large and growing <u>demand</u> for <u>high-tech products</u>. Science parks can help develop new technology for these products.
- The UK has a high number of respected <u>research universities</u> for businesses on science parks to form links with.
- Clusters of <u>related businesses</u> in one place can boost each other.

Manchester Science Park

Economic Change in the UK has Three Main Causes

De-industrialisation

1) The UK's industrial base declined as increased <u>automation</u> (use of machines) led to <u>job losses</u> in manufacturing industries.
2) As other countries industrialised, they could produce goods more <u>cheaply</u> than the UK — this increased competition forced some UK manufacturing industries to <u>close</u>.

Globalisation

1) A lot of <u>manufacturing</u> has moved <u>overseas</u>, where <u>labour costs</u> are <u>lower</u>, e.g. <u>Marks and Spencer</u> manufactures clothes in India and China.
2) Some <u>TNCs</u> have moved some of their <u>tertiary</u> and <u>quaternary</u> operations to the UK — e.g. <u>Apple</u>® employs nearly 6500 people in the UK.
3) Trade with other countries is an increasingly important part of UK GDP. The <u>proportion</u> of the UK's <u>GDP</u> that comes from <u>foreign trade</u> increased from 38% in 1965 to 62% in 2017.

Government Policies

1) Government <u>decisions</u> on investment and <u>support</u> for businesses (e.g. tax breaks) affect the economy.
2) In the 1980s, several key manufacturing industries that had been owned and run by the government were <u>privatised</u>, e.g. steel and ship-building, leading to major <u>job losses</u> but increased efficiency.
3) Since the 1980s, the government has carried out a lot of <u>deregulation</u> — removing restrictions and taxes on businesses to encourage entrepreneurs and investors to move to the UK. This has helped attract tertiary and quaternary industries, e.g. <u>financial institutions</u>.
4) Membership of <u>trade agreements</u> and organisations, e.g. the <u>World Trade Organisation</u>, makes it easier for companies in the UK to operate across the world and move their manufacturing overseas.

Economic Development in the UK

Industry has Impacts on the Physical Environment

1) Industry can have <u>negative</u> effects on the <u>environment</u>. Factories may release <u>pollutants</u> or <u>greenhouse gases</u>, and running them uses lots of <u>energy</u> and <u>water</u>. Extracting raw materials, e.g. mining, can also damage the environment by destroying habitats and releasing toxic chemicals into water courses.

2) <u>Modern</u> industrial developments are more <u>environmentally sustainable</u> than older industrial plants due to increasing energy and waste disposal <u>costs</u>, stricter environmental <u>regulations</u> and better <u>awareness</u>.

The <u>Unicorn Group</u> manufactures various products (e.g. bins and floor tiles) in Lisburn, Northern Ireland. It's made its production more <u>sustainable</u> by installing <u>solar panels</u> and <u>biomass boilers</u> in its factory and getting <u>100%</u> of its electricity from <u>renewable</u> sources. Unicorn Group has also reduced <u>waste</u> by <u>recycling</u> left over steel and plastic.

EXAMPLE

The UK has a Good but Improving Transport Network

<u>Congested</u> transport networks can <u>slow</u> economic development, so the UK is improving its:

Roads — <u>capacity</u> on motorways is being increased by <u>upgrading</u> to "<u>smart motorways</u>" with extra lanes, e.g. the M4. Between 2015 and 2020, Highways England plans to create 400 miles of new road capacity, e.g. building a new dual carriageway to link the A5 to the M1 near Luton.

Railways — <u>Crossrail</u> will increase central London's rail capacity by 10% when it opens fully (expected to happen in 2019). The proposed <u>HS2</u> line linking London, Birmingham, Leeds and Manchester would increase capacity and allow faster journeys between <u>major English cities</u>.

Airports — the UK Government has agreed that a <u>new runway</u> is needed in the south east. One proposal is for a third runway at <u>Heathrow</u> airport, which would allow an extra <u>700 planes</u> a day. However, this would increase <u>noise</u> and <u>air pollution</u> in the area and increase <u>greenhouse gas emissions</u>.

Ports — a new port, <u>London Gateway</u>, opened at the mouth of the River Thames in 2013. It can handle the world's largest container ships and it is hoped that it will become a hub for <u>global trade</u>. Other major ports, such as Felixstowe, are increasing their capacity.

The UK has Strong Links to Other Countries

The UK is connected to the <u>wider world</u> in many ways, including:

1) **Trade** — the UK trades <u>globally</u>, and its overseas <u>exports</u> are worth over <u>£160 billion</u> per year. Links to the USA, Europe and Asia are particularly significant.

2) **Culture** — the UK's strong <u>creative industries</u> mean that UK culture is exported worldwide, e.g. the <u>Shaun the Sheep</u>™ TV series made by Aardman Animations in Bristol is shown in 170 countries. <u>Immigration</u> has helped shape the UK's culture, leading to cultural <u>diversity</u> in food, art, music etc.

3) **Transport** — the <u>Channel Tunnel</u> links the UK to France, providing a <u>route</u> to <u>mainland Europe</u>. Large <u>airports</u> like Heathrow act as an international <u>hub</u>, linking the UK to the rest of world.

4) **Electronic Communications** — <u>telephones</u> and the <u>internet</u> make it easier for people in the UK to communicate with people in other countries, strengthening the UK's overseas links. <u>Trans-Atlantic cables</u> (carrying phone lines and internet connections) linking Europe with the USA are <u>routed</u> via the UK.

The UK has also formed <u>economic</u> and <u>political</u> links with other countries:

1) **European Union (EU)** — the EU is an <u>economic</u> and <u>political partnership</u> of 27 countries. Goods and people can <u>move freely</u> between EU countries, <u>strengthening</u> links between members. The UK is due to <u>leave</u> the EU in 2019.

2) **The Commonwealth** — the Commonwealth is an <u>association</u> of 53 states, including the UK and many of its former <u>colonies</u>. It promotes <u>co-operation</u> between member countries, e.g. through, trade, aid and sport.

Commonwealth Games, 2014

Economic Development in the UK

Changes in the UK Economy are Changing Rural Areas

Changes in the UK economy cause population growth or decline
in rural areas — this can have economic and social effects:

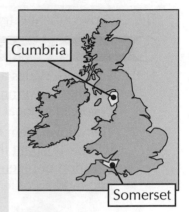

Cumbria

Population Decline — South Lakeland, Cumbria

1) Cumbria is a rural county in north west England that includes the
   Lake District National Park. South Lakeland is a district in the south
   of the county that includes the borough of Barrow-in-Furness.

2) The population of South Lakeland decreased by 0.8% from 2005 to 2015,
   with some places seeing a higher drop (e.g. 4.3% in Barrow). This is partly
   due to a decline in jobs — agriculture and manufacturing are big industries
   in Cumbria but they're both in decline.

Somerset

3) Population decline has economic impacts. In Barrow, shops such as
   Gamestation have closed, while others, including Marks and Spencer,
   are at risk of closure. This affects employment and the local economy.

4) It also has social impacts. Younger people have left, leaving a higher
   proportion of older people, which puts strain on medical services and
   social care. With continued decline, schools and other services may close.

Population Growth — North Somerset

1) North Somerset is a mainly rural area in south west England.

2) The area's population increased by about 7.8% between 2005 and 2015. Many people
   have moved to towns and villages that have easy access to the centre of Bristol.

3) Population growth has economic impacts — house prices in the area rose
   by 6.7% in 2017-18, pricing out some locals. The area has seen economic
   benefits too — employment and wages are above the national average.

4) It also has social impacts — roads are congested with commuters to Bristol,
   and some services (e.g. schools) are oversubscribed. Many people moving
   to the area are elderly, which increases pressure on healthcare.

There is Some Evidence for a North-South Divide in the UK

1) The decline of heavy industry has had more of a negative impact on the north
   of the UK (including Wales, Scotland and Northern Ireland), but the growth
   of the post-industrial service industry has mostly benefited the south.

2) Economic and social indicators tend to be more positive for the south
   than the north — this is the north-south divide. For example:

Bath

Baaath

Bath

Baaath

- Wages are generally lower in the north than the south, e.g. the 2014
  average weekly wage in Huddersfield was 40% lower than in London.

- Health is generally worse in the north than the south, e.g.
  life expectancy for male babies born in Glasgow in 2012
  was 72.6 years, but in East Dorset it was 82.9 years.

- Education — GCSE results are generally better in the south
  of England than they are in the Midlands or the north.

3) There are exceptions — there are wealthy areas in the north, e.g. parts of Cheshire,
   and places with high deprivation in the south, e.g. some areas of Cornwall.
   Some cities don't fit the trends, and not everything is worse in the north.

Unit 2B — The Changing Economic World

Economic Development in the UK

The Government is Trying to Resolve Regional Differences

The UK government is trying to <u>reduce</u> the <u>north-south divide</u> by:

1 Devolving More Powers

1) Scotland, Wales and Northern Ireland have their own <u>devolved governments</u>, and some powers are being devolved to local <u>councils</u> in England too.

2) This allows them to use money on schemes they feel will best <u>benefit</u> the local community, e.g. better <u>public transport</u> or <u>regeneration</u> projects to turn disused buildings into modern office spaces to attract businesses to the area.

Y Senedd, the Welsh National Assembly

2 Creating Enterprise Zones

1) Around 50 <u>Enterprise Zones</u> have been created across England, Scotland and Wales.

2) Companies get a range of <u>benefits</u> for locating in enterprise zones, including:

- <u>Reduced taxes</u> — business rates are reduced by up to 100%.

- <u>Simpler planning rules</u> — certain developments (e.g. new industrial buildings) are automatically allowed within enterprise zones.

- <u>Financial benefits</u> — in some enterprise zones, businesses who invest in buildings or equipment can <u>reduce</u> future <u>tax</u> bills.

- <u>Improved infrastructure</u> — the government ensures <u>superfast broadband</u> is available.

3) These measures can be used to <u>encourage</u> companies to locate in areas of high unemployment, bringing <u>jobs</u> and <u>income</u> which could help to reduce the north-south divide.

Example — Sheffield City Region Enterprise Zone

In 2011, the UK government approved the creation of an <u>enterprise zone</u> in the <u>Sheffield</u> region. Projects which have been set up as part of the Enterprise Zone include:

- <u>McLaren Composites Technology Centre</u> — car manufacturers McLaren worked with researchers from the University of Sheffield to build facilities for developing cutting-edge materials. They estimate that this could bring £100 million to the local economy.

- <u>Great Yorkshire Way</u> — a major new <u>road</u> is being built to connect the Sheffield City Region with Doncaster Sheffield <u>Airport</u>, making it easier for people to travel to the region.

By 2017, the Enterprise Zone had already helped to create <u>16 000 new jobs</u> in the area and brought in <u>£318 million</u> of investment from private companies.

3 The Northern Powerhouse

1) The Northern Powerhouse is the <u>government's plan</u> to reduce the inequality between the north and south by attracting <u>investment</u> into the north and improving <u>transport links</u> between northern cities. The plan includes working to extend the coverage of superfast <u>broadband</u> and spending <u>£70 million</u> on improving schools.

2) It has been <u>criticised</u> for being more of a <u>concept</u> than an actual <u>plan</u> — it's not always clear how the money promised is going to be spent. Critics have also pointed out that it focuses on <u>Manchester</u> and other big cities but <u>ignores</u> smaller towns and cities in the north.

The real north-south divide — chips and gravy...

It's easy to assume you know everything on these three pages because it's about the UK and you probably know the UK quite well. But you might need to know details for the exam, so don't be tempted to cut corners.

Revision Summary

Hurrah, another section bites the dust. Hopefully you've now developed a good understanding of the changing economic world — luckily I've got a big stack of revision summary questions so you can be sure. All the answers are in the section you've just revised, so if you're struggling for an answer, head back to the page and learn it again. Once you've got all of them right, you can head onwards and upwards for some lovely resource management.

Development (p.81-83) ☑

1) What is development?
2) What is meant by the development gap?
3) List five measures of development.
4) Give one way countries can be classified.
5) What do HIC, LIC and NEE stand for?
6) Describe the five stages of the demographic transition model.
7) How is a country's level of development linked to the different stages of the DTM?

Uneven Development (p.84-87) ☑

8) How can climate result in uneven development?
9) Explain how debt can cause uneven development.
10) Give two historical factors that can affect how developed a country is.
11) What are the consequences of uneven development?
12) a) Explain how debt relief can reduce the global development gap.
    b) Give four other strategies to reduce the global development gap.
13) a) Name one country that is trying to grow tourism to close the development gap.
    b) Give one positive and one negative effect for the country of this increase in tourism.

Economic Development in India (p.88-90) ☑

14) What is India's current level of development?
15) How is India's industrial structure changing?
16) What is a TNC?
17) a) Name a TNC that operates in India.
    b) Describe the advantages and disadvantages of TNCs to India.

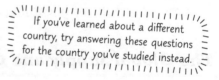
If you've learned about a different country, try answering these questions for the country you've studied instead.

18) Explain how India's trading relationship with the wider world is changing.
19) What is the difference between short-term and long-term aid?
20) Explain the difference between top-down and bottom-up aid.
21) Describe the impact of India's economic development on quality of life.
22) Describe the environmental impacts of India's economic development.

Economic Development in the UK (p.91-94) ☑

23) What sort of industry has become more important as the UK becomes post-industrial?
24) Why has there been an increase in the number of science parks in the UK?
25) What are the main causes of economic change in the UK?
26) How can the effect of industry on the environment be reduced?
27) Why is it important that the UK continues to improve its transport networks? How is it doing so?
28) Give three examples of the UK's strong links with other countries.
29) Give two contrasting ways that changes in the UK's economy are affecting rural areas.
30) a) What is the north-south divide?
    b) How is the UK government trying to reduce the north-south divide?

Global Distribution of Resources

A <u>resource</u> is just something that we <u>use</u> — and in this case we're talking about food, water and energy.

Everyone Needs Food, Water and Energy

1) Resources, such as food, water and energy, are needed for <u>basic human development</u>.
2) Access to these three resources affects the <u>economic</u> and <u>social well-being</u> of people and countries:

Food

1) When people <u>can't access</u> enough <u>safe</u>, nutritious food, they can't eat the right balance of <u>nutrients</u>. This can cause <u>malnourishment</u>. Malnourishment includes <u>undernourishment</u> — where people don't get enough food of any kind.
2) Malnourishment can limit children's development (e.g. by causing <u>iron deficiency</u>). It also increases the likelihood of getting <u>ill</u> — globally, one third of all under-5s die from diseases linked to malnourishment.

Water

1) People need <u>clean</u>, <u>safe</u> water for drinking, cooking and washing.
2) Without proper <u>sanitation</u>, water sources get <u>polluted</u> by raw sewage.
3) <u>Water-borne diseases</u> such as cholera and typhoid kill many people each year.
4) Water is needed to produce food, clothes and many other products, so it has a <u>big impact</u> on people's <u>lifestyles</u>.

Energy

1) Countries need energy for <u>industry</u> and <u>transport</u>, as well as for use in homes.
2) Electricity can allow countries to <u>develop</u> industry, creating jobs and <u>wealth</u>.
3) Lifestyles in higher income countries (HICs) depend on a large, <u>stable</u> supply of energy.
4) Without electricity, people in lower income countries (LICs) and newly emerging economies (NEEs) may use other resources. Burning wood can lead to <u>local deforestation</u>, so people have to walk further to find fuel. Kerosene stoves can release <u>harmful fumes</u>.
5) Electricity can also power <u>pumps</u> for wells and provide more <u>safe water</u> for communities.

3) A <u>lack</u> of any one of these resources can affect a person's ability to <u>attend school</u> or <u>work</u>. This can prevent people from <u>learning</u> and <u>using skills</u> needed to help their country's economic development.

The Global Supply and Consumption of Resources is Unequal

1) The global distribution of resources is very <u>uneven</u>. Some countries don't have their own energy reserves. Others have dry climates or environments that are <u>not suitable</u> for food production.
2) To access more resources, these countries have to <u>import</u> them or find <u>technological solutions</u> to produce more, e.g. building desalination plants can produce fresh water from saltwater. This is <u>expensive</u>.
3) So <u>consumption</u> of resources depends on a country's <u>wealth</u>, as well as resource <u>availability</u>:

HICs

Consumption of resources is <u>greater</u> in <u>HICs</u> because they can afford to <u>buy</u> the resources they need and expect a <u>higher standard of living</u>. Countries such as Luxembourg <u>import</u> much of the energy they use.

NEEs

Consumption is <u>increasing rapidly</u> in <u>NEEs</u> such as China. Industry is <u>developing</u> quickly (which requires lots of energy) and population and wealth are also <u>increasing rapidly</u>.

LICs

Consumption is <u>lower</u> in <u>LICs</u> such as Uganda, because they <u>can't afford</u> to either:
- <u>exploit</u> available resources OR
- <u>import</u> lacking resources

There's more about resource consumption on pages 100, 107 and 113.

Global food consumption — keep eating till you're a perfect sphere...
Get your head around the main ideas on this page and you'll be off to a flying start with the rest of the topic.

Food in the UK

Jet-setting pineapples and fields so big you can't see the other side — <u>food production</u> in the UK is <u>changing</u>.

Different Types of Food are Becoming More Popular

The types of food that are in <u>demand</u> in the UK have <u>changed</u>. Before the 1960s, most of the fruit and vegetables on sale in the UK were <u>locally produced</u> and <u>seasonal</u>. Now, there's a greater demand for a wider <u>range</u> of products:

High-value Foods

As people's incomes have increased, <u>exotic fruits</u>, <u>vegetables</u>, <u>spices</u> and <u>coffee</u> have become more popular. These foods are often grown in <u>LICs</u>, e.g. Ethiopia, and then <u>exported</u> to HICs, e.g. the UK.

Seasonal Products

Seasonal food is <u>only available</u> during the months that it grows. Fruit and vegetables are <u>imported</u> to meet the demand for seasonal produce <u>all year round</u> — e.g. strawberries from Mexico.

Organic Produce

People are becoming more <u>concerned</u> about the <u>environmental impacts</u> of food production, and how <u>chemicals</u> can <u>affect</u> their <u>health</u>. As organic food production is <u>strictly regulated</u> (e.g. no artificial fertilisers are used), demand is growing. Some organic food is produced in the UK, but lots is <u>imported</u>.

The Carbon Footprint of Our Food is Growing

1) The growing, processing and packaging of food <u>produces CO_2</u> and other greenhouse gases (see p.16). Up to <u>10%</u> of the UK's total greenhouse gas emissions in 2017 came directly from <u>agriculture</u>.

2) <u>Transporting</u> food from where it is grown to where it is sold also produces CO_2. The <u>distance</u> food is transported to the market is called its <u>food miles</u>. More food miles mean more CO_2 is produced.

3) The amount of greenhouse gas produced whilst growing, packing and transporting a food is called its <u>carbon footprint</u>. A larger carbon footprint means more greenhouse gases and more <u>global warming</u>.

4) <u>Imported foods</u> have to be transported a <u>long way</u>, so have many food miles and a large carbon footprint.

5) People are becoming <u>aware</u> of the <u>environmental issues</u> caused by transporting food over long distances. This is leading people to look for <u>local sources</u> of food, such as farmers' markets, farm shops and locally produced vegetable boxes.

Farming is Becoming More Industrialised

Since the 1960s, there has been a growth in <u>agribusiness</u> in the UK. Agribusiness is <u>large-scale</u>, <u>industrial</u> farming where all processes, from the production of seeds and fertilisers to the processing and packaging of the food, are <u>controlled</u> by <u>large firms</u>. This means that farms in the UK have been <u>changing</u>:

- Farm sizes have <u>increased</u> — many small farms have been <u>taken over</u> and <u>field sizes increased</u> so that food can be produced more <u>cheaply</u>.

- The amount of <u>chemicals</u> used in food production has been increasing — large quantities of <u>artificial fertilisers</u> and <u>pesticides</u> are applied to crops, and animals are given <u>special feed</u> to encourage growth.

- The number of <u>workers</u> employed in agriculture <u>fell</u> to just over <u>1.1%</u> of the UK's <u>total employment</u> in 2017. This is partly because of the greater use of <u>machinery</u>, e.g. in planting and harvesting.

Think what the food miles of those flying saucer sweets must be...

Farming is no longer a local business — make sure you know the main trends in UK food production.

1) Explain how changing food demand in the UK has created environmental challenges. [4]

Managing the UK's Water

The UK may be famous for being grey and wet, but apparently the <u>rain</u> doesn't fall in the <u>right places</u>...

The Demand for Water Varies Across the UK

In the UK, the places with a <u>good supply</u> of water aren't the same as the places with the <u>highest demand</u>:

<u>UK average annual rainfall</u>

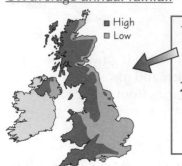

■ High
□ Low

<u>UK population density</u>

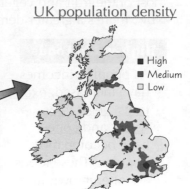

■ High
■ Medium
□ Low

1) The <u>north</u> and <u>west</u> of the UK have <u>high rainfall</u>. These are areas of <u>water surplus</u> (there's a greater supply than demand).

2) The <u>south east</u> and the <u>Midlands</u> have <u>high population densities</u>, so there's a high demand for water. They are areas of <u>water deficit</u> (there's a greater demand than supply).

The demand for water in the UK is <u>increasing</u>:

1) Since 1975, the amount of water used by households in the UK has gone <u>up</u> by about <u>70%</u>. This is partly because people have more <u>appliances</u> that use lots of water, e.g. dishwashers and washing machines.

2) The UK <u>population</u> is predicted to <u>increase</u> by over 6 million people by 2040, to total nearly <u>73 million</u>.

3) Population densities are also <u>changing</u> — there are plans to build lots of <u>new homes</u> in the south east where there is already a <u>water deficit</u>.

Water Pollution Needs to be Managed

1) <u>Polluted</u> or <u>low quality</u> water <u>reduces</u> the amount available for use, putting <u>pressure</u> on water resources.

2) Overall, the <u>quality</u> of river water in the UK has been <u>improving</u>. However, there are still some problems:

> • Nitrates and phosphates from <u>crop fertilisers</u> are washed into <u>rivers</u> and <u>groundwater</u>.
> • <u>Pollutants</u> from vehicles are washed into water sources through <u>runoff</u> when it rains.
> • <u>Chemical</u> and <u>oil spills</u> from factories can <u>pollute</u> local water sources and groundwater.

3) Up to <u>80%</u> of water in parts of southern England comes from <u>groundwater</u>, but <u>pollution</u> is affecting the water quality of nearly <u>50%</u> of groundwater used for public supply in the UK. Many groundwater sources have <u>closed</u> or have needed <u>expensive treatment</u> to make them safe to use.

4) Strategies to manage water quality include <u>improving drainage systems</u> and imposing <u>regulations</u> on the amount and types of fertilisers and pesticides used.

Groundwater is water found underground in cracks and pores in rock, and in soil.

Water Transfers Can Help Maintain Supplies

One solution to the supply and demand problem is to <u>transfer</u> water from areas of <u>surplus</u> to areas of <u>deficit</u>. For example, Birmingham (an area of deficit) is supplied with water from parts of Wales (an area of surplus).

Water Transfer can cause a Variety of Issues

1) The <u>dams</u> and <u>aqueducts</u> that are needed are <u>expensive</u> to build (e.g. the Birmingham Resilience Project, which will supply extra water to Birmingham, has estimated costs of about <u>£300 million</u>).

2) It can affect the <u>wildlife</u> that lives in the rivers, e.g. fish migration can be <u>disrupted</u> by dams.

3) There might be <u>political issues</u>, e.g. people may not want their water transferred to another area.

Water management techniques — cross your legs and jiggle...

Remember, the availability of water depends on how much there is and how many people want to use it. If there's a deficit, one way to solve the problem is to transfer in water from somewhere with a water surplus.

Energy in the UK

We get most of our energy from <u>coal</u>, <u>oil</u> and <u>gas</u> — but some comes from more <u>renewable</u> energy sources.

The UK's Energy Mix Has Changed

1) Traditionally, the UK has relied on <u>fossil fuels</u> (coal, oil and gas) to supply its energy. In 1970, <u>91%</u> of our energy came from <u>coal</u> and <u>oil</u>.

2) The discovery of large <u>gas reserves</u> under the North Sea meant that by 1980, <u>22%</u> of the UK's energy was supplied by <u>gas</u>.

3) Recently there has been a <u>shift</u> away from burning fossil fuels, and towards <u>renewable</u> energy sources (i.e. ones that won't run out). All coal-fired power stations in the UK are due to close by 2025, and in 2014, <u>19%</u> of <u>all electricity</u> in the UK was generated from renewable sources.

4) <u>Wind</u> and <u>bioenergy</u> (energy from the break down or burning of biological matter) are the biggest sources of renewable energy, but the use of <u>solar</u> and <u>hydroelectric</u> power has also increased.

The UK's Supplies of Coal, Oil and Gas are Running Out

1) North Sea oil and gas reserves are being swiftly <u>used up</u> and production has been <u>declining</u> since 2000.

2) The UK still has coal reserves, but coal production has <u>significantly decreased</u> since the mid-20th century. There has been <u>less demand</u> due to an effort to reduce CO_2 emissions, and the cost of mining the remaining reserves is increasing. The last deep coal mine in the UK closed in December 2015.

3) In the UK, the use of <u>shale gas</u> from underground is being considered as a way of adding to resources. It's extracted using a process called <u>fracking</u>.

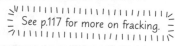
See p.117 for more on fracking.

Exploiting Energy Sources Causes Economic and Environmental Issues

The <u>extraction</u> of fossil fuels and <u>production</u> of electricity can cause <u>problems</u>:

Economic Issues

1) <u>Extracting</u> fossil fuels can be <u>expensive</u> and the cost of extraction increases as reserves are used up.

2) North Sea oil is especially <u>expensive to produce</u>. If the price of oil on the world market drops, it may cost more to produce than it can be sold for.

3) The <u>cost</u> to the consumer of electricity from <u>nuclear</u> and <u>renewable</u> energy sources is relatively <u>high</u>.

4) <u>Money</u> is needed for <u>research</u> into alternative energy sources, e.g. shale gas, and for <u>initial investment</u>, e.g. the new nuclear power station at Hinkley Point, which is going to cost around £20.3 billion.

5) Domestic sources don't currently provide enough energy to meet <u>demand</u>, so the UK has to <u>pay</u> to <u>import energy</u> from other countries.

Environmental Issues

1) The burning of fossil fuels releases <u>CO_2</u> and other <u>greenhouse gases</u>.

2) Fracking may <u>pollute groundwater</u> and cause <u>mini-earthquakes</u> — some people in the UK are campaigning to ban it.

3) Accidents, such as oil spills or nuclear disasters, can leak <u>toxic chemicals</u> into water sources, soils and the atmosphere.

4) Natural <u>ecosystems</u> can be <u>damaged</u> by renewable energy generators like large <u>wind farms</u> or the <u>tidal power project</u> planned for Fleetwood in Lancashire.

5) Power stations and wind farms are often considered to be <u>eyesores</u>.

I wish my brother's gas supplies would run out — he's such a stinker...

Don't panic if you're to asked interpret data on energy in the exam — just read it carefully and try to link it to what you know from this page. That does, however, require learning this page... so what are you waiting for?

Global Demand for Food

Ah, my favourite topic — <u>grub</u>. Finally a topic you can get your teeth into...

Global Food Supply is Uneven

The amount of food that countries <u>produce</u> <u>varies</u>. This map shows the production of <u>cereals</u> by country from 2012 to 2014. The production of other food follows a <u>similar pattern</u>.

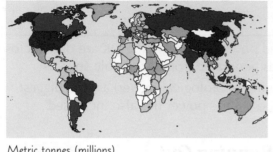

Metric tonnes (millions)
- ■ >410
- ■ 90-410
- ■ 50-90
- ■ 16-50
- ▨ 2.8-16
- □ <2.8
- ▨ No data available

1) North America and East Asia produce <u>a lot</u> of food.

2) Central America and Africa only produce <u>small amounts</u> of food.

The factors that affect how much food can be produced are explained on the next page.

The amount of food people <u>eat</u> also <u>varies</u> across the world. This map shows <u>daily calorie intake</u>.

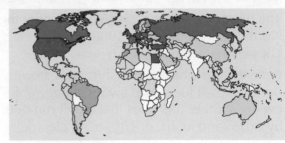

Daily calorie (kcal) intake per person (2011-2013)
- ■ Over 3539
- ■ 3358 to 3539
- ■ 3266 to 3358
- ▨ 3095 to 3266
- ▨ 2546 to 3095
- □ Less than 2546
- □ No data available

1) <u>HICs</u>, such as the USA, <u>eat a lot</u>. They can afford to <u>import</u> a large variety of foods, and many people have a <u>high income</u> so can buy more food.

2) <u>LICs</u>, such as Ethiopia, <u>consume less</u> food — less is <u>available</u> and people can't <u>afford</u> as much.

3) <u>NEEs</u>, such as China, are <u>consuming more</u> as their wealth increases.

1) <u>Food security</u> is when people are able to eat enough nutritious food to stay <u>healthy</u> and <u>active</u>. Countries that <u>produce a lot</u> of food or are rich enough to <u>import</u> what they need have food security.

2) <u>Food insecurity</u> is when people can't get enough food to stay healthy and active. Countries that <u>don't grow enough</u> to feed their population and <u>can't afford</u> to import the food they need have food insecurity.

Global Food Consumption is Increasing

Food <u>consumption</u> around the world is <u>increasing</u>. This is down to two main reasons:

1 Rising Population

The global population is <u>increasing</u> and is expected to reach 9 billion by 2040 — <u>more people</u> require <u>more food</u>.

2 Economic Development

1) Economic development means that countries are getting <u>wealthier</u>. Wealthier people have more <u>disposable income</u> to spend on food. They often buy a greater variety of food and <u>more</u> than they <u>need</u>.

2) Wealthy countries can afford to <u>import</u> food all year round, so people no longer eat just what is <u>seasonally available</u>.

3) <u>Industrialisation</u> of agriculture means some countries are able to <u>produce more</u> food at <u>lower cost</u>. Food becomes <u>cheaper</u>, so people can afford to <u>eat more</u>.

EXAM QUESTION

Secure food supply — living next door to a chippy...

Have a good chew through this page — understanding this lot will help with the rest of the topic.

1) *Compare the global patterns of food production and consumption.*   [2]

Food Insecurity

Food insecurity is a pretty complex issue — there are loads of <u>factors</u> that affect <u>how much</u> food is available.

Food Supply is Affected by Physical and Human Factors

Food insecurity occurs for two reasons — not enough food is being <u>produced</u>, or people are unable to <u>access</u> food supplies. Food production and accessibility are affected by both <u>physical</u> and <u>human</u> factors:

Physical Factors

1) <u>Climate</u> — countries with climates that are <u>unsuitable for farming</u> (e.g. too cold) can't grow much food. <u>Extreme weather events</u>, such as floods and droughts, can also <u>affect food supply</u>.

2) <u>Water stress</u> — areas with <u>low rainfall</u> or little water for <u>irrigation</u> struggle to grow enough food.

3) <u>Pests and diseases</u> — pests <u>reduce yields</u> by consuming crops (e.g. locust swarms eat all the vegetation in their path). <u>Diseases</u> can cause a lot of <u>damage</u> if they spread through crops and livestock, e.g. 37% of the world's wheat crops are under threat from wheat rust.

Human Factors

1) <u>Poverty</u> — people living in poverty often don't have their <u>own land</u> to grow food. Poverty can also affect people's ability to <u>farm effectively</u>, e.g. they may not be able to buy fertilisers or pesticides. At a global scale, some countries can't afford to <u>import</u> food.

2) <u>Technology</u> — <u>mechanisation</u> of equipment (e.g. tractors) increases productivity by making farming more <u>efficient</u>. <u>New technologies</u> (e.g. genetic engineering, see p.96) can <u>increase yields</u> and help <u>protect</u> plants from disease.

3) <u>Conflict</u> — fighting may <u>damage agricultural land</u> or make it <u>unsafe</u>. Access to food becomes difficult for people who are <u>forced</u> to <u>flee</u> their homes. Conflicts also make it difficult to <u>import</u> food because trade routes are <u>disrupted</u> and political relationships with supply countries may <u>break down</u>.

Food Insecurity has Negative Impacts

Food insecurity doesn't just mean that people go hungry — it can lead to a whole load of <u>other problems</u> too:

1) **Famine** — this is a <u>serious lack of food</u> across a <u>large area</u>. It can lead to <u>starvation</u> and <u>death</u>. Between 2010 and 2012, nearly <u>260 000</u> people died in <u>Somalia</u> as a result of a famine caused by a <u>drought</u>.

2) **Undernutrition** — to stay healthy, people need a <u>balanced diet</u>. Undernutrition is when you don't get <u>enough nutrients</u> to keep your body <u>healthy</u>. Undernutrition can cause <u>development problems</u> such as <u>stunted growth</u>. In sub-Saharan Africa, stunted growth affects around <u>40%</u> of children under 5.

3) **Soil erosion** — people who are struggling to produce enough food may not use the best <u>agricultural practices</u> (e.g. they may <u>over-cultivate</u> or <u>overgraze</u> the land). Over-cultivation and overgrazing can <u>reduce</u> plant cover, leaving soil <u>exposed</u> to wind and rain. This can lead to <u>soil erosion</u>.

Over-cultivation is where crops are grown repeatedly without giving the soil time to recover its nutrients.

4) **Rising prices** — when there isn't <u>enough</u> food available, food prices usually <u>increase</u> because demand <u>exceeds</u> supply. Rising prices tend to <u>worsen</u> food insecurity in LICs.

5) **Social unrest** — food shortages and rising food prices can cause <u>riots</u> and may contribute to <u>civil wars</u>. Between 2016 and 2019, food shortages in Venezuela led to <u>protests</u>, <u>looting</u> of supermarkets and <u>riots</u>.

Any food I try to eat using chopsticks is pretty insecure...

Food insecurity is a complex issue, usually caused by a combination of these factors. Knowing the factors and impacts on this page won't help solve world hunger I'm afraid, but it will help you write lovely exam answers.

Increasing Food Production

If you've read the previous page you'll know why <u>food insecurity</u> can make things go seriously pear-shaped. We need to <u>produce</u> more grub — and there are some pretty interesting ways people are doing just that.

New Technologies can Increase Food Supply

1) With <u>global demand</u> for food <u>increasing</u>, new ways of <u>increasing food supplies</u> are urgently needed.

2) There are many techniques that can be used to increase <u>yields</u>. Here are some examples:

Irrigation

Irrigation involves <u>artificially watering</u> the land. It can be used to make dry areas more <u>productive</u>, or to increase the <u>number of harvests</u> and the <u>yield</u> of crops.

There are three main types of irrigation:

1) <u>Gravity flow</u> — digging <u>ditches</u> and <u>channels</u> to transport ground or surface water to fields (there's an example of this on p.103).

2) <u>Sprinklers</u> — <u>spraying</u> water across fields.

3) <u>Drip systems</u> — dripping water from <u>small holes</u> in pipes directly onto the soil around the roots of crop plants.

Hydroponics and Aeroponics

Hydroponics and aeroponics are methods of growing plants <u>without soil</u>:

1) In hydroponics, plants grow in a <u>nutrient solution</u>, supported by materials like rockwool, gravel or clay balls.

2) In aeroponics, plants are <u>suspended in air</u>. Water containing nutrients is sprayed onto the roots. The water drips off the roots and is <u>used again</u>.

3) Plants are <u>monitored closely</u> and nutrients <u>adjusted</u> to maximise crop yield.

4) <u>Less water</u> is required than plants grown in soil. <u>Reduced risk</u> of disease and pests means less need for <u>pesticides</u>.

5) Hydroponics and aeroponics are very <u>expensive</u>, so these methods are currently only used for <u>high-value crops</u>, such as tomatoes or lettuce.

Biotechnology

Biotechnology involves <u>genetically engineering crops</u> to improve production. Genetically modified (GM) crops allow <u>more</u> to be grown in <u>smaller areas</u> with <u>fewer resources</u>. GM crops can be designed to have:

1) <u>Higher yields</u>, e.g. a C4 breed of rice is being developed which could increase yields by up to 50%.

2) <u>Resistance to drought</u>, <u>disease</u> or <u>pests</u> (so less of the crop is killed or eaten before it is harvested).

3) <u>Higher nutritional values</u>, e.g. potatoes with more protein, rice with more vitamin A.

However, there are <u>ethical</u> and <u>environmental</u> concerns:

1) GM crops may <u>reduce biodiversity</u> because <u>fewer varieties</u> of crops are planted.

2) GM plants may <u>interbreed</u> with wild plants and pass on their <u>genes</u> or <u>disrupt ecosystems</u>.

The New Green Revolution

The new green revolution aims to increase yields using <u>sustainable</u> methods, including:

1) <u>GM crops</u>, including varieties with pest and disease resistance. These need <u>fewer resources</u> (such as pesticides) and so can be grown more <u>cheaply</u> and with <u>less</u> environmental <u>damage</u>.

2) <u>Traditional</u> and <u>organic</u> farming methods, including <u>soil nutrient recycling</u>, <u>crop rotation</u> and using <u>natural predators</u> to control pests. This helps to limit the environmental impact of food production.

Increasing Food Production

Appropriate Technology

1) <u>High-tech</u> methods like hydroponics and GM crops can be <u>expensive</u>, so they're not always a <u>practical</u> choice for LICs. Appropriate technologies are often a better option.

2) Using appropriate technologies involves choosing ways of increasing food production that are <u>suited</u> to <u>local environments</u> and the <u>needs</u>, <u>skills</u>, <u>knowledge</u> and <u>wealth</u> of the people in those areas.

3) For example, in LICs:

*   <u>Individual wells</u> with easy to maintain, <u>mechanical pumps</u> are more suitable than larger, diesel-powered pumps.

*   A <u>drip irrigation system</u> constructed from <u>local materials</u> is more appropriate than an imported, high-tech sprinkler system.

*   Planting a <u>variety</u> of <u>local species</u> that can cope with local environmental conditions and have seeds that can be collected and re-planted may be more appropriate than planting a single GM variety that may have to be <u>repurchased</u> each year.

Irrigation Helps Farming in Burkina Faso

EXAMPLE

1) <u>Burkina Faso</u> is an LIC in <u>West Africa</u>. Around <u>30%</u> of the population rely on <u>agriculture</u> for employment.

2) The climate in Burkina Faso is <u>hot</u> and generally <u>dry</u>, with a short <u>rainy season</u>. There is limited water for <u>irrigation</u>, and <u>malnutrition</u> is widespread. The <u>population</u> is <u>rising</u>, putting more <u>pressure</u> on water and food resources.

3) Several <u>dams</u> and <u>reservoirs</u> have been built in Burkina Faso to provide a reliable water supply for irrigation. One of these is the <u>Bagrè Dam and Irrigation System</u>:

*   The dam was built in 1993 on the White Volta River, about <u>150 km</u> from the country's capital, Ougadougou. It can store up to <u>1.7 billion m³</u> of water.

*   From the late 1990s, <u>canals</u> were built to carry water from the reservoir for <u>irrigation</u>. The government hoped that the scheme would increase agricultural <u>productivity</u> and <u>reduce food insecurity</u>.

Advantages

*   By 2017, gravity-based <u>irrigation systems</u> were providing a <u>reliable</u> year-round water supply to over <u>3300 hectares</u> of land.

*   By 2012, <u>1800 hectares</u> of paddy fields had been created, producing over <u>12 500 tonnes</u> of rice that year.

*   <u>Hydropower</u> from the dam now supplies <u>10%</u> of Burkina Faso's electricity.

*   The project created more than <u>1500 jobs</u>.

Disadvantages

*   The project aimed to irrigate around <u>30 000 hectares</u>, but by 2009 the irrigated area was only around <u>10%</u> of this.

*   The irrigation canals have not been <u>well-maintained</u>, leading to <u>water loss</u> and decreased productivity.

*   Expensive <u>water charges</u> make it difficult for farmers to make a living. Only <u>22%</u> live above the poverty threshold.

*   Many people were <u>displaced</u> during the <u>construction</u> of the irrigation system, and some were <u>not compensated</u> for the loss of their land.

*   The dam is sometimes <u>opened</u> to <u>manage water levels</u>, which can lead to severe <u>flooding</u> in neighbouring Ghana. In 2018, over <u>11 000 hectares</u> of land were flooded and <u>15 people</u> were <u>killed</u>.

EXAM QUESTION

Finding ways to increase food supply can be really irrigating...

This is important stuff — re-read this lot 'til you find discussing these methods as easy as GM pie...

1) Using a named example, evaluate one large-scale method used to increase food production. [6]

Sustainable Food Supply

It's no good if we just go around <u>trashing</u> the planet — we're gonna have to look after it, if we want to eat.

Industrial Agriculture is Bad for the Environment

1) There are <u>two challenges</u> in making sure that food supplies are <u>sustainable</u>:
   - Growing <u>enough</u> food now to feed a <u>rising population</u>.
   - Making sure that the <u>environment</u> isn't <u>damaged</u> in the process, so that enough food can <u>continue</u> to be grown to feed <u>future generations</u>.

2) <u>Industrial agriculture</u> is intensive, large-scale food production. The practice has become more widespread since the 1940s, particularly in the USA. It does a good job of producing lots of food <u>now</u>, but it has a <u>negative impact</u> on the environment, affecting our ability to produce food in the <u>future</u>.

3) For example, industrial agriculture uses <u>70%</u> of the world's <u>fresh water supply</u>, and relies on <u>chemical pesticides</u> and <u>artificial fertilisers</u>. It can make soil less productive by <u>permanently</u> removing nutrients.

Low Impact Farming Makes Food Supplies More Sustainable

To make food supplies <u>sustainable</u>, <u>alternative methods</u> are needed which don't damage the <u>environment</u>.

Organic Farming

1) Organic farming uses <u>natural processes</u> to return <u>nutrients</u> to the soil, so that crops can continue to be grown. E.g. crops, animals and empty (fallow) areas are <u>rotated</u> and <u>natural fertilisers</u> (such as cow manure) are used — this can be <u>less damaging</u> to the environment.

2) <u>Artificial herbicides</u> and <u>pesticides</u> are <u>restricted</u>, and animals aren't given <u>extra supplements</u> or <u>vaccinations</u>. This reduces the <u>reliance</u> on unsustainable resources and can protect <u>biodiversity</u>.

3) Organic farmers are encouraged to <u>sell</u> their produce <u>close</u> to where it is produced, reducing the amount of road and air <u>transport</u> required.

Permaculture

1) Permaculture aims to produce food in a way that <u>recreates natural ecosystems</u> in an effort to <u>protect</u> the soil, insects and other wildlife.

2) Food production is designed to be <u>low maintenance</u> and to keep soils <u>healthy</u> so that crops can continue to be grown. There are several different methods that can be used, including:

   - <u>Mixed cropping</u> — plants of <u>different heights</u> and different <u>types</u> are grown in one area. This means the available <u>space</u> and <u>light</u> are used better, there are <u>fewer pests</u> and <u>diseases</u>, and <u>less watering</u> is required.

   - <u>Natural predators</u> — introducing natural predators <u>reduces</u> the need for <u>pesticides</u>, e.g. <u>frogs</u> can be used to control <u>slugs</u>.

Urban Farming Initiatives

1) Urban farming initiatives use <u>empty land</u>, <u>roof tops</u> and <u>balconies</u> to grow food and raise animals in <u>towns</u>, e.g. urban residents use allotments to grow fruit and vegetables.

2) Urban farming makes food <u>locally available</u>, reducing the need to transport it long distances. This means it is often <u>fresher</u> and <u>more nutritious</u> and can also be <u>cheaper</u> — improving the food security of poorer residents.

3) It adds <u>greenery</u> to cities, making them <u>healthier</u> and more <u>attractive</u> places to live and makes urban areas <u>less dependent</u> on industrial agriculture.

Sustainable Food Supply

Eating Seasonally and Reducing Waste is More Sustainable

Making food supplies more sustainable is not just about using better growing techniques — changing how we consume food can also have an effect.

Fish and Meat from Sustainable Sources

1) Many fish species are at risk from over-fishing, due to increased consumption. Sustainable fishing includes catch quotas that limit the amount of fish taken and fishing methods that are less harmful to the environment. Labelling allows consumers to choose fish that have been fished sustainably.

2) Raising animals for meat is bad for the environment — e.g. forests are often cleared to make space for cattle, and animals produce methane (a greenhouse gas). However, meat production can be made more sustainable, for example by feeding animals on locally sourced rather than imported food, and by ensuring that all edible parts of the animal are eaten. Research suggests that adding a small amount of seaweed to normal cattle feed can decrease their methane emissions.

Seasonal Food Consumption

1) In many HICs, people expect to be able to get the foods they like all year round. These foods have to be imported when they are not available locally, e.g. peaches are harvested in the UK from July to September, but are imported all year round from warmer countries, such as Spain and Greece.

2) Importing food is not sustainable. Transport adds food miles and increases the food's carbon footprint (see p.97), adding to global warming.

3) Eating seasonally means only eating the foods that grow locally at that time of year, reducing the amount of food that is imported.

Reduced Waste and Losses

1) Globally, one third of food that is produced is lost or wasted — reducing this will mean that less needs to be grown.

2) Schemes such as 'Think.Eat.Save' and 'Love Food Hate Waste' encourage individuals, businesses and governments to waste less food, e.g. by helping people plan their meals better and sharing recipe ideas for using up leftovers. Many supermarkets in the UK also work with charities to distribute waste food to those in need.

Mali Uses Agroforestry to Produce a Sustainable Food Supply

1) In the Koutiala region of Mali (an LIC), many local farmers have begun to use agroforestry techniques to make their food supply more sustainable.

2) Mali is a very dry country. Intensive use of land for farming is causing desertification (see p.33), making land less fertile.

3) To combat this, farmers have started planting staple crops like maize in amongst trees and nitrogen-fixing plants.

4) The plants add nitrogen to the soil so artificial fertilisers aren't needed. The trees provide shade and prevent soil erosion. They also increase the nutrient and water content of the soil — leaf fall increases the organic content of the soil so that it holds water better.

5) This system increases maize yield at the same time as protecting the soil. The system is sustainable because farmers can produce food without damaging the local environment.

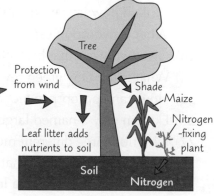

EXAM QUESTION

Agro-forestry — really angry trees...

We can all do our bit — small changes to eating habits can make food supplies more sustainable.

1) Outline how reducing food waste can make food supplies more sustainable. [2]

Unit 2C — Food

Revision Summary

Mmmm, what a fantastic feast of facts that was. Remember, you only have to study <u>one</u> topic out of Food, Water and Energy, so the good news is that if you <u>haven't</u> studied Food, you only have half a page of questions to answer. And the bad news is that after that, you need to keep on reading.

If Food is your chosen topic then you've reached the end of the topics in this book — congratulations. You win the amazing prize of going straight to the Issue Evaluation section on p.121. Do not pass Go, do not collect £200. You can have a biscuit first though — reading about food has made me pretty hungry too.

Global Distribution of Resources (p. 96) ☐

1) Give two ways that food is important to people's social well-being.
2) Give two ways that energy is important to people's economic well-being.
3) How might a lack of access to water affect the economic development of a country?
4) Which category of country consumes the most resources?

Resources in the UK (p. 97-99) ☑

5) Describe how demand for seasonal food has changed in the UK.
6) Why has demand for organic food increased in the UK?
7) What are food miles?
8) Describe three ways that farming in the UK has changed.
9) Which areas in the UK have a high demand for water?
10) Why is the demand for water increasing in the UK?
11) Why does water pollution need managing?
12) Give one solution to problems of water deficit.
13) Describe how the UK's energy mix has changed since 1970.
14) Why has coal production in the UK declined?
15) Give two environmental issues caused by the exploitation of energy resources.

Food Demand, Supply and Insecurity (p. 100-101) ☐

16) Give a definition of food security.
17) Explain why global food consumption is increasing.
18) Give two physical factors that affect the availability of food.
19) Explain how conflict can affect food security.
20) List five impacts of food insecurity.

Increasing Food Supplies (p. 102-105) ☑

21) Explain how irrigation can increase food production.
22) What is hydroponics?
23) Give two ways that biotechnology can increase food production.
24) What is the new green revolution?
25) How can appropriate technology be used to increase food production?
26) Explain why a named large-scale agricultural development was necessary.
27) Describe three different methods of sustainable farming.
28) How does eating food that is in season help to make food supplies more sustainable?
29) a) Give an example of a local scheme in an LIC or an NEE to increase sustainable supplies of food.
    b) Explain how the scheme works.

Global Demand for Water

You may well wish it wouldn't <u>rain</u> so blimmin' much but many people around the world would disagree. The <u>availability</u> of water <u>varies</u> from place to place and the world keeps requiring <u>more</u> and <u>more</u>...

Water Insecurity is Not Having Enough Clean Water

1) It's important to have a <u>reliable</u>, <u>sustainable</u> source of enough <u>good quality</u> water to meet people's needs.

2) Having <u>excess</u> water is known as a <u>water surplus</u>. Places with a water surplus have <u>water security</u> — they have <u>enough</u> water to meet everyone's <u>needs</u> (e.g. industry, agriculture and personal health).

3) Having <u>too little</u> water is called a <u>water deficit</u>. This can cause <u>water insecurity</u> — not having enough clean water for everyone (e.g. to drink, water crops or provide energy).

4) Water security depends on factors like the <u>amount</u> of water available (e.g. from rainfall, rivers and groundwater), the number of people <u>using</u> the water, and <u>access</u> to the water — which can be <u>limited</u> in poverty-stricken areas.

5) When <u>demand</u> for water <u>exceeds supply</u> during a certain period, or when water is not of high enough <u>quality</u> to use, places are said to experience <u>water stress</u>.

Global Patterns of Water Security and Insecurity Vary

This map shows <u>global water security</u>. Using a high percentage of supplies increases <u>vulnerability</u> to <u>water stress</u>.

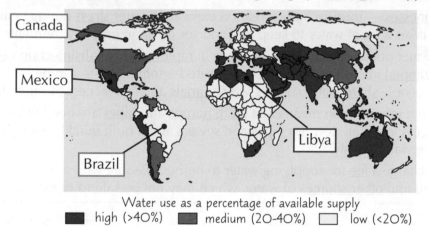

Canada

Mexico

Brazil

Libya

Water use as a percentage of available supply
■ high (>40%) ■ medium (20-40%) □ low (<20%)

<u>Water insecurity</u> — areas with <u>low rainfall</u> and / or a <u>high population density</u>, e.g. Libya, Mexico.

<u>Water security</u> — areas with <u>high rainfall</u> and / or a <u>low population density</u>, e.g. Canada, Brazil.

Water Demand is Rising because there are More People with More Money

The <u>global demand</u> for water is <u>rising</u> for two main reasons:

1 Rising population

1) Global <u>population</u> is <u>increasing</u> — each person needs water for <u>drinking</u>, <u>washing</u>, <u>cooking</u> etc.

2) More people require <u>more food</u> — <u>irrigation</u> for agriculture uses <u>70%</u> of the world's freshwater resources.

2 Economic development

Water use increases as the world becomes <u>increasingly developed</u>.

1) <u>Industrialisation</u> — as countries become more developed, they <u>produce</u> more goods. <u>Manufacturing</u> uses a lot of water.

2) <u>Energy production</u> — developed countries require more energy. Some estimates suggest that over <u>50 billion m³</u> of fresh water is used annually to produce energy.

3) <u>Rising living standards</u> — as countries develop, people become wealthier and are able to afford a <u>higher standard of living</u>. This increases water use, as more people can afford flushing toilets, showers, dishwashers, etc.

Aaah, so THAT's what the locks on canals are for...

Lots of terms to learn here. Let the definitions soak in before you move on — it'll make the rest of the topic flow a lot better. You need to know the global patterns of water security too, so take a good look at the map above.

Water Insecurity

You need to know the <u>causes</u> and <u>effects</u> of water insecurity. By a lucky chance, here's just the page for you...

Water Availability is Affected by Many Factors

Water <u>availability</u> isn't just about <u>how much</u> rainfall you get — lots of <u>other factors</u> affect it too:

Physical Factors

1) <u>Climate</u> — most places <u>rely</u> on <u>rainfall</u> to feed lakes and rivers for their water supply. In hotter climates, more water <u>evaporates</u> from these stores. <u>Climate change</u> is <u>altering</u> the total amount of rainfall places receive, as well as causing global <u>temperatures</u> to <u>rise</u>. This means that many dry areas are getting <u>drier</u>, increasing the <u>risk</u> of <u>droughts</u>.

2) <u>Geology</u> — when rain falls on <u>impermeable rock</u>, e.g. clay, it <u>runs off</u> into rivers and lakes. These are <u>easy</u> to get water from. When rain falls on <u>permeable rock</u>, e.g. sandstone, it <u>infiltrates</u> the rock and can form <u>underground water stores</u> (<u>aquifers</u>), which are <u>harder</u> to get water from. However, <u>groundwater</u> can make water <u>available</u> in very <u>dry</u> places, e.g. the Sahara desert.

Economic and Social Factors

1) <u>Over-abstraction</u> — this is when <u>more</u> water from natural sources (e.g. rivers, lakes and groundwater) is used than is <u>replaced</u>. It is caused by:
   - <u>Population growth</u> and <u>economic development</u> (see previous page).
   - <u>Improvements</u> in <u>sanitation</u> and <u>hygiene</u> — e.g. people shower more frequently.
   - High <u>demand</u> from <u>businesses</u> — tourism and recreation can cause <u>water stress</u> during peak holiday seasons, e.g. it takes a lot of water to keep golf courses green in arid environments.

2) <u>Polluted</u> water <u>sources</u> — water pollution is a major <u>problem</u> in <u>rapidly industrialising countries</u>, where <u>industrial waste</u> is <u>dumped</u> into rivers without being treated. Animal waste can be <u>hazardous</u> in places where people <u>share water</u> sources with <u>animals</u> and lack access to sanitation.

3) <u>Limited infrastructure</u> — rapid urbanisation means that <u>more pumps</u> and <u>pipes</u> are needed to ensure <u>safe</u> and <u>reliable access</u> to water. If water pipes and sewers aren't built quickly enough, <u>sewage</u> can <u>contaminate</u> the water supply.

4) <u>Poverty</u> — water <u>providers</u> charge a <u>fee</u> for supplying water to homes. People who are <u>too poor</u> to pay for it have to find <u>other sources</u> of water, which may not be safe to drink.

Water Insecurity Can Have a Wide Range of Impacts

<u>Water insecurity</u> leads to lots of <u>problems</u>. For example:

1) <u>Pollution</u> and <u>disease</u> — water that's polluted (e.g. by <u>sewage</u> or industrial <u>chemicals</u>) can be more dangerous in areas where water is scarce, as people may have no alternatives to the polluted water. Some waterborne <u>diseases</u>, e.g. cholera, are caused by bacteria in <u>sewage-contaminated</u> water.

2) <u>Reduced food production</u> — agricultural <u>irrigation</u> uses a lot of water, so when there's a water <u>shortage</u>, crop growth can be limited. This can lead to <u>starvation</u>.

3) <u>Reduced industrial output</u> — manufacturing industries are hugely <u>water-intensive</u>, so can't <u>produce</u> as many products during water shortages. This <u>reduces</u> workers' <u>incomes</u> and affects the <u>economy</u>.

4) <u>Conflict</u> — when countries with water insecurity <u>share</u> the same water sources, such as rivers or aquifers, <u>water shortages</u> can trigger <u>conflicts</u>. One country may try to <u>improve</u> its own water security by <u>taking more</u> water from a river, which can <u>reduce</u> the water security of countries <u>downstream</u>. E.g. <u>Afghanistan</u> has tried to support recent developments by using the <u>Helmand River</u>, which borders <u>Iran</u>. This could <u>threaten water security</u> in northeast Iran, so the two countries may come into conflict.

I'm too shy to drink in public — I have water insecurity...

Standard geography fare here — a load of factors and a load of impacts. Lovely.

1) *Outline one impact of water insecurity.* [2]

Increasing Water Supply

There are some pretty <u>large-scale</u> technological solutions that can <u>improve</u> water supply...

Water Supplies Can be Increased in Several Ways

Dams and Reservoirs

Rainfall can be <u>unpredictable</u> or prone to <u>seasonal variation</u> — this can cause <u>water deficits</u> at certain times of the year. One solution that provides a reliable water source all year round is <u>increasing storage</u>.

1) Building a <u>storage dam</u> across a <u>river</u> traps water behind the dam, creating a reservoir.

2) During times of <u>water surplus</u> the reservoir will be <u>filled</u>. This water can then be <u>released</u> when there's a <u>water deficit</u>, ensuring that there is a <u>consistent flow</u> of water in the river all year round. E.g. Llyn Clywedog reservoir in Wales is used to <u>regulate</u> the water levels in the River Severn.

3) Reservoirs can cause <u>conflict</u> because they <u>flood</u> agricultural land. They may also <u>drown settlements</u>, forcing people to relocate.

4) Dams are <u>expensive</u> to build and maintain — repairs to Chasewater in Staffordshire cost £5.5 million.

Water Diversion

Imperial Dam

1) Water diversion is when a <u>dam</u> is built to <u>raise</u> a river's water level and <u>redirect</u> water to a chosen location.

2) This type of dam is typically <u>less</u> disruptive than a <u>storage dam</u> as it <u>redirects</u> water instead of storing it in a reservoir.

3) Diversion dams can be used to <u>irrigate</u> farmland or produce <u>hydroelectric power</u>.

4) E.g. Arizona's Imperial Dam <u>diverts</u> water from the Colorado River to the All-American Canal.

© National Geographic Image Collection / Alamy Stock Photo

Water Transfer

1) Water transfer schemes are large-scale <u>engineering projects</u> that <u>move</u> water from an area of <u>surplus</u> to an area of <u>deficit</u>.

2) Water is usually transferred in <u>canals</u> and <u>pipes</u>, but <u>pumping stations</u> and <u>aqueducts</u> (artificial channels) are sometimes used to move water across hills and valleys.

3) Water transfer has the potential to <u>reduce</u> water insecurity in the receiving area, but can cause massive <u>environmental</u>, <u>social</u> and <u>economic</u> problems (see next page).

Water transfer has definitely improved my commute...

Desalination

<u>Desalination</u> removes the <u>salt</u> from <u>seawater</u> so it can be used.

1) There are two main processes — seawater is either <u>heated</u> until it <u>evaporates</u> (leaving the salt behind) and is <u>condensed</u> as freshwater, or seawater is passed through a <u>membrane</u> that removes salt.

2) Wealthy <u>desert</u> countries often use desalination as the main source of clean, drinking water, e.g. <u>98.8%</u> of Dubai's water is supplied through desalination. It has the region's <u>largest</u> supply plant, which produces up to <u>140 million gallons</u> of desalinated water every day.

3) Desalination is <u>expensive</u> because <u>energy</u> is needed to heat seawater or to force it through the <u>membranes</u>. Most desalination plants are also powered by <u>fossil fuels</u>, though Saudi Arabia is building the world's first large-scale, <u>solar-powered</u> plant.

The constant drip of revision is making me need a water transfer...

... but you need to make sure you can describe some of these marvellous water supply strategies in the exam. Remember, large-scale schemes like these often cost a lot of money and have social and environmental costs.

Water Transfer — China

Water insecurity problems? Just build a massive, ambitious and extremely expensive water transfer project...

China is Transferring Water from the Wetter South to the Drier North

1) Northern China is home to two cities with over 10 million people — Beijing and Tianjin.

2) High population densities, combined with expanding industry and an increasing need for agricultural land in the north has led to a high demand for water.

3) In the past, groundwater was used to help meet the demand. This led to water shortages in rural areas, along with land subsidence and sandstorms, as soil dried out and became unstable.

4) To combat water insecurity in the north, the Chinese government planned a South-North water transfer project to reroute water across the country:

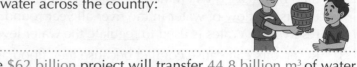

- The $62 billion project will transfer 44.8 billion m³ of water from the south to the north of the country every year.

- Work began in 2002 and since then, the Central and Eastern Routes have been completed (in 2013 and 2014 respectively). The Western Route's completion is planned for 2050.

- The project will transfer water along three routes from China's main rivers to areas of water deficit. This is made possible by various pumping stations and tunnels — the Eastern route alone has nearly 9 km of tunnels and 23 pumping stations.

Advantages

1) The water transfer scheme provides clean water to people in Beijing and Tianjin.

2) Industrial development can continue in the north, bringing more wealth to the country.

3) The scheme provides water that can be used to irrigate farmland, so crops can be grown.

4) It should prevent over-abstraction (p.108) in the north, helping to stop land subsidence.

The Central Route

Disadvantages

1) Large areas have been flooded, destroying natural habitats. The huge construction works are damaging fragile ecosystems.

2) Diverting so much water will increase water stress in the south, e.g. a drought in 2010-2011 significantly reduced China's wheat yields.

3) Raising the dam of the Danjiangkou Reservoir flooded productive farmland and forced 345 000 people to move. Most of them now have less land and poorly built housing. Many received little compensation and are now unemployed.

4) The water supplied to Beijing is very expensive due to the project's high cost and it's only available in urban areas. The urban poor and many people in rural areas have no access to the diverted water.

Danjiangkou Reservoir

© Newscom / Alamy Stock Photo

Crying over revision? It's just a bit of water transfer...

There are many advantages and disadvantages to moving water from one area to another. Make sure you've transferred all of the information on this page to your brain — you'll need to know an example for the exam.

Sustainable Water Supply

Massive engineering works aren't <u>always</u> the answer to water insecurity. We can <u>all</u> do our bit to make sure that we use water resources <u>sustainably</u>, to help make sure that there's enough for <u>everyone</u>.

Sustainable Water Supplies — Use Less and Re-Use More

Water needs to be used more <u>sustainably</u> to make sure there is <u>enough</u> to meet everyone's <u>current needs</u> without preventing <u>future generations</u> from meeting their needs. There are several strategies to help with this:

Water Conservation

Water conservation is about using <u>less</u> water. For example by:

1) <u>Fixing leaks</u> in reservoirs, pipes and taps to stop water <u>wastage</u> — 20% of water in the UK is lost to leaks before it reaches consumers.

2) Fitting <u>dual-flush toilets</u> or <u>devices</u> in the toilet <u>cistern</u> — these can save up to <u>3.5 litres</u> of water with every flush.

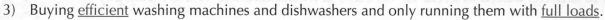

Drip pipe irrigation

3) Buying <u>efficient</u> washing machines and dishwashers and only running them with <u>full loads</u>.

4) <u>Irrigating</u> farmland using <u>drip pipes</u> or <u>sprays</u> that direct water to exactly where it is <u>needed</u>, instead of more wasteful irrigation techniques (e.g. traditional channels or ditches).

5) Fitting homes and businesses with <u>water meters</u>. Charging for metered water raises awareness of water use, and makes people more likely to <u>reduce</u> their usage — homes with meters tend to use <u>10-15%</u> less water.

6) <u>Educating</u> people to have <u>shorter</u> showers and <u>turn off</u> taps when they aren't in use — Los Angeles' "<u>Save the Drop</u>" campaign used a video to highlight some common ways that people waste water.

Groundwater Management

Groundwater needs to be managed to prevent <u>over-abstraction</u> (see p.108) and <u>pollution</u>:

1) The <u>amount</u> of groundwater being extracted can be <u>monitored</u> to ensure it is not removed <u>faster</u> than it is naturally <u>replaced</u>. <u>Laws</u> can be passed to prevent too much groundwater being extracted, e.g. in the UK, you need a <u>license</u> to extract more than 20 m³ of water a day.

2) To prevent <u>polluting</u> groundwater and making it <u>unusable</u>, farmers can be encouraged to apply fewer <u>artificial fertilisers</u> and <u>pesticides</u> to farmland, and companies that leak <u>toxic industrial waste</u> can be <u>fined</u>.

3) When groundwater supplies are <u>shared</u> between countries, <u>international agreements</u> are needed to prevent one country from taking an <u>unsustainable</u> amount of water, leaving the others <u>unable</u> to meet the needs of their populations. For example, in 2010, Argentina, Brazil, Paraguay and Uruguay all signed an agreement regarding the sharing of water from the Guarani aquifer — they agreed to use water <u>fairly</u> and <u>sustainably</u>, to share <u>research</u> on the aquifer, and to avoid <u>environmental damage</u>. However, <u>agreeing</u> how much water each country can take and how a groundwater resource should be managed can be very <u>difficult</u>.

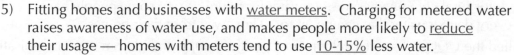

Bra.

Para.

Arg.

Uru.

Guarani Aquifer

Recycling

Recycling water involves taking water that has already been <u>used</u> and using it <u>again</u>.

1) Water from <u>homes</u> and <u>industries</u> can be piped to <u>water treatment plants</u> where it is treated to make it <u>safe</u> enough to <u>reuse</u>.

2) Recycling water is more <u>sustainable</u> because <u>less</u> water needs extracting to meet demands. E.g. recycled water could <u>increase</u> water supplies by <u>27%</u> in some cities in the USA.

3) Most recycled water is used for <u>irrigation</u>, <u>industry</u>, <u>power plants</u> and <u>toilet flushing</u>, though it can also be <u>treated</u> more extensively to make it safe to <u>drink</u>.

Sustainable Water Supply

'Grey' Water

1) 'Grey' water is a type of recycled water that is usually reused immediately without being treated. It is mostly waste water from peoples' homes, e.g. from washing machines, showers, or sinks, but doesn't include water from toilets — this water is contaminated.

2) Because it is relatively clean, it can be safely used for irrigating gardens or farmland, washing cars and flushing toilets. It's not safe for washing hands or drinking though.

3) Grey water also helps to conserve energy, as less energy is used treating water.

4) However, household grey water systems can be expensive to install, and the water must be reused quickly to stop bacteria from developing.

Kenya is Using Sand Dams to Create a Sustainable Water Supply

EXAMPLE

1) Kenya is a hot, dry country in East Africa. Most rain falls in just a few downpours each year.

2) Most rivers only flow during the rainy season — in the dry season the water evaporates. This makes it difficult for rural communities to store water for future use, so some people have to travel 6-9 hours every day for water that can be up to 10 km away from their homes.

3) An organisation called the UDO (Utooni Development Organisation), with aid from other organisations, has worked to reduce water insecurity in Kenya by installing sand dams in several rural areas, such as Machakos and Kitui. These dams give the local community access to water all year round:

Sand Dams

- A low dam (about 1 m high) is built across the river.
- During the rainy season, when water is flowing in the river, coarse material (e.g. sand) is trapped behind the dam.
- Water gets trapped between the sand particles (about a third of what is trapped behind the dam is actually water).
- The sand prevents the water from evaporating in the hot sun during the dry season.
- When the river stops flowing, water can be extracted from the sand by digging a well, by piping water through the dam to a tap, or by simply digging holes and scooping it out.

Diagram labels: River bank, Dam, Accumulated sand, river flow, Trapped water, Rock

Advantages

- The dams are cheap to build, use local materials and don't require much maintenance.
- The height of the dam can be raised each year to trap more sand and more water.
- The water can be used for irrigation to grow crops.
- Members of the community do not have to walk as far to get water. The Kya Kimew dam in Machakos has helped reduce the distance travelled each day by up to 9 km.

Sand dam in Kenya
© iStock.com / SimplyCreativePhotography

Oh no, my water is full of sand — dam...

Lots of facts about sustainable water supplies to soak up — study them until your brain's saturated.

EXAM QUESTION

1) Outline how recycling water can help to make water supplies more sustainable. [2]

Energy Supply and Demand

Fire up the generator — it's time to talk about energy... It's enough to make your hair stand on end.

Energy Security Depends on Energy Production and Consumption

1) Energy security means having a reliable, uninterrupted and affordable supply of energy.

2) A country's energy security depends on the supplies available (either produced or imported), the size of the population, and the amount of energy that a typical person uses.

3) An energy surplus is when a country produces more energy than its population requires — the extra energy can be exported. An energy surplus gives a country energy security.

4) Having less energy than required is called an energy deficit — this can cause energy insecurity.

Global Energy Production is Unevenly Distributed

The map on the right shows the total amount of energy produced, per country, in 2012.

Some countries produce lots of energy because they have large energy reserves and the money to exploit them. For example:

- Iran, Saudi Arabia — large oil reserves.

- China, Australia — large coal reserves.

- UK, Russia — large oil and gas reserves.

Some countries produce little energy because they have few resources, and some are unable to exploit the resources they do have due to poverty or political instability. For example:

- Ireland — has few resources to exploit.

- Sudan — politically unstable, has little money.

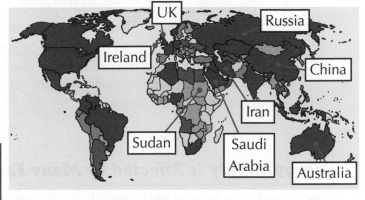

Energy production (million tonnes oil equivalent)

- ■ 200 and over
- ■ 100-199
- ■ 50-99
- ■ 20-49
- ■ 2-19
- □ Less than 2

Global Energy Consumption is also Unevenly Distributed

The map below shows the average energy consumption per person, in each country, in 2014.

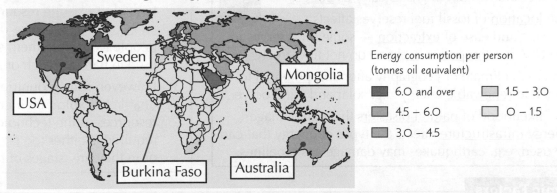

Energy consumption per person (tonnes oil equivalent)

- ■ 6.0 and over
- ■ 4.5 – 6.0
- ■ 3.0 – 4.5
- □ 1.5 – 3.0
- □ 0 – 1.5

There's a strong relationship between wealth and energy consumption:

1) Wealthy, developed countries (e.g. Australia, Sweden and the USA) tend to consume lots of energy per person because people expect a higher standard of living and they can afford it. Most people have access to electricity and heating, and use energy-intensive devices, e.g. cars.

2) Poorer, less developed countries (e.g. Burkina Faso and Mongolia) consume less energy per person as people are less able to afford it. Less energy is available and lifestyles are less dependent on high energy consumption than in wealthier countries.

Energy Supply and Demand

The Global Demand for Energy is Increasing

There are <u>three</u> main reasons why the global <u>demand</u> for energy is <u>increasing</u>:

1 Rising Population

1) Global <u>population</u> is projected to <u>increase</u> to over <u>9 billion</u> by 2040.

2) More <u>people</u> means more <u>energy</u> is needed, e.g. to heat homes.

2 Economic Development

Recent economic development has increased the <u>wealth</u> of some poorer countries.

1) People use this wealth to buy more <u>material possessions</u>. Lots of these things <u>use energy</u>, e.g. cars and televisions.

2) As countries develop, their <u>industry</u> expands — industry uses a lot of energy, so global demand for energy increases.

3 Technological Advances

1) Technological advances have created all sorts of new <u>devices</u> that need <u>energy</u>, e.g. computers, mobile phones and tablets. As these become more popular, <u>more</u> energy is needed to <u>power</u> them.

2) Some advances have made energy <u>more affordable</u> — the use of <u>wind</u> energy in <u>Texas</u> has prevented consumers' energy costs from rising. However, this means people can afford to <u>use more</u> energy, so demand increases.

Amarillo, Texas

Energy Supply is Affected by Many Factors

Energy supply can be affected by the <u>physical environment</u>, <u>technology</u>, the <u>economy</u> and <u>politics</u>:

Physical Factors

1) The <u>global distribution</u> of fossil fuels is unequal — some countries have <u>few</u> resources, and others have <u>inaccessible</u> resources, e.g. Antarctic oil reserves.

2) Fossil fuels are <u>non-renewable</u>, so supplies will <u>run out</u> eventually — South Africa's Mossel Bay plant could run out of gas as early as <u>2020</u>.

3) The <u>location</u> of fossil fuel reserves affects the cost and ease of <u>extraction</u> — some oil reserves in the USA are <u>trapped</u> in <u>rocks</u> so do not flow freely.

4) An area's climate or geography affects its <u>potential</u> to generate <u>renewable</u> energy, e.g. solar and wind power.

5) The likelihood of <u>natural disasters</u> that can damage energy <u>infrastructure</u> affects the types of energy that can be used, e.g. earthquakes may damage gas pipelines.

Technological Factors

1) Technological advances mean that it is possible to exploit <u>new resources</u>, e.g. the UK can access previously inaccessible gas reserves by <u>fracking</u> (p.117).

2) Some technology makes it <u>easier</u> to exploit <u>existing</u> resources, e.g. <u>autonomous machines</u> don't need people to operate them so can be used in hard-to-reach or <u>risky</u> areas.

3) However, some countries are still <u>unable</u> to exploit their energy resources as the technology required is either <u>too expensive</u> or in the early stages of testing.

Economic Factors

1) Remaining <u>non-renewable</u> energy sources are becoming <u>harder</u> to <u>reach</u> and more <u>costly</u> to <u>extract</u>.

2) The <u>prices</u> of fossil fuels such as oil and gas are very <u>volatile</u> — they can <u>vary</u> a lot due to complex <u>economic</u> and <u>political</u> factors, such as world <u>exchange rates</u> and <u>trade deals</u> between countries. Countries that <u>rely</u> on energy imports might not always be able to <u>afford</u> them.

3) Some <u>LICs</u> may have potential energy sources but too little wealth to <u>exploit</u> them.

4) Building new energy infrastructure (e.g. nuclear power stations or wind farms) can be very <u>expensive</u>. E.g. <u>Niger</u> has large <u>uranium reserves</u> but <u>lacks</u> the <u>money</u> to develop nuclear <u>technology</u>.

Energy Supply and Demand

Political Factors

1) <u>Political instability</u> in countries with large energy reserves can affect their ability to <u>export</u> resources, e.g. oil exports from the Middle East <u>decreased</u> during the Gulf War (1990-1991).

2) <u>Climate change</u> linked to burning fossil fuels (p.16) has resulted in <u>international agreements</u> to <u>reduce</u> the concentration of <u>greenhouse gases</u> in the atmosphere, e.g. many countries pledged to reduce their CO_2 emissions as part of the Paris Agreement (p.18).

3) Concerns over the <u>safety</u> of nuclear power and nuclear waste disposal have resulted in <u>stricter regulations</u>. This means it's become <u>harder</u> to build nuclear power stations.

Energy Insecurity has a Range of Impacts

If demand for energy exceeds supply, <u>people</u>, the <u>environment</u> and the <u>economy</u> can all suffer:

Environmental and Economic Costs

1) As fossil fuels are <u>used up</u>, reserves in less <u>accessible</u> and more <u>environmentally sensitive</u> areas are <u>exploited</u>.

2) This <u>increases</u> the cost of producing energy and risks <u>environmental damage</u>.

EXAMPLE: The <u>UK</u> has begun fracking (see p.117) near Blackpool to exploit shale gas reserves. The impacts of this process are <u>unclear</u>, but people fear that it could cause <u>earthquakes</u> or <u>contaminate</u> the water table.

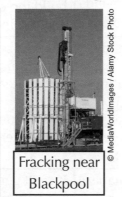

Fracking near Blackpool

© MediaWorldImages / Alamy Stock Photo

Food Production

1) Energy insecurity can <u>limit</u> how many <u>agricultural machines</u> can be used.

2) Demand for <u>cleaner</u> and <u>cheaper</u> energy sources increases <u>demand</u> for <u>biofuels</u>.

3) Growing biofuel crops takes up <u>land</u> that could be used to grow <u>food</u>. This can lead to food <u>shortages</u> and may <u>increase</u> food prices.

EXAMPLE: It's predicted that <u>168 million acres</u> of land would be needed to grow enough <u>sugarcane</u> to meet all the <u>USA's</u> energy needs with <u>biofuel</u>.

Harvesting sugarcane

Industrial Output

1) <u>Energy shortages</u> and <u>higher</u> energy costs <u>reduce</u> industrial output — factories have to <u>produce less</u> or <u>relocate</u> somewhere with better energy security to minimise costs. This can <u>threaten jobs</u> as factories may be forced to reduce employee hours or shut down.

2) <u>Higher costs</u> are often passed on to the <u>consumer</u>, as producers are forced to raise their prices.

EXAMPLE: In 2017, some companies in the <u>UK</u> (such as <u>Tata Steel</u>) had to shut down during <u>peak hours</u> because of <u>high energy costs</u>.

Potential for Conflict

1) There is the potential for political <u>instability</u> when energy <u>demand</u> exceeds energy <u>supply</u>.

2) This can cause <u>conflict</u> between countries with an energy <u>surplus</u> and those with an energy <u>deficit</u>.

EXAMPLE: In 2012, <u>Sudan</u> and <u>South Sudan</u> came into conflict over ownership of the <u>Heglig oil field</u>, which lies on the <u>border</u> of the two countries. South Sudan attempted to claim the oil field from Sudan to prevent energy insecurity, and a short <u>war</u> was fought.

Insecure but don't know what for? Check it's not a political factor...

Be careful — political instability and conflict can be both causes and impacts of energy insecurity. Be sure to get the details clear in your head so you don't get yourself muddled up if you're asked about it in the exam.

Increasing Renewable Energy Supplies

Finding ways to <u>increase</u> energy <u>supply</u> is pretty important, given all the shenanigans on the previous page...

Renewable Energy Sources will Never Run Out

Renewable energy can be a good option for increasing energy supply — the sources <u>won't run out</u>, they produce few or <u>no waste</u> products, and generally require <u>less maintenance</u> than non-renewable power stations.

Costa Rica ran entirely off renewable energy for 300 days in 2018.

There are lots of <u>renewable energy sources</u> — these are the ones you need to know about:

Energy Type	How does it work?	Advantages	Disadvantages	Example
Solar	Energy from the <u>Sun</u> is used to <u>heat water</u> or to generate <u>electricity</u> using <u>photovoltaic cells</u>.	Solar cookers and water heaters are <u>cheap</u>. Excess energy can be sold, making extra money.	<u>Photovoltaic cells</u> are <u>expensive</u>. They depend on sunlight, so are unreliable.	<u>Morocco</u> is home to the world's largest <u>solar farm</u>, the Noor Complex. It is expected to provide electricity for over <u>1 million</u> people.
Hydro (HEP)	Hydroelectric power is created from <u>falling water</u>. Water <u>trapped</u> by a <u>dam</u> is allowed to <u>fall</u> through tunnels. The <u>force</u> of the falling water turns <u>turbines</u> and generates <u>electricity</u>.	HEP is <u>flexible</u> and <u>efficient</u> — water flow and electrical output can be <u>adjusted</u> to match demand and limit <u>waste</u>.	Building dams can <u>destroy habitats</u> and <u>communities</u>. It's <u>expensive</u> to build the dams and turbines.	The <u>Three Gorges Dam</u> in China is the largest HEP station in the world. In 2016, <u>China</u> produced more HEP than Brazil, Canada and the USA combined.
Geothermal	<u>Water</u> is <u>pumped</u> into the ground and turned into steam by <u>heat</u> from the Earth's crust. The steam turns a <u>turbine</u>, which generates <u>electricity</u>. The steam can also be piped to houses for <u>heating</u>.	It is <u>cheap</u> and <u>reliable</u> — generally, little construction needs to take place to harness this energy.	It works best in <u>tectonically active</u> areas, which aren't found everywhere.	<u>87%</u> of <u>Iceland's</u> heating and hot water for homes comes from geothermal energy, thanks to its position on a <u>plate boundary</u>.
Tidal	<u>Currents</u> or changes in <u>water level</u> caused by <u>tides</u> are used to turn <u>turbines</u> and generate electricity.	It can be reliably <u>predicted</u> — tidal cycles are very <u>regular</u>.	It can't generate <u>constant</u> energy. The turbines are <u>expensive</u>.	The proposed <u>Swansea Bay Tidal Lagoon</u> would generate enough power for <u>120 000</u> homes.
Wave	<u>Wind</u> blowing across water makes <u>waves</u>. The changing water level drives air through <u>turbines</u> to generate <u>electricity</u>.	It's <u>usable</u> during the winter, so it works well with <u>solar</u> power.	It's <u>expensive</u> to build and install the turbines.	Wave energy projects are being tested in the UK, e.g. in <u>Orkney</u>, <u>Cornwall</u> and <u>Wales</u>.
Wind	Wind turbines use wind energy to generate electricity. They can be built on <u>land</u> or at <u>sea</u>, often in large <u>wind farms</u> with lots of turbines.	There are <u>no greenhouse gas</u> emissions once the turbines have been built.	Wind is <u>variable</u> — wind farms can't generate electricity all the time.	For one day in 2017, <u>Denmark</u> ran <u>solely</u> on wind power, producing enough energy to power <u>10 million</u> homes.
Biomass	<u>Biomass</u> is wood, plants or animal waste that's <u>burnt</u> for power or used to produce <u>biofuels</u>.	It doesn't require much <u>technology</u> — a good choice for LICs.	Biomass is only <u>renewable</u> if managed <u>sustainably</u>.	The <u>USA</u> produced over <u>1 million</u> barrels of biofuel a day in <u>2015</u>, mainly from <u>ethanol</u>.

I use wave power every time I say goodbye...

1) Identify a renewable source of energy and discuss its ability to meet energy demands. [4]

Increasing Non-Renewable Energy Supplies

HICs are finding <u>newer</u> and more <u>technologically advanced</u> ways of getting to the last reserves of fossil fuels...

Non-renewable Energy Sources Will Run Out Eventually

1) <u>Fossil fuels</u> have traditionally supplied most of our energy, but reserves will eventually <u>run out</u> or become <u>too difficult</u> to <u>extract</u>.

2) The use of <u>nuclear energy</u> has been <u>increasing</u> since the 1950s, but nuclear energy comes from <u>uranium</u> and will also eventually <u>run out</u>.

3) However, we can <u>increase energy supplies</u> from non-renewable sources:

© Aflo Co., Ltd. / Alamy Stock Photo

Fossil Fuels

1) The supply of fossil fuels can be increased by searching for <u>new reserves</u>, or by <u>exploiting</u> reserves that have been <u>discovered</u> but not yet <u>used</u>.

2) As <u>technology</u> develops, it has become possible to extract resources that were previously <u>too difficult</u> or <u>costly</u> to access, e.g. by fracking.

Nuclear

1) Nuclear technology can be used to generate a <u>large</u> amount of <u>energy</u> from a <u>small</u> amount of <u>fuel</u>.

2) However, nuclear power stations are <u>expensive</u> to build and to <u>decommission</u> — nuclear <u>waste</u> must be safely <u>stored</u> for <u>1000s of years</u>. Accidents can be <u>disastrous</u> and cause global panic, e.g. the Fukushima disaster, 2011.

3) More energy can be extracted by developing new <u>technology</u> to improve the <u>efficiency</u> of nuclear reactors.

4) New <u>breeder reactors</u> can generate more fuel as they operate — making nuclear energy more <u>renewable</u>.

Extracting Fossil Fuels has Advantages and Disadvantages

EXAMPLE

1) <u>Fracking</u> is a way of extracting <u>shale gas</u> — natural gas <u>trapped</u> underground in <u>shale rock</u>. In <u>2017</u>, work began at a site on Preston New Road, near <u>Blackpool</u> in Lancashire.

2) <u>Liquid</u> is pumped into shale rock at <u>high pressure</u>. This causes the rock to <u>crack</u> (fracture), <u>releasing</u> the <u>gas</u>, which is then collected as it comes back out of the well.

3) There are a range of <u>advantages</u> and <u>disadvantages</u> to fracking:

Advantages

1) <u>Lots</u> of shale gas is available in the UK. It's thought there is at least <u>5 trillion m³</u> of gas at the fracking sites in Lancashire.

2) Fracking increases the UK's <u>energy security</u> as other fossil fuel supplies start to decline.

3) Gas is <u>less polluting</u> than other fossil fuels. It releases <u>half</u> the CO_2 of coal when burned.

4) Fracking is <u>cheaper</u> than some renewable energy sources but it can cost more to <u>extract</u> than gas from other sources.

5) The <u>technology</u> has already been <u>tested</u>, e.g. in Texas, USA, and shown to work.

Disadvantages

1) Gas is <u>not</u> a <u>sustainable</u> energy source. It's <u>non-renewable</u>, and releases CO_2 when it's burned — contributing to <u>global warming</u>.

2) Fracking risks <u>polluting</u> groundwater, drinking water and the air.

3) It uses lots of <u>water</u> (a limited resource).

4) It's known to cause small <u>earthquakes</u> — a <u>1.5 magnitude</u> earthquake was triggered by the work in Lancashire in December <u>2018</u>.

5) It's an issue that people feel <u>strongly</u> about — several people were <u>arrested</u> after <u>protesting</u> against the Lancashire site.

6) Investment in fracking may <u>slow down</u> the investment in <u>renewable</u> energy.

Not for Shale

My favourite energy supply is non-renewable — I've run out of pie...

This stuff is a hot topic at the moment — turn on the news and there's likely to be something about fracking or nuclear power stations. Examiners really love to test relevant geographical topics, you know. Just sayin'...

Sustainable Energy

Sustainable energy is about making sure there's <u>enough</u> energy for your dog to be scared by a vacuum cleaner <u>today</u>, while making sure your children's children's children's cat can lounge by a radiator in <u>years to come</u>.

Sustainable Energy means Future Generations can Meet their Energy Needs

1) <u>Sustainable</u> energy provides energy <u>today</u> without preventing <u>future generations</u> from meeting their energy needs.

2) It's important because <u>demand</u> for energy is <u>increasing</u> as the world's population increases, but <u>non-renewable</u> energy resources (such as coal, oil and gas) are <u>running out</u>.

3) Humans need to exploit <u>existing</u> resources better, find <u>new</u> renewable energy sources and <u>use</u> energy more <u>efficiently</u>.

A Carbon Footprint is a Measure of Energy Use

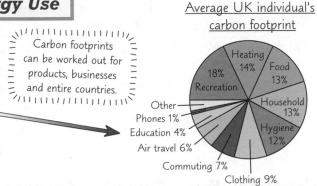

1) A <u>carbon footprint</u> is a measure of the amount of <u>greenhouse gases</u> an individual's activities <u>produce</u>. It includes both <u>direct</u> and <u>indirect</u> emissions.

2) <u>Direct</u> emissions are those produced from things that <u>use</u> energy, e.g. having the <u>heating</u> on, using <u>electrical appliances</u>, <u>commuting</u> and <u>air travel</u>.

3) <u>Indirect</u> emissions are those produced when <u>making</u> the things that we <u>buy</u>, like <u>food</u> or <u>clothing</u>.

Carbon footprints can be worked out for products, businesses and entire countries.

Average UK individual's carbon footprint

Recreation 18%, Heating 14%, Food 13%, Household 13%, Hygiene 12%, Clothing 9%, Commuting 7%, Air travel 6%, Education 4%, Phones 1%, Other

Pie chart based on the data from a study by the government-funded Carbon Trust.

Energy can be Conserved in Various Ways

There are lots of ways that <u>energy use</u> can be <u>reduced</u>:

Sustainable Design

Buildings can be <u>designed</u> to use energy more <u>sustainably</u>, for example:

1) <u>Insulation</u> — <u>less</u> energy is needed to <u>heat</u> homes and workplaces that are well-insulated.

2) Modern <u>boilers</u> — new boilers are more <u>efficient</u> than older models, so less energy is wasted.

3) <u>Solar panels</u> — these are fitted to <u>roofs</u> to provide <u>renewable</u> energy with a low carbon footprint.

<u>Transport</u> can also be designed to use energy more sustainably:

1) Switching to <u>electric</u> — electric cars, vans and trains are more <u>efficient</u> than <u>petrol</u> or <u>diesel</u> versions.

2) <u>Biofuel</u> — <u>waste</u> products can be converted into biofuel and <u>re-used</u>. Buses in London have been using biofuel made from <u>coffee beans</u> since 2017.

Demand Reduction

1) <u>Demand</u> can be reduced by giving people <u>incentives</u> to <u>lower</u> their <u>energy use</u>. E.g. the UK government can offer <u>tax relief</u> and exemptions to businesses that use energy efficient technology.

2) Improving <u>public transport</u> and encouraging <u>walking</u> or <u>cycling</u> reduces the demand for energy used to power transport. <u>Congestion charges</u> in London encourage people to reduce how frequently they drive in certain areas.

3) Fitting <u>smart energy meters</u> in people's homes helps them to be more <u>aware</u> of how much energy they are consuming and can encourage them to find ways to <u>reduce</u> their energy usage (and their electricity bills).

Congestion charging — Central ZONE — Mon - Fri 7am - 6pm

Congestion charge sign, London

Sustainable Energy

Using Technology to Increase Efficiency

Doing the <u>same</u> job but using <u>less</u> fuel <u>conserves</u> energy:

1) Energy saving <u>light bulbs</u> — CFL light bulbs can last <u>ten times</u> longer and are up to <u>four times</u> more <u>efficient</u> than incandescent light bulbs, which have been <u>banned</u> in the EU since 2009.

2) <u>Hybrid</u> cars, vans and trains combine diesel and electric power to <u>increase</u> efficiency. E.g. hybrid trains between London and the south west use <u>electricity</u> when possible and diesel when there are no overhead electric wires.

3) <u>Regenerative braking</u> — road vehicles and trains can be fitted with devices to <u>store</u> the energy lost when braking so it can be <u>used later</u> or <u>returned</u> to the <u>national grid</u>.

4) Manufacturers are making <u>more efficient</u> engines in response to new <u>laws</u> and rising <u>fuel costs</u>.

5) <u>Power stations</u> are <u>switching</u> to gas and using <u>Combined Cycle Gas Turbine</u> technology — energy that used to be lost as heat is now recovered and used to create steam, which turns additional turbines to generate up to <u>50%</u> more electricity from the <u>same</u> amount of fuel.

Rice Husks are used to Generate Sustainable Power in Bihar

EXAMPLE

1) <u>Bihar</u> is a <u>rural</u> state in north-east <u>India</u> (an <u>NEE</u>).

2) Around <u>85%</u> of people who live in Bihar are not <u>connected</u> to the <u>electricity grid</u>, particularly those in the most <u>rural</u> areas. People that are connected often have an <u>unreliable</u> energy supply.

3) In <u>2007</u>, a scheme began to use <u>local biomass</u> (a renewable energy source) to supply more homes in Bihar with <u>electricity</u>.

4) The scheme uses <u>rice husks</u> — a <u>waste product</u> from producing rice for food:

- Rice husks are <u>collected</u> and used to generate electricity in <u>small</u>, <u>local</u> power plants.
- Each power plant has a <u>simple</u> design and contains a <u>rice husk gasifier</u>, <u>filters</u> to clean the gas, a <u>gas turbine</u>, a <u>generator</u> and a <u>distribution system</u> that can supply electricity to homes within a <u>1.5 km</u> range.
- Producing electricity <u>locally</u> is very <u>efficient</u>, as the rice husks don't need to travel long distances and the electricity does not need to be <u>transferred</u> very far.

5) The scheme was very <u>successful</u>:

- By 2015, <u>84</u> rice husk power plants were operating in Bihar, supplying electricity to around <u>200 000 people</u>.
- Generating electricity from biomass <u>reduced</u> the need for <u>diesel generators</u> and <u>kerosene lamps</u>, reducing <u>fossil fuel</u> use.
- As well as supplying electricity, the power plants provide <u>jobs</u> for local people. They are trained in <u>management</u>, <u>operations</u> or <u>maintenance</u>. This keeps the scheme <u>sustainable</u> as it reduces <u>reliance</u> on external organisations and expertise.
- The government now offers <u>financial support</u> to help set up further biomass plants.

EXAM QUESTION

Hybrid brains — increasing revision efficiency...

1) *With reference to the pie chart on page 118, explain how designing sustainable homes could help to reduce the average UK person's carbon footprint.*　[6]

Revision Summary

Hope you're still well hydrated and full of energy, because here's a lovely page of revision summary questions. Remember, you only need to do <u>one</u> option from Food, Water and Energy. If you chose Food, then the revision summary questions you need are back on p.106, but if you're a Water or Energy sort of person, you've come to exactly the right place. As always, all the answers you need are on the pages you (should) have just learnt — if you get stuck on a question, go back and revise the page again.

<u>Water Supply and Demand (p.107-108)</u> ☑

1) Give a definition of water security.
2) Describe the global pattern of water security.
3) Explain how economic development is increasing the demand for water.
4) Explain how geology can affect water availability.
5) Give three economic or social factors that can lead to water insecurity.
6) Describe how water insecurity can lead to conflict.

<u>Increasing Water Supplies and Sustainable Water Supply (p.109-112)</u> ☑

7) Describe how dams and reservoirs increase water supply.
8) How might creating reservoirs lead to conflict?
9) What is desalination?
10) Describe two methods of desalination.
11) a) Give an example of a large-scale water transfer scheme.
    b) Give two advantages and two disadvantages of the scheme.
12) List six ways that water can be conserved.
13) Describe how managing groundwater can provide more sustainable water supplies.
14) a) What is 'grey' water?
    b) How is using 'grey' water sustainable?
15) a) Give an example of a local scheme to increase sustainable supplies of water in an LIC or NEE.
    b) Give three advantages of the scheme.

<u>Energy Supply and Demand (p.113-115)</u> ☑

16) Give a definition of energy insecurity.
17) Describe the global distribution of energy production.
18) Why is global energy consumption unevenly distributed?
19) Give three reasons why the global demand for energy is changing.
20) Give two physical, economic, technological and political factors that affect energy security.
21) What are the impacts of energy insecurity?

<u>Increasing Energy Supplies and Sustainable Energy (p.116-119)</u> ☑

22) Give seven renewable energy sources that could be used to increase energy supplies.
23) Describe one way that energy supplies from non-renewable energy sources can be increased.
24) Give one advantage and one disadvantage of fracking.
25) What does the 'sustainable use of energy' mean?
26) What does a person's carbon footprint measure?
27) How can energy be conserved by sustainable design?
28) How can demand for energy be reduced?
29) Give examples of how technology can improve efficiency and help to conserve energy.
30) a) Give a named example of local renewable energy scheme in an LIC or NEE.
    b) Describe how the scheme works.

Issue Evaluation

Imagine being able to see your exam paper <u>12 weeks</u> before the exam. Well, guess what — you (almost) can.

Issue Evaluation is All About Analysing and Interpreting Information

<u>Part A</u> of <u>Paper 3</u> is an issue evaluation. You have to answer questions based on a <u>geographical issue</u>.

1) You'll be given a resource booklet <u>12 weeks</u> before the exam to let you get your head round the topic. It will contain loads of material about a geographical issue:
   - The issue could be based in the <u>UK</u> or <u>elsewhere</u> and vary in scale from <u>local</u> to <u>international</u>.
   - It might be about <u>physical</u> or <u>human</u> geography topics, or a <u>mix</u> of the two.
   - It could cover any of the <u>compulsory</u> content you've studied during the course.
   - It might extend into <u>new</u> contexts that you haven't studied before.

   Your teacher will probably help you with this.

2) You need to study <u>all</u> the information carefully, work out what it all <u>means</u> and how it <u>fits</u> together.

3) In the exam, you'll have to answer questions about the issue, using the <u>resources</u> you've been given, as well as your <u>existing knowledge</u> of Geography.

4) You'll also have to write a <u>longer</u> answer where you'll have to make a <u>decision</u> about something <u>related</u> to the issue you've been presented with, and <u>justify</u> that decision (see below).

There'll be Lots of Different Information Sources in the Resource Booklet

1) The booklet could include several different <u>types</u> of information, such as maps, graphs, photographs, diagrams, statistics, newspaper articles and quotes from people involved.

2) All the information will be <u>related</u> in some way — e.g. you might be given a newspaper article on a non-governmental organisation, photos of a city in an LIC and a data table about measures of development in that LIC.

3) The information you're given will give you some <u>clues</u> about the <u>type</u> of questions that might come up, e.g. if the booklet has a table of development indicators in two countries, it's pretty likely that you'll have to compare them in some way.

4) You <u>won't</u> be able to take <u>your</u> copy of the resource booklet into the exam — you'll get a fresh, <u>clean</u> copy. You can <u>write notes</u> about the topics covered on <u>your</u> copy of the booklet but you'll need to <u>learn</u> them for the exam.

Use All the Information to Form Opinions About the Issue

1) You'll be asked to <u>argue</u> a point of view using the information, e.g. suggesting how an area could best be managed to meet the needs of everyone involved. There's no single <u>right</u> or <u>wrong</u> answer — but you need to be able to <u>justify</u> your argument, so make sure you can use the <u>data</u> to support it.

2) Whatever your view is, you need to give a <u>balanced</u> argument. Try to think of potential economic, political, social and environmental <u>impacts</u> of the different sides of the argument, and how any <u>negative impacts</u> could be <u>reduced</u>.

3) It's likely to be a complex issue with lots of different parties involved. So think about possible <u>conflicts</u> that your solution might cause between different groups of people, or between people and the environment, and how they could be <u>resolved</u>.

Well, mine are size ten, brown and made of leather...

There's no excuse for not preparing — you have 12 weeks to work out what will come up. So when you get your resource booklet, try writing some questions you think might come up — and then try answering them.

Fieldwork

Ah, fieldwork. Time to venture into the <u>outside world</u> armed only with a clipboard and a geographical hat*...

*Geographical hat not
always supplied.

You Have to Write About Two Geographical Enquiries in the Exam

1) Fieldwork is assessed in the <u>second</u> part (<u>Part B</u>) of <u>Paper 3</u>. There's no assessed coursework, but in the exam you need to be able to write about at least one <u>human</u> and one <u>physical</u> geographical enquiry.

'Geographical enquiry' is just fancy exam-speak for fieldwork.

2) The fieldwork section of the exam is split into <u>two</u> parts:

- In one part you'll be asked about <u>fieldwork techniques</u> in <u>unfamiliar</u> situations. You might have to answer questions about techniques for <u>collecting data</u>, how to <u>present data</u> you've been given or how <u>useful</u> the different techniques are.

- In the other part you have to answer questions about <u>your investigations</u> — you might be asked about your <u>question</u> or <u>hypothesis</u>, <u>methods</u>, what <u>data</u> you collected and <u>why</u>, how you <u>presented</u> and <u>analysed</u> it, how you could <u>extend</u> your research and so on.

Your Research Question and Data Collection Methods Could Come Up

1) You need to be able to <u>explain</u> why your research question or hypothesis is <u>suitable</u> for a geographical enquiry.

2) You'll also need to know the geographical <u>theory</u> behind your question.

3) You might be asked <u>how</u> and <u>why</u> you collected your data. Make sure you can:

- <u>Describe</u> and <u>justify</u> what data you collected. This includes whether it was <u>primary</u> data (data that you collected yourself) or <u>secondary</u> data (data that someone else collected and you used).

- <u>Explain</u> why you <u>collected</u> or <u>used</u> it, how you <u>measured</u> it and how you <u>recorded</u> it. You may have used different <u>sampling techniques</u> to collect your primary data:

  1) <u>Random sampling</u> is where samples are chosen at random, e.g. picking pebbles on a beach.

  2) <u>Systematic sampling</u> takes samples at <u>regular</u> intervals, e.g. measuring river discharge every 10 m.

  3) <u>Stratified sampling</u> is where you choose samples from <u>different groups</u> to get a good overall representation, e.g. collecting the views of people in different age groups about a local issue.

- <u>Explain</u> the <u>risks</u> associated with your data collection methods, how you <u>reduced</u> them, and why the <u>location</u> you chose was <u>suitable</u>.

You May Need to Write About How You Presented and Analysed Your Data

1) The way you <u>presented</u> your data, and <u>why</u> you chose that option, could come up in the exam.

2) You might need to write about <u>what</u> you did, why it was <u>appropriate</u>, and how you <u>adapted</u> your presentation method for your data.

3) You could also be asked how <u>effective</u> your presentation techniques were or if there was a <u>different</u> way you could have <u>presented</u> your data.

4) You're likely to be asked about what your data showed. Make sure you can:

Describe Your Data

- You need to be aware of any <u>patterns</u> and <u>correlations</u> in your data as well as any <u>anomalies</u>.
- In the exam, include <u>specific</u> points from your data.
- You might need to <u>compare</u> different sets of data.
- Use <u>statistical techniques</u> to help you spot patterns and make comparisons.

There's more on statistics on p.134.

Explain the Results

- You might need to explain <u>why</u> there are patterns and why different data sets are <u>linked</u>.
- Use your <u>geographical knowledge</u> to help you explain the results.
- Remember to use <u>geographical terms</u>.

Fieldwork

Conclusions are a Summary of the Results

1) A <u>conclusion</u> sums up what you found out in relation to your original question.

2) You might need to <u>refer</u> to your conclusion in the exam, so before the big day make sure you can confidently write:

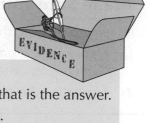

- A brief <u>summary</u> of what your <u>results</u> show.
- An <u>answer</u> to the question you are investigating, and an <u>explanation</u> of why that is the answer.
- An explanation of how your results provide <u>evidence</u> to answer the question.
- An explanation of <u>how</u> your conclusion fits into the <u>wider geographical world</u> — think about how your conclusion and results could be <u>used</u> by other people or in further investigations.

Make Sure You Can Evaluate Your Investigation

Evaluation is all about <u>self assessment</u> — looking back at how <u>good</u> or <u>bad</u> your study (or the data you are given in the exam) was. You might be asked to:

1) Identify any <u>problems</u> with the data collection <u>methods</u> used and suggest how they could be <u>improved</u>. Think about things like the <u>size</u> of the data sets, if any <u>bias</u> (unfairness) slipped in and if other methods would have been more <u>appropriate</u> or more <u>effective</u>.

2) Suggest possible <u>limitations</u> of your data. Think in advance about whether your data allowed you to <u>answer</u> your research question and whether there may be <u>other</u> data that would have been <u>useful</u>.

3) Describe how <u>accurate</u> the results are and link this to the <u>methods</u> — say whether <u>errors</u> in the methods affected the results.

4) Comment on the <u>validity</u> of your conclusion. Think about how problems with the methods used can lead to less <u>reliable</u> and <u>accurate</u> results, and how this affects the <u>validity</u> of the conclusion.

EVALUATION
☑ Best Research EVER
☐ Excellent
☐ Good
☐ Average
☐ Poor
☐ Forgot how to do Geography

> <u>Accurate</u> results are as near as possible to the <u>true</u> answer — they have <u>few errors</u>.
> <u>Reliable</u> results can be <u>reproduced</u>.
> <u>Valid</u> means that the data <u>answers</u> the original question and is <u>reliable</u>.

Here's an <u>example</u> exam question with a worked answer:

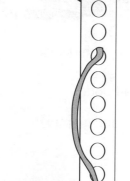

Q: Evaluate how effective your data collection methods were in helping you to reach a valid conclusion.

A: I <u>concluded</u> that the river flowed faster further downstream. However, one <u>problem</u> with my data collection <u>method</u> was that it was difficult to put the float in at exactly the same point each time. This reduced the <u>accuracy</u> of my <u>measurements</u>. To make my investigation <u>more accurate</u>, I could have placed a tape measure across the river to mark the exact point of entry. Another <u>problem</u> was that I only took two <u>readings</u> at each site and I only used one upstream site and one downstream site. To make my data <u>more reliable</u>, I could have taken more readings at each site, and used a larger number of sites both upstream and downstream. These improvements would have produced a more <u>valid</u> conclusion.

No, you can't get a tractor to do your field work for you...

Don't worry if your fieldwork doesn't go to plan. It's more important that you can write about it and say why things went wrong. It helps if you try to make it work though — and reading these pages again won't hurt.

Answering Questions

Here are some lovely <u>techniques</u> and <u>skills</u> you'll need for your exams. First, answering questions properly...

Make Sure you Read the Question Properly

It's easy to <u>misread</u> the question and write about the wrong thing. Here are some tips to help you <u>avoid</u> this:

1) Figure out if it's a <u>case study</u> question — if the question wording includes 'using named examples' or 'with reference to one <u>named</u> area' you need to include a case study or an example you've learnt about.

2) Underline the <u>command words</u> in the question (the ones that tell you what to do):

When writing about differences, '<u>whereas</u>' is an excellent word to use in your answers, e.g. 'New Zealand is an HIC whereas Nepal is an LIC'.

These questions don't normally have a <u>right</u> or <u>wrong</u> answer — the important thing is that you <u>explain</u> your answer.

Command word	Means...
Describe	what it's <u>like</u>
Explain	<u>why</u> it's like that (i.e. give <u>reasons</u>)
Compare	the <u>similarities</u> AND <u>differences</u>
Discuss	give <u>both sides</u> of an argument
Suggest why	give <u>reasons</u> for
Outline	give <u>main</u> points
Assess	make an <u>informed</u> decision
Evaluate	give <u>positives</u> and <u>negatives</u>
Justify	give <u>reasons</u> for your decision
To what extent	<u>how far</u> an argument is <u>true</u>

If you're asked to describe a pattern (e.g. from a map), first identify the <u>general pattern</u>, then refer to any <u>anomalies</u>.
E.g. to answer 'describe the global distribution of volcanoes', first say that they're mostly on plate margins, then mention that a few aren't (e.g. in Hawaii).

3) Underline the <u>key words</u> (the ones that tell you what it's about), e.g. volcanoes, tourism, immigration.

4) If the question says '<u>using Figure 2</u>', make sure you've talked about what Figure 2 shows. Don't just give lots of geographical knowledge and <u>forget</u> about the photo you were supposed to be talking about. <u>Re-read</u> the question and your answer when you've <u>finished</u>, just to check.

Some Questions are Level Marked

Questions worth <u>4 marks</u> or more with longer written answers are <u>level marked</u>, which means you need to do these things to get the <u>top level</u> and a <u>high mark</u>:

1) Read the question <u>properly</u> and figure out a <u>structure</u> for your answer before you start. Your answer needs to be well organised and structured, and written in a logical way.

2) If it's a case study question, include plenty of <u>relevant details</u>:

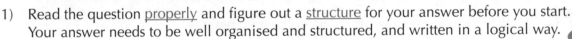

- This includes things like <u>place names</u>, <u>dates</u>, <u>statistics</u>, names of <u>organisations</u> or <u>companies</u>.
- Don't forget that they need to be <u>relevant</u> though — it's no good including the exact number of people killed in a flood when the question is about the causes of a flood.

3) <u>9 mark questions</u> sometimes have <u>3 extra marks</u> available for <u>spelling</u>, <u>punctuation</u> and <u>grammar</u>. To get top marks you need to:

- Make sure your spelling, punctuation and grammar are consistently <u>correct</u>.
- Write in a way that makes it <u>clear</u> what you mean.
- Correctly use a wide range of <u>geographical terms</u> (e.g. sustainable development).

Outline the similarities and differences between compare and discuss...

It may seem a bit simple to you, but it's really important to understand exactly what you're being asked to do. This can be tricky — sometimes the differences between command words can be quite subtle, so get learning.

Labelling and Comparing

These next few pages give you some advice on what to do for <u>specific types</u> of questions.

You Might Have to Label Photos, Diagrams or Maps

If you're asked to <u>label</u> something:

1) Figure out from the question what the labels should <u>do</u>, e.g. describe the effects of an earthquake, label the characteristics of a waterfall, describe the coastal defences, etc.

2) Add <u>at least</u> as many labels as there are <u>marks</u>.

3) When describing the features, talk about things like the <u>size</u>, <u>shape</u> and <u>relief</u>. Make sure you use the correct <u>geographical names</u>, e.g. arête, wave cut platform, meander.

Q: Label the <u>major landforms</u> of this coastline.

A:
- Stack formed from a collapsed arch.
- Sandstone cliffs
- Arch caused by wave erosion
- Cave
- Beach formed by deposition of sand and shingle.

Identify Common Features If You Compare Figures in the Exam

You might be given <u>two figures</u>, like a map and a photograph, or a plan and an aerial photograph, and be asked to use them <u>together</u>. Here are some tips for this kind of question:

1) The figures might <u>not</u> be the <u>same way up</u>.

2) Work out how the photo <u>matches</u> the plan or map — look for <u>major</u> features like a lake, a big road or a mountain, and then try to find them on the other figure.

3) Look at what's <u>different</u> between the photo and the map or plan and think about <u>why</u> it might be different.

Area A

Seaview Apartments

KEY
= Road
■ Building
♠♠ Parkland
〜 Sea

Madeleine Park

Q: Look at the <u>development plan</u> for Crystal Bay (2012) and the photo taken <u>after</u> development in 2017.

   a) <u>Name</u> the area labelled A in the photo.

   b) Give one <u>difference</u> between the photo and the plan.

A: a) Madeleine Park

   b) There's a small harbour area in front of the apartments.

It isn't only fashionistas that are interested in labels...

You might have to compare figures in your exam to answer all sorts of questions — take your time and read the question carefully so you know exactly what you should be doing. Coming up next is maps, whoop whoop.

Maps

Maps, glorious maps... there's nothing better. OS® maps are my personal favourite, but these aren't bad.

Latitude and Longitude are Used for Global Coordinates

1) Lines of <u>latitude</u> run <u>horizontally</u> around the Earth. They measure how far <u>north</u> or <u>south</u> of the <u>equator</u> a place is.

2) Lines of <u>longitude</u> run <u>vertically</u> around the Earth. They measure how far <u>east</u> or <u>west</u> of the <u>Prime Meridian</u> (a line of longitude running through Greenwich in London) a place is.

3) Latitude and longitude are measured in <u>degrees</u>.

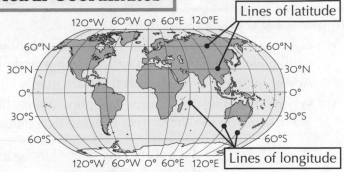

Describing Distributions on Maps — Describe the Pattern

1) In your exam you could get questions like, 'use the map to <u>describe</u> the <u>distribution</u> of water security' or '<u>explain</u> the <u>distribution</u> of deforestation'.

2) Describe the <u>general pattern</u> and any <u>anomalies</u>.

3) Make at least as many <u>points</u> as there are <u>marks</u>, and use <u>names</u> of places and figures if they're given.

4) If you're asked to give a <u>reason</u> or <u>explain</u>, you need to <u>describe</u> the distribution first.

Population density of Britain

Key

■ 600 to 5000 persons per km²

■ 400 to 599 persons per km²

□ 200 to 399 persons per km²

□ 0 to 199 persons per km²

Q: Use Figure 1 to <u>explain</u> the pattern of population density in Britain.

A: The <u>London</u> area has a <u>very high</u> population density (600 to 5000 per km²). There are also areas of <u>high</u> population density (400 to 599 per km²) in the <u>south east</u>, the <u>Midlands</u> and <u>north west</u> of England. These areas include major <u>cities</u> (e.g. Birmingham and Manchester). More people live in and around cities because there are <u>better services</u> and more <u>job</u> opportunities than in <u>rural</u> areas. Scotland and Wales have the <u>lowest</u> population densities in Britain (less than 199 per km²)...

Describing Locations on Maps — Include Details

1) In your exam you could get a question like, '<u>describe</u> the <u>location</u> of cities in the area shown'.

2) When you're asked about the <u>location</u> of something, say <u>where</u> it is, what it's <u>near</u> and use <u>compass</u> points.

3) If you're asked to give a <u>reason</u> or explain, you need to <u>describe</u> the location first.

You could be given two maps to use for one question — link information from the two maps together.

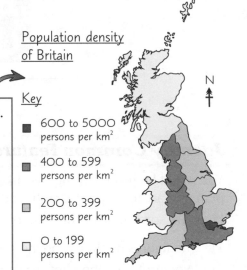

Q: Use the maps to describe the location of the National Parks.

Spondovia

Key:
■ National Parks

Spondovia

Dub
Liet
Strava

Key: ■ Mountains
● Cities

A: The National Parks are found in the <u>south west</u> and <u>north east</u> of Spondovia. They are all located in <u>mountainous</u> areas. Three of the parks are located near to the city of <u>Strava</u>.

Describing maps — large, cumbersome, impossible to fold...

...but I love them really. Give me a paper map over some digital device — or worse, a GPS sat-nav type thing. Make sure you're happy with latitude and longitude, then practise describing a map using lots of lovely details.

Geographical Skills

Maps

This page has more <u>dots</u> and <u>lines</u> than the Morse code highlights of the last footy match of the season...

Dot Maps Show Distribution and Quantity Using Identical Symbols...

1) <u>Dot maps</u> use identical <u>dots</u> to show how something is <u>distributed</u> across an area.

2) Use the <u>key</u> to find out what <u>quantity</u> each dot represents.

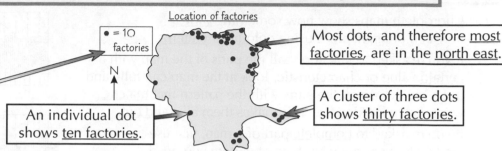

Location of factories

• = 10 factories

Most dots, and therefore <u>most factories</u>, are in the <u>north east</u>.

A cluster of three dots shows <u>thirty factories</u>.

An individual dot shows <u>ten factories</u>.

...Proportional Symbol Maps use Symbols of Different Sizes

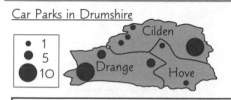

Car Parks in Drumshire

Cilden
Orange
Hove

• 1
• 5
● 10

Q: Which area has most car parks?
A: Drange, with 20.

1) <u>Proportional symbol maps</u> use symbols of different <u>sizes</u> to represent different <u>quantities</u>.

2) A <u>key</u> shows the quantity each different sized symbol <u>represents</u>. The bigger the <u>symbol</u>, the larger the <u>amount</u>.

3) The <u>symbols</u> might be circles, squares, semi-circles or bars, but a larger symbol <u>always</u> means a larger amount.

Isolines on Maps Link up Places with Something in Common

1) <u>Isolines</u> are lines on a map <u>linking</u> up all the places where something's the <u>same</u>, for example:
   • <u>Contour lines</u> are isolines linking up places at the same <u>altitude</u>.
   • <u>Isolines</u> on a weather map (called <u>isobars</u>) link together all the places where the <u>pressure's</u> the same.

2) The <u>closer</u> together the lines are, the <u>steeper</u> the <u>gradient</u> (how quickly the thing is changing) at that point.

1 Reading Isoline Maps

<u>Find</u> the place you're interested in on the map. If it's <u>on</u> a line, just <u>read</u> off the value. If it's <u>between</u> two lines, <u>estimate</u> the value.

2 Completing Isoline Maps

<u>Drawing</u> an isoline map is like doing a <u>dot-to-dot</u> — you just <u>join</u> up all the dots with the <u>same</u> numbers. Make sure you <u>don't cross</u> any other isolines though.

Q: Find the average annual rainfall in <u>Port Portia</u> and on <u>Mt. Mavis</u>.

A: Port Portia is between 200 mm and 400 mm, so the rainfall will be around 300 mm per year. Mt. Mavis is on an isoline, so the rainfall is 1000 mm per year.

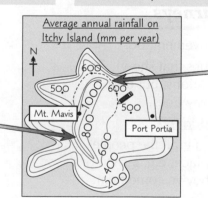

Average annual rainfall on Itchy Island (mm per year)

Mt. Mavis
Port Portia

Q: Complete the isoline for an average rainfall of <u>600 mm</u> per year.
A: See the red line.

When it comes to maps, the key is, er, key...

Whether you've got identical dots, proportional symbols or wavy lines, the key to correctly interpreting the map is to understand what each symbol means. To do this correctly, you really need to check the key carefully.

Geographical Skills

Maps

More ludicrously named maps. Well, the last two are OK, but <u>choropleth</u> sounds like a dental treatment.

Choropleth Maps show How Something Varies Between Different Areas

1) <u>Choropleth</u> maps show how something <u>varies</u> between different areas using <u>colours</u> or <u>patterns</u>.

2) If you're asked to talk about all the parts of the map with a <u>certain</u> value or characteristic, look at the map carefully and put a big <u>tick</u> on all the parts with the pattern that <u>matches</u> what you're looking for. This makes them all <u>stand out</u>.

3) If you're asked to <u>complete</u> part of a map, first use the <u>key</u> to work out what <u>type</u> of pattern you need. Then carefully <u>draw</u> on the pattern, e.g. using a ruler.

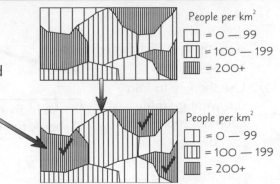

Flow Lines show Movement

1) <u>Flow line</u> maps have <u>arrows</u> on, showing how things <u>move</u> (or are moved) from one place to another.

2) They can also use <u>proportional symbols</u> — the <u>width</u> of the arrows can show the <u>quantity</u> of things that are moving.

Just go with the flow, man.

Q: Which area do the <u>greatest</u> number of people entering the UK come from?

A: The USA, as this arrow is the largest.

Q: The number of people entering the UK from the <u>Middle East</u> is roughly half the number of people entering from the <u>USA</u>. Draw an <u>arrow</u> on the map to show this.

A: Make sure your arrow is going in the right direction and its size is appropriate (i.e. half the width of the USA arrow).

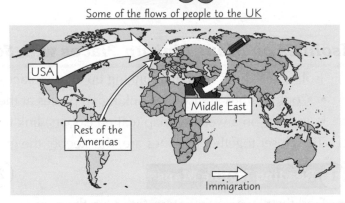

Some of the flows of people to the UK

Desire Lines show Journeys

1) <u>Desire line</u> maps show movement too.

2) Desire lines are <u>straight</u> lines that show <u>journeys</u> between <u>two</u> locations, but they don't follow roads or railway lines.

3) One <u>line</u> represents one <u>journey</u>.

4) They're used to show <u>how far</u> all the people have <u>travelled</u> to get to a place, e.g. a shop or a town centre, and where they've come <u>from</u>.

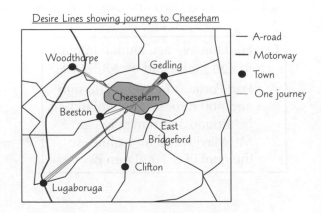

Desire Lines showing journeys to Cheeseham

Desire lines — I'm sure my palm reader mentioned those...

...unfortunately I'm not as good as seeing the future as she is* so I can't predict if any of these maps are going to come up in your exam. They could though, so make sure you know what they are and how to read them.

*If you're wondering, I'm going to meet a short, hairy stranger very soon...

Ordnance Survey® Maps

Next up, the dreaded <u>Ordnance Survey</u>® maps. Don't worry, they're easy once you know how to use them.

Learn These Common Symbols

<u>Ordnance Survey</u> (OS®) maps use lots of <u>symbols</u>. It's a good idea to learn some of the most <u>common</u> ones — like these:

▬	Motorway
▬	Main (A) road
▬	Secondary (B) road
⌣	Bridge
—	Railway

–·–·–	County boundary
▬▬ ▬▬	National Park boundaries
▭	Building
●—	Bus station

⠒⠒⠒⠒	Footpaths *
⋇	Viewpoint
i	Tourist information centre
P	Parking
+▪ ▐ ●	Places of worship

You Have to be Able to Understand Grid References

You need to be able to use <u>four figure</u> and <u>six figure</u> grid references for your exam.

Q: Give the four figure and six figure grid reference for the place of worship.

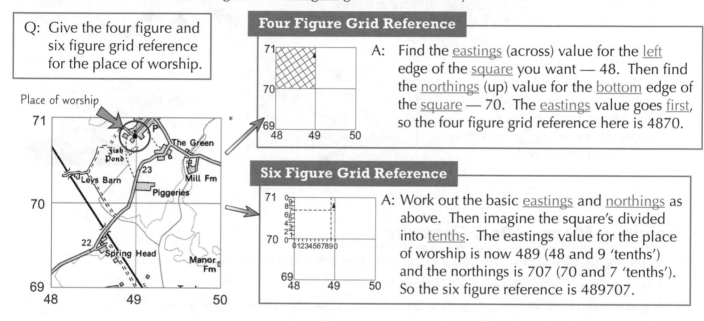

Four Figure Grid Reference

A: Find the <u>eastings</u> (across) value for the <u>left</u> edge of the <u>square</u> you want — 48. Then find the <u>northings</u> (up) value for the <u>bottom</u> edge of the <u>square</u> — 70. The <u>eastings</u> value goes <u>first</u>, so the four figure grid reference here is 4870.

Six Figure Grid Reference

A: Work out the basic <u>eastings</u> and <u>northings</u> as above. Then imagine the square's divided into <u>tenths</u>. The eastings value for the place of worship is now 489 (48 and 9 'tenths') and the northings is 707 (70 and 7 'tenths'). So the six figure reference is 489707.

You Need to Know your Compass Points

You've got to know the <u>compass</u> — for giving <u>directions</u>, saying which <u>way</u> a river's <u>flowing</u>, or knowing what they mean if they say 'look at the river in the <u>NW</u> of the map' in the exam.

North, West, East, South **OR** *Never, Wheat, Eat, Soggy*

You Might have to Work Out the Distance Between Two Places

To work out the <u>distance</u> between <u>two</u> places on a map, use a <u>ruler</u> to measure the distance in cm then <u>compare</u> it to the <u>scale</u> to find the distance in km.

Q: What's the distance from the bridge (482703) to the church (489707)?

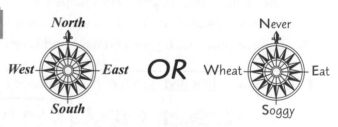

A: They're 2.2 cm apart on the map...

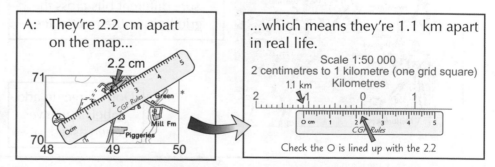

...which means they're 1.1 km apart in real life.

Scale 1:50 000
2 centimetres to 1 kilometre (one grid square)
1.1 km   Kilometres

Check the O is lined up with the 2.2

Learn the common cymbals — and really annoy your neighbours...

I told you that OS® maps aren't so bad. If a bedraggled walker who's been out in the rain for nearly five hours with only a cup of tea to keep them going can read them, then so can you. Get ready for some more map fun...

Ordnance Survey® Maps

Almost done with map skills now. Just this final page looking at <u>contour lines</u> and <u>sketching</u> from OS® maps.

The Relief of an Area is Shown by Contours and Spot Heights

1) <u>Contour lines</u> are the <u>browny-orange</u> lines on maps — they join points of equal <u>height</u> above sea level (<u>altitude</u>).

2) They tell you about the <u>relief</u> of the land, e.g. whether it's hilly or flat.

3) They show the <u>height</u> of the land by the <u>numbers</u> marked on them. They also show the <u>steepness</u> of the land by how <u>close together</u> they are (the <u>closer</u> they are, the <u>steeper</u> the slope).

4) For example, if a map has <u>lots</u> of contour lines on it, it's probably hilly or <u>mountainous</u>. If there are only a <u>few</u> it'll be flat and often <u>low-lying</u>.

5) A spot height is a <u>dot</u> giving the height of a particular <u>place</u>. A <u>trigonometrical</u> point (trig point) is a blue <u>triangle</u> plus a <u>height</u> value. They usually show the <u>highest</u> point in that area (in metres).

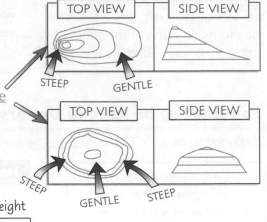

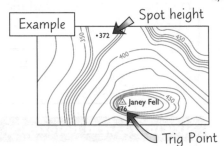

Spotty Trig Point

Sketching Maps — Do it Carefully

1) In the exam, they could give you a map or photograph and tell you to <u>sketch</u> part of it.

2) Make sure you figure out what <u>bit</u> they want you to <u>sketch</u>, and <u>double check</u> you've got it right.

3) If you're sketching an <u>OS® map</u>, it's a good idea to copy the <u>grid</u> from the map onto your sketch paper — this helps you to copy the map <u>accurately</u>.

4) Draw your sketch in <u>pencil</u> so you can rub it out if it's wrong.

5) Look at how much <u>time</u> you have and how many <u>marks</u> it's worth to decide how much <u>detail</u> to add.

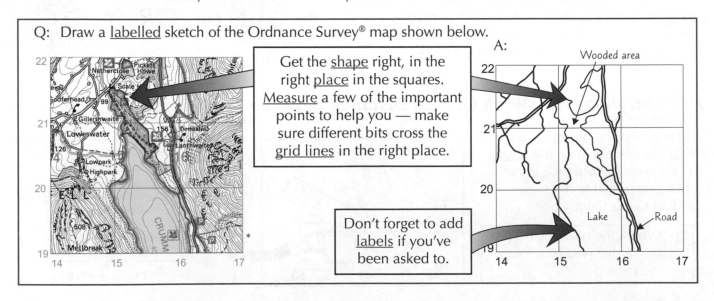

Q: Draw a <u>labelled</u> sketch of the Ordnance Survey® map shown below.

Get the <u>shape</u> right, in the right <u>place</u> in the squares. <u>Measure</u> a few of the important points to help you — make sure different bits cross the <u>grid lines</u> in the right place.

Don't forget to add <u>labels</u> if you've been asked to.

A:

Wooded area

Lake — Road

What a relief that's over...

When you're sketching a map or photo, see if you can lay the paper over it — then you can trace it (sneaky). Anyway, that's about it for maps, but you're not free yet. It's time to rock the charts and graphs. What a treat.

* © Crown copyright 2019 OS 100034841

Charts and Graphs

Stand by for charts and graphs. Make sure you can <u>interpret</u> (read) and <u>construct</u> (draw) each of them...

Describing what Graphs Show — Include Figures from the Graph

When <u>describing</u> graphs, make sure you mention the general <u>pattern</u> — when it's going <u>up</u> and <u>down</u>, and any <u>peaks</u> and <u>troughs</u>. You should also mention any <u>anomalies</u> and refer to <u>specific</u> data points.

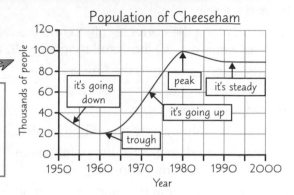

Q: Use the graph to describe population change in Cheeseham.

A: The population halved between 1950 and 1960, from 40 thousand people to 20 thousand people. It then increased to 100 thousand by 1980, before falling slightly and staying steady at 90 thousand from 1990 to 2000.

Bar Charts — Draw the Bars Straight and Neat

1) To <u>read</u> a bar chart, go from the <u>top</u> of the correct bar across to the <u>scale</u>, and read off the <u>number</u>.

2) To find the value of <u>part</u> of the bar in a <u>divided</u> bar chart — find the number at the <u>top</u> of the part of the bar you're interested in, and <u>subtract</u> the number at the <u>bottom</u> of it.

3) To <u>complete</u> a bar chart, find the number you want on the <u>vertical</u> scale and trace a <u>line</u> across to where the <u>top</u> of the bar will be with a ruler. Draw in a <u>bar</u> of the right size using a ruler.

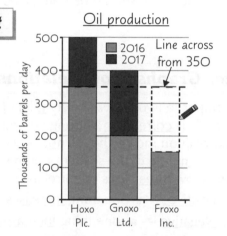

Q: How many barrels of oil did Hoxo Plc. produce per day in 2017?

A: 500 000 – 350 000 = 150 000 barrels per day

Q: Complete the chart to show that Froxo Inc. produced 200 000 barrels of oil per day in 2017.

A: 150 thousand (2016) + 200 thousand = 350 000 barrels. So draw the bar up to this point.

Histograms are a Lot Like Bar Charts

1) Histograms are <u>similar</u> to bar charts, but they have a <u>continuous</u> scale of numbers on the <u>bottom</u> and there <u>can't</u> be any <u>gaps</u> between the bars.

2) You can use histograms when your data can be <u>divided</u> into <u>intervals</u>, like this:

3) You <u>draw</u> and <u>plot</u> them just like a <u>bar chart</u>, but you have to make sure that the bars are all the correct <u>width</u>, as well as the correct <u>height</u>.

Time	Cars
0700-0800	334
0800-0900	387
0900-1000	209
1000-1100	121
1100-1200	?

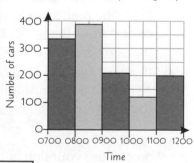

Q: How many cars were recorded between 1100 and 1200?

A: Trace a line from the top of the 1100-1200 bar and read the answer off — 200 cars.

The top forty for sheep — the baaaaaaaaaaaaa chart...

Something to watch out for with bar charts (and line graphs on the next page) is reading the scale — check the value of each division before reading or completing them. Don't assume that every division is worth just one...

Charts and Graphs

'More charts and graphs' I hear you cry — well OK, your weird wishes are my command.

Line Graphs — the Points are Joined by Lines

To read a line graph:

1) Read along the correct <u>scale</u> to find the value you want, e.g. 20 thousand tonnes or 1920.

2) Read <u>across</u> or <u>up</u> to the line you want, then read the <u>value</u> off the <u>other</u> scale.

To complete a line graph:

1) Find the value you want on <u>both</u> scales.

2) Make a <u>mark</u> (e.g. ×) at the point where the two values <u>meet</u> on the graph.

3) Using a ruler, <u>join</u> the mark you've made to the <u>line</u> that it should be connected to.

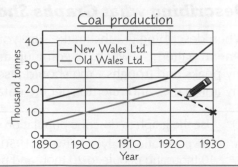

Q: Complete the graph to show that Old Wales Ltd. produced 10 thousand tonnes of coal in 1930.

A: Find 1930 on the bottom scale, and 10 thousand tonnes on the vertical scale. Make a mark where they meet, then join it to the blue line with a ruler.

Scatter Graphs Show Relationships

Scatter graphs tell you how closely <u>related</u> two things are, e.g. altitude and air temperature. The fancy word for this is <u>correlation</u>. <u>Strong</u> correlation means the two things are <u>closely related</u> to each other. <u>Weak</u> correlation means they're <u>not</u> very closely related. The <u>line of best fit</u> is a line that goes roughly through the <u>middle</u> of the scatter of points and tells you about what <u>type</u> of correlation there is. Data can show <u>three</u> types of correlation:

1) <u>Positive</u> — as one thing <u>increases</u> the other <u>increases</u>.

2) <u>Negative</u> — as one thing <u>increases</u> the other <u>decreases</u>.

3) <u>None</u> — there's <u>no</u> relationship between the two things.

Line of best fit

Positive   Negative   None

1 Reading Scatter Graphs

1) If you're asked to describe the relationship, look at the <u>slope</u> of the graph, e.g. if the line's moving <u>upwards</u> to the right it's a <u>positive</u> correlation. You also need to look at how <u>close</u> the points are to the line of best fit — the <u>closer</u> they are, the <u>stronger</u> the correlation.

2) If you're asked to <u>read</u> off a specific point, just follow the rules for a <u>line graph</u>.

Relationship between altitude and rainfall

Line of best fit

Rainfall / mm
Altitude / m

2 Completing Scatter Graphs

1) You could be asked to draw a <u>line of best fit</u> — just draw it roughly through the middle of the scatter of points.

2) If you're asked to <u>add</u> a point, just follow the rules for adding a point to a <u>line graph</u>.

Q: Describe the relationship shown by the scatter graph.

A: Altitude and rainfall show a strong, positive correlation — as altitude increases, so does the amount of rainfall.

- You can use your line of best fit to make <u>predictions</u> by reading off values from the graph.

- If you're confident your best fit line will <u>continue</u>, you can <u>extend</u> it beyond the data you have collected. This means you can make predictions <u>outside</u> the range of data.

Sorry darling, we've got no relationship — look at our scatter graph...

Line graphs and scatter graphs with a line of best fit are pretty similar, but whatever you do, don't mix them up — however much you might want to, it's not always okay to join all the dots up willy-nilly. They may not like it.

Charts and Graphs

Yep, you guessed it — there are even more <u>charts</u> and <u>graphs</u> to learn. These are the last ones, I promise.

Pie Charts Show Amounts or Percentages

The important thing to remember with pie charts is that the <u>whole pie = 360°</u>.

1 **Reading Pie Charts**

1) To work out the <u>%</u> for a <u>wedge</u> of the pie, use a <u>protractor</u> to find out its angle in <u>degrees</u>.

2) <u>Divide</u> that number by <u>360</u> and <u>multiply</u> by <u>100</u>.

3) To find the <u>amount</u> a wedge of the pie is <u>worth</u>, work out your <u>percentage</u> then turn it into a <u>decimal</u>. Then multiply the decimal by the <u>total</u> amount of the pie.

<u>Pie Chart of Transport Type</u>

Q: Out of 100 people, how many used a pogostick?
A: $126 - 90 = 36°$, so $(36 \div 360) \times 100$
= 10%, so $0.1 \times 100 = 10$ people.

2 **Completing Pie Charts**

To draw on a new <u>wedge</u> that you <u>know</u> the % for, turn the <u>%</u> into a <u>decimal</u> and multiply it by <u>360</u>. Then draw a wedge of that many <u>degrees</u>.

Q: Out of 100 people, 25% used a bicycle. Add this to the pie chart.
A: $25 \div 100 = 0.25$, $0.25 \times 360 = 90°$.

To add a new <u>wedge</u> that you know the <u>amount</u> for, <u>divide</u> your amount by the <u>total</u> amount of pie and multiply the answer by <u>360</u>. Then draw on a wedge of that many <u>degrees</u>.

Q: Out of 100 people, 55 used a car. Add this to the pie chart.
A: $55 \div 100 = 0.55$, 0.55×360
= 198° (198° + 126° = 324°).

Dispersion Diagrams Show the Frequency of Data

<u>Percentage of household waste recycled</u>

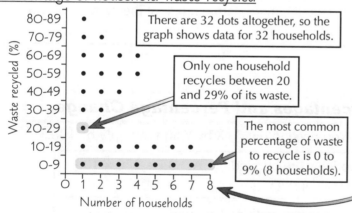

There are 32 dots altogether, so the graph shows data for 32 households.

Only one household recycles between 20 and 29% of its waste.

The most common percentage of waste to recycle is 0 to 9% (8 households).

1) Dispersion diagrams are a bit like a cross between a <u>tally chart</u> and a <u>bar chart</u>.

2) The <u>range</u> of data that's measured goes on one <u>axis</u>. <u>Frequency</u> goes on the <u>other</u> axis.

3) Each <u>dot</u> represents <u>one</u> piece of information — the <u>more</u> dots there are in a particular category, the more <u>frequently</u> that event has happened.

4) The dispersion diagram on the <u>left</u> shows the percentage of household waste that's recycled for households in a particular village.

Population Pyramids Show the Structure of a Population

1) Population pyramids are a bit like two <u>bar charts</u> on their <u>sides</u>.

2) They show the <u>population</u> of a country by <u>age</u> and <u>gender</u>.

3) The <u>number</u> of people goes on the <u>horizontal</u> axis, and the <u>age groups</u> go on the <u>vertical</u> axis. The <u>left</u> side is the <u>male</u> population and the <u>right</u> side is the <u>female</u> population.

There are a few people over 80.

There are lots of people aged 0-9.

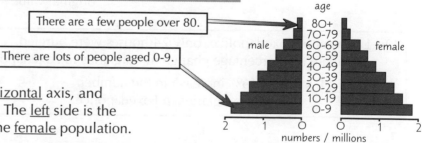

Pie charts aren't bad, but I prefer cake...

*Who'd have thought pie could be so complicated. Don't panic though — a bit of practice and you'll be sorted. And don't worry, there's only one page of this section to go. Congratulations. I'm so proud of you. *weeps*.*

Statistics

EEEK, it's a page about <u>maths</u>. In a geography book. Still, it should all be very familiar from maths lessons...

Learn the Definitions for Mode, Median, Mean and Range...

Mode, median and mean are measures of <u>average</u>, and the range is how <u>spread out</u> the values are:

<u>MO</u>DE = <u>MOST</u> common	<u>MED</u>IAN = <u>MIDD</u>LE value (when they are in size order)
<u>MEAN</u> = <u>TOTAL</u> of items ÷ <u>NUMBER</u> of items	<u>RANGE</u> = DIFFERENCE between highest and lowest

Sample	1	2	3	4	5	6	7
River discharge (cumecs)	184	90	159	142	64	64	95

Q: Calculate the mean, median, mode and range for the river discharge data shown in the table above.

A:
- The mode is the most common value = <u>64</u>.
- To find the median, put all the numbers in order and find the middle value:
  64, 64, 90, <u>95</u>, 142, 159, 184. So the median is <u>95</u>.

  When there are two middle numbers, the median is halfway between the two.
- Mean = $\dfrac{\text{total of items}}{\text{number of items}}$ = $\dfrac{184 + 90 + 159 + 142 + 64 + 64 + 95}{7}$ = $\dfrac{798}{7}$ = <u>114</u>
- The range is the difference between highest and lowest value, i.e. 184 − 64 = <u>120</u>

As well as finding the <u>median</u>, you can also find the <u>upper</u> and <u>lower</u> quartiles —
the values a <u>quarter</u> (25%) and <u>three-quarters</u> (75%) of the way through the ordered data.

Q: The number of shoppers in each shop in a village were counted. Find the median and the quartiles of the data set.

A: 2, 3, 6, 6, 7, 9, 13, 14, 17, 22, 22

| Lower quartile | Median | Upper quartile |

The <u>interquartile range</u> is the <u>difference</u> between the <u>upper</u> quartile and the <u>lower</u> quartile. It contains the middle 50% of values.

Q: Find the interquartile range of the number of shoppers.
A: 17 − 6 = <u>11</u>

You Need to be Able to Calculate Percentages and Percentage Change...

To give the amount X as a <u>percentage</u> of a sample Y, you need to <u>divide</u> X by Y and <u>multiply</u> by 100.

Q: This year, 35 out of the 270 houses in Foxedapolice were burgled. Calculate the percentage of houses burgled in Foxedapolice.

A: 35 ÷ 270 × 100
= <u>13%</u>

Calculating <u>percentage change</u> lets you work out how much something has <u>increased</u> or <u>decreased</u>.
You use this formula:

$$\text{Percentage change} = \frac{\text{final value} - \text{original value}}{\text{original value}} \times 100$$

A <u>positive</u> value shows an <u>increase</u>, and a <u>negative</u> value shows a <u>decrease</u>.

Q: Last year in Foxedapolice, only 24 houses were burgled. Calculate the percentage change in burglaries in Foxedapolice.

A: $\dfrac{35 - 24}{24} \times 100$ = 46% increase in the number of burglaries in Foxedapolice.

This page is mean — grab me a camomile tea, stat...

Sheesh, I wasn't expecting so much maths in a geography book. But here it is, so you might as well learn it before your exams. Anyway, this is the last page on exam stuff, so once you've cracked it you can celebrate...

Glossary

abiotic factors	The <u>non-living</u> components of an ecosystem, e.g. climate, soil, water.
abrasion	When bits of eroded rock in water or ice <u>scrape</u> against rock, eroding it.
agribusiness	Large-scale, <u>industrial farming</u> that is usually controlled by large companies.
appropriate technology	Materials and methods that are <u>cheap</u>, <u>sustainable</u> and easily <u>available</u> to local people, enabling them to meet their basic needs, e.g. sand fences and hand-pumped wells.
attrition	When bits of eroded rock in water <u>collide</u>, break into smaller pieces and become more <u>rounded</u>.
beach nourishment	Adding <u>sand</u> or <u>shingle</u> from elsewhere to the upper part of a <u>beach</u>, often to prevent erosion.
biodiversity	The <u>variety</u> of <u>organisms</u>, both plants and animals, living in a particular area.
biomass	Natural <u>material</u> (e.g. wood, animal waste) that can be burnt as <u>fuel</u> or used to make biofuels.
biotechnology	<u>Genetically engineering</u> crops, e.g. to increase nutritional value, yield or disease resistance.
biotic factors	The <u>living</u> components of an ecosystem, e.g. plants, animals, people.
brownfield site	Land that has previously been <u>developed</u>, but is no longer in use.
carbon footprint	The amount of <u>greenhouse gases</u> produced by a particular product or an individual's activities.
climate change	Any significant <u>change</u> in the Earth's climate over a <u>long period</u> of time.
commercial farming	<u>Farming</u> crops or livestock <u>to sell</u>, e.g. to retailers or large food companies, for a profit.
conservative plate margin	A tectonic plate boundary where two plates are <u>moving sideways</u> past each other, or in the <u>same direction</u> but at different speeds. No crust is created or destroyed.
constructive plate margin	A tectonic plate boundary where the two plates are <u>moving away</u> from each other. <u>Magma rises</u> from the mantle to fill the gap created and then cools, forming <u>new crust</u>.
consumer	An organism that gets its energy by <u>eating</u> other <u>organisms</u>, e.g. a rabbit eats grass.
Coriolis effect	The apparent <u>curve of winds</u> across the Earth's surface due to the planet's <u>rotation</u>.
decomposer	An organism, e.g. fungus, that gets its <u>energy</u> by breaking down <u>dead material</u>.
deforestation	The <u>clearance</u> of large areas of <u>forest</u>.
deposition	The process of water <u>dropping material</u> as it slows down and loses energy. Ice can also deposit material when it melts.
desertification	A decline in the quality of <u>land</u> as it becomes drier and <u>less productive</u>.
destructive plate margin	A tectonic plate boundary where two plates are <u>moving towards</u> each other. The denser oceanic plate <u>subducts</u> beneath the less dense continental plate and is destroyed. If two continental plates meet, the ground is <u>forced up</u>, creating fold mountains.
discharge	The <u>volume</u> of water flowing in a river, measured in <u>cumecs</u> — cubic metres per second (m³/s).
drought	A long period of time with <u>little</u> or no <u>precipitation</u>. Can cause areas to experience water stress.
ecosystem	A <u>community</u> of <u>plants</u> and <u>animals</u> and the <u>environment</u> in which they live.

Glossary

ecotourism	Tourism that does minimal environmental damage, promotes conservation and benefits locals.
erosion	The gradual wearing away of material, e.g. by moving water or ice.
food chain	A diagram showing what organisms in an ecosystem eat, usually in the form of a flow chart.
food web	A diagram showing how several food chains interact and overlap.
fossil fuel	A non-renewable energy source, e.g. coal, oil or gas, formed from the remains of organisms.
fragile environment	An environment that is easily disrupted and hard to restore to its natural state.
global atmospheric circulation	The transfer of heat from the equator to the poles by the movement of air.
global warming	The sharp rise in global temperatures over the last century.
globalisation	The process of countries becoming more economically, politically and culturally connected.
greenfield site	Undeveloped land, e.g. farmland or forest.
greenhouse effect	The warming of the planet as greenhouse gases (e.g. carbon dioxide (CO_2) and methane) absorb outgoing heat, so less is lost to space.
gross domestic product (GDP)	The total value of goods and services a country produces in a year. Often given in US$.
gross national income (GNI)	The total value of goods and services a country produces in a year, including income from overseas. Often given in US$.
higher income country (HIC)	A country with a high GNI per capita, e.g. the UK.
human development index (HDI)	A way of measuring and comparing countries' development level. Income, life expectancy and education level are used to produce a value between 0 (least developed) and 1 (most developed).
hydraulic action / power	Erosion caused by sea or river water colliding with rocks.
indigenous people	People born in or originating from an area, e.g. the Inuit people are indigenous to the Arctic.
infrastructure	Basic structures, facilities and services needed in society, e.g. buildings, roads and water supply.
longshore drift	The gradual zigzag movement of sediment along a coast. Caused by waves carrying material up the beach at an oblique angle and back down the beach at a right angle.
lower income country (LIC)	A country with a low GNI per capita, e.g. Uganda.
managed retreat	Removing flood defences to let land flood naturally.
mass movement	The shifting of rocks and loose material down a slope by sliding, slumping and rockfalls.
megacity	An urban area with over 10 million residents, e.g. Mumbai, Tokyo, London.
migration	The movement of people from one area to another.
mitigation	Action taken to reduce the long-term risk or impacts from a natural hazard.
natural increase	The growth in population when birth rate exceeds death rate.

Glossary

newly emerging economy (NEE)	A country that is undergoing rapid economic development, e.g. Brazil, India, China. They tend to be moving from an agriculture-based economy to an industrial one.
non-renewable energy	Energy from sources that will eventually run out, e.g. fossil fuels.
nutrient cycling	The cyclical movement of nutrients through an ecosystem.
orbital changes	Changes in the way the Earth moves around the Sun.
over-abstraction	When more water is removed from natural sources, e.g. rivers, than is replaced.
permaculture	A food production method that aims to reproduce natural ecosystems and keep soil healthy.
permafrost	A layer of permanently frozen ground underneath the soil in polar and tundra areas.
primary effects	Immediate impacts caused directly by a natural hazard, e.g. an earthquake destroys buildings.
producer	An organism, e.g. grass, that uses energy from sunlight to produce food.
renewable energy	Energy from sources that can be replenished, e.g. solar and wind energy.
saltation	When pebble-sized particles are bounced along the sea or river bed by the force of water.
secondary effects	Indirect impacts of a natural hazard, e.g. an earthquake can trigger a tsunami.
soil erosion	The loss of nutrient-rich, fertile topsoil due to natural processes or human activity.
solution	When soluble materials, e.g. limestone, dissolve in water and are transported.
squatter settlement	Poor quality, often illegal, housing that may lack amenities, e.g. a water or electricity supply.
subduction	The process by which a tectonic plate is forced down into the Earth's mantle by another plate.
subsistence farming	A type of agriculture where the farmer only produces food for themselves and their family.
suspension	When small particles, e.g. silt and clay, are transported by water.
sustainability	Meeting the needs of the present, without reducing the ability of people to do so in the future.
traction	When large particles, e.g. boulders, are pushed along the river or sea bed by the force of water.
transnational corporation (TNC)	A large company with operations in multiple countries.
transportation	The movement of eroded material.
tropical storm	An intense low pressure weather system that brings heavy rain and strong winds. Also known as a hurricane, typhoon or cyclone.
tsunami	A series of large and powerful waves caused by the displacement of a large volume of water.
urbanisation	The increase in the proportion of a country's population living in urban areas.
water stress	When the demand for water in an area exceeds the usable supply.
water transfer	The deliberate movement of water from an area of surplus to an area of deficit.
weathering	The breaking down of rock in situ.

Index

Index

Index